WHAT THE BIBLE *REALLY* SAYS ABOUT MONEY AND GIVING

IT'S NOT WHAT YOU THINK!

Dr. Michael Davis

Copyright © 2020 Dr. Michael Davis.

All rights reserved. No part of this book may be used or reproduced by any means, graphic, electronic, or mechanical, including photocopying, recording, taping or by any information storage retrieval system without the written permission of the author except in the case of brief quotations embodied in critical articles and reviews.

This book is a work of non-fiction. Unless otherwise noted, the author and the publisher make no explicit guarantees as to the accuracy of the information contained in this book and in some cases, names of people and places have been altered to protect their privacy.

WestBow Press books may be ordered through booksellers or by contacting:

WestBow Press
A Division of Thomas Nelson & Zondervan
1663 Liberty Drive
Bloomington, IN 47403
www.westbowpress.com
1 (866) 928-1240

Because of the dynamic nature of the Internet, any web addresses or links contained in this book may have changed since publication and may no longer be valid. The views expressed in this work are solely those of the author and do not necessarily reflect the views of the publisher, and the publisher hereby disclaims any responsibility for them.

Any people depicted in stock imagery provided by Getty Images are models, and such images are being used for illustrative purposes only. Certain stock imagery © Getty Images.

ISBN: 978-1-9736-7752-9 (sc)
ISBN: 978-1-9736-7754-3 (hc)
ISBN: 978-1-9736-7753-6 (e)

Library of Congress Control Number: 2019916468

Print information available on the last page.

WestBow Press rev. date: 12/23/2019

Scripture quotations marked NIV are taken from The Holy Bible, New International Version®, NIV® Copyright © 1973, 1978, 1984, 2011 by Biblica, Inc.® Used by permission. All rights reserved worldwide.

Scripture quotations marked ESV taken from The Holy Bible, English Standard Version® (ESV®), Copyright © 2001 by Crossway, a publishing ministry of Good News Publishers. All rights reserved.

Scripture quotations marked NASB are taken from The New American Standard Bible®, Copyright © 1960, 1962, 1963, 1968, 1971, 1972, 1973, 1975, 1977, 1995 by The Lockman Foundation. Used by permission.

Scripture quotations marked NKJV are taken from the New King James Version®. Copyright © 1982 by Thomas Nelson. Used by permission. All rights reserved.

Scripture quotations are taken from The Living Bible, copyright © 1971 by Tyndale House Foundation. Used by permission of Tyndale House Publishers Inc., Carol Stream, Illinois 60188. All rights reserved. The Living Bible, TLB, and the The Living Bible logo are registered trademarks of Tyndale House Publishers.

Scripture quotations are from the New Revised Standard Version Bible, copyright © 1989 the Division of Christian Education of the National Council of the Churches of Christ in the United States of America. Used by permission. All rights reserved.

Scripture quotations marked ASV are taken from the Holy Bible, American Standard Version (The Revised Version, American Standard Edition of the Bible). Public domain.

Scripture quotations marked WEB are taken from the World English Bible.

Scripture quotations marked KJV are taken from the King James Version.

Scripture quotations marked YLT are from Young's Literal Translation of the Bible. Public domain.

Wycliff Bible Copyright © 2001 by Terence P. Noble.

The New Testament in Modern English by J.B Phillips copyright © 1960, 1972 J. B. Phillips. Administered by The Archbishops' Council of the Church of England. Used by Permission.

Scripture quotations marked GNT are taken from the Good News Translation® (Today's English Version, Second Edition). Copyright © 1992 American Bible Society. All rights reserved.

Complete Jewish Bible Copyright © 1998 by David H. Stern. All rights reserved. No portion of this book may be reproduced, stored in a retrieval system, or transmitted in any form or by any means without prior written permission of the publisher.

Scripture quotations marked MSG are taken from The Message. Copyright © 1993, 1994, 1995, 1996, 2000, 2001, 2002. Used by permission of NavPress Publishing Group.

Scripture quotations marked AMP are taken from the Amplified® Bible, Copyright © 2015 by The Lockman Foundation. Used by permission.

The Passion Translation®. Copyright © 2017 by Passion & Fire Ministries, Inc. Used by permission. All rights reserved. thePassionTranslation.com

Scripture quotations marked ERV are taken from the Easy to Read Version. Copyright © 2006 by Bible League international.

Scripture quotations marked NET are taken from NET Bible® copyright ©1996-2006 by Biblical Studies Press, L.L.C. http://netbible.com All rights reserved.

For *Sandi*:

If only …

CONTENTS

Acknowledgements v
Preface vii

Chapter 1 God's Foundation for Viewing Money 1
Chapter 2 Managing Mammon 29
           Appendix 2a – Developing Your Personal
           Financial Roadmap 72
           Appendix 2b - How to Become a Christ-Follower 81
Chapter 3 The Sermon on the Amount 86
           Appendix 3: Additional Comments on Giving 134
Chapter 4 Is Debt a Dirty Four-Letter Word? 138
           Appendix 4: Common Questions regarding
           Debt and Borrowing 177
Chapter 5 Managing Mammon for The Long-Term 191
Chapter 6 Retirement: Is it Even Biblical? 245
Chapter 7 When You Go to be with the Lord 273

Seminar and Author Contact Information 305
Endnotes 307

ACKNOWLEDGEMENTS

Amazingly, this book has been over forty years in the making, dating all the way back to 1976 when I attended an early seminar presented by the late Larry Burkett. That seminar aroused in me a desire to somehow combine my secular training in business with teaching God's people how to manage money. Little did I know at that time how much guidance is in His Word and how little was—and still is—taught from the pulpit.

Over the years since, I have periodically presented a seminar on this topic to various churches and non-profit organizations. But always in the background was a desire to present it in book format, allowing for wider dissemination and easier access to the timeless and life-altering guidance in God's 2,000+ year-old manual on how He wants us, His followers, to live and conduct our lives here on His earth.

What the Bible **Really** *Says about Money and Giving* is the end result of three streams of input. First, there were many valuable and insightful comments from participants at the seminars that helped clarify and simplify many of the concepts presented. Second, in the actual preparation of this book, two of my long-time friends, Barbara Brown and Thomas Hill, spent innumerable hours reviewing early drafts, helping to hone and refine the material into an easy-to-read yet rememberable format. Beth Harris then took that material and applied her excellent editorial skills to yield a professional and grammatically correct final copy. Finally, the people at WestBow Press—especially Venus Gamboa and Bob DeGroff—provided the all-important guidance and advice necessary to shepherd the manuscript through the publishing process.

This book is motivated by the extensive guidance on financial issues contained in God's Word. I have done my best to present that guidance in as clear and understandable a manner as possible. Moreover, I have striven, to the best of my ability, to have carefully considered the context of that Godly guidance in order to draw the proper inferences and correct conclusions that He intended. Of course, any failure in that process is on my shoulders, not His.

PREFACE

Yet another book on how to handle money? Well, yes and no. God's Word does indeed talk a lot about money and financial issues—in fact, it is the most discussed topic in the Bible. Yet so little of that wisdom is taught from the pulpit ... or in Sunday School ... or seminary ... or even in many Christian-based financial books and seminars. Whether due to a lack of practical knowledge on some financial issues or an uneasy fear of talking too much about money, many pastors neglect a significant portion of timeless and relevant guidance of how God desires for us to live our lives here on earth ... guidance that has been ignored far too long.

Moreover, what little of His guidance has been taught, especially in the area of giving, has been misrepresented. What God desires as a free-flowing and honor-endowing expression of our love for Him and thankfulness for guiding and blessing every facet of our lives has instead been presented as an inaccurate and legalistic requirement. As a result, giving is often devoid of true heartfelt motivation, lacking in cheerful willingness and enthusiasm, and rarely being viewed as a *privilege* in being able to participate in this heavenly purpose. No wonder there is so little appetite to hear more about what God has to say about money.

And yet, His Word—and even Jesus Himself—deals with no issue in more depth than money and how to manage it. Besides giving, the Biblical guidance covers detailed topics like borrowing, investing, retirement, even estate planning. More importantly, the Bible provides a grand design of how He desires for us, His redeemed people, to truly live life during our brief time here on His earth. Understanding that design sets the context for how to view and implement His detailed guidance on money and financial issues.

As just a brief overview of that grand design, in God's realm, money is simply a tool and a test of where our hearts are. No matter how much wealth we possess, His Word makes abundantly clear that none of it—no matter how hard we worked to obtain it—belongs to us. In fact, His Word even tells us that it is God who gives us the ability *to* produce wealth in the first place. As a result, learning His desires and guidance on this all-important issue—one that constitutes such a considerable portion of our daily lives—should be a top priority, don't you think?

Get ready to learn what God *really* has to say about managing money. Though written well over 2,000 years ago, the Bible's guidance is as relevant as today's news. As a result, be prepared to be both amazed and challenged by what God's Book has to tell you about managing your finances in today's world … it might even upend your long-held beliefs on how to earn, manage, and give away your—really *His*—money.

1

GOD'S FOUNDATION FOR VIEWING MONEY

In the total expanse of human life there is not a single square inch of which the Christ, Who alone is sovereign, does not declare, 'That is mine!' - Abraham Kuyper

My home is in Heaven; I'm just traveling through this world – Billy Graham

We are here on God's earth for such a brief time. And yet, during that time, He has a spectacular plan for our lives—one that we could never conceive on our own. Day by day, we should do everything within our power to seek, understand, and most of all, live that plan. For in doing so, we will live lives that are dynamic, extraordinary, and supernatural in their impact.

That plan is lovingly and clearly communicated to us through His Word—we need only to be willing to open our hearts and minds to it. Within its pages is guidance for nearly every facet of our lives. One of those facets—in fact as you'll learn, one of the most important—is how God wants us to view and use this thing called money. To get us started, during my many years as an accounting professor, I used to tell a lot of jokes in class, always to try to make a point. Here's one of my favorites:

> A company needed to hire an accountant, so they placed an ad in the newspaper. They received a flock of resumes, whittled them down to the top three, and invited those three people in for an interview. With the first candidate, after going over their resume and asking pertinent questions, the interviewer told the candidate that he had one final question. The candidate said "fine," and the interviewer asked, "OK, how much is one minus one?" Without hesitation, the candidate said "zero," and the interviewer said "OK—we'll be in touch." The process and the answer to the final question was the same with candidate number two. But in response to that final question, candidate number three paused thoughtfully and then replied, "how much would you like it to be?" "You're hired!" the interviewer immediately responded.

So, let me turn that around and ask you: "how much would *you* like this book to be, in other words, how much would you like to learn of what God *really* has to tell us about money?" Because His Word *does* have so much to teach us and because, unfortunately, so little of it is taught from the pulpit, I'm going to make a few guarantees. Here's the first one: I guarantee that if you allow this material to sink into your heart and mind, you *are* going to learn a lot. But, to borrow an analogy from the gym, while a personal trainer can show you how to use the machines and properly lift the weights, they can't do the training for you. If you are to get any benefit from those workouts, *you* must do the work—the heavy lifting—yourself. And not just one time or one week; no, to have long-lasting benefits, working out must become a lifestyle. For me, I go first thing in the morning, and I call it "job one." From there, I go to "job two," whatever that is that day.

CONCEPT FOR SUCCESS

There is a word—really a concept—which is relevant in the gym, or with weight loss, or stopping smoking, but especially with our handling of money, which is absolutely essential for success that I will use over and over. I know some of you will not like this word, but without putting this word into practice, your answer to the question "how much would you like this book to be?" will be just like the answers of the first two job candidates: "zero" as far as its lasting impact on your life. To motivate you into implementing this word, let me share a short but enlightening passage from the book of James, 1:23-24:

> *Anyone who listens to the word but does not do what it says is like someone who looks at his face in a mirror* [24] *and, after looking at himself, goes away and immediately forgets what he looks like.*

As crazy as this might seem, here's an analogy: Have you ever had trouble remembering the name of someone you just met? Believe me, I do—and it is so frustrating. Unless I say that person's name over and over, it will be gone. Over time, I've gotten better but I still have to work at it.

So, what's that nasty word? *Discipline.* It is going to be very easy to forget much of what you read in this book. In order to, as James says, "do what *it*—the Word—says," you are going to have to *work* at it—to have discipline.

For example: Some readers may be in moderate to severe financial distress right now. I will be blunt with you: it is going to take time and discipline to work your way out. Others might be feeling anxious about how little they have saved for their kid's education or for their planned retirement. Again, it is going to take time and discipline to reach those goals. In the gym, big muscles, six-pack abs, and a trim waist are not produced in a week or two. It's not rocket science how to achieve the desired results—it is mostly time, discipline, and sticking with the program. Such will be the case with getting your finances on what I term a "firm Biblical foundation." I will be sharing a lot of Scripture passages and will do my best as your personal financial trainer to help you see what they mean. Ultimately, it will be up to you to put what you learn into practice, to—as James says—"look in a mirror" occasionally. Hopefully you will really like what you see.

A Caution

There is also a caution I must share with you. Continuing with the gym analogy, if, for example, you work only your biceps and abs without working on the rest of your body, you're going to get some strange looking results. In fact, some guys will do just about anything for bigger biceps, even using illegal substances like steroids, and look how out of balance things can get:[1]

As appalling as those pictures might look, our finances can look just as bad unless we understand how the issue of managing money fits within the overall context of how God wants us to live life here on His earth—which is the whole purpose of His Word. Only then will you be able to understand the specific guidance it provides on how to increase your "money muscles" or obtain your "six pack ab" investment portfolio.

STAGE-SETTING QUESTIONS

To set the stage for understanding that overall context, let me first ask you to take a little time to ponder your answers to a few questions.

Question #1: *Why **are** you here on God's earth?* In essence, what is your purpose here? Is it to "go for the gusto?" and "he who has the most toys wins?"

As a preface to the second question, appreciate that God has placed you into one of *the* most materialistic societies that has ever existed. So:

Question #2: *How do you live within such an environment and not be affected by it?* For example: If you grew up in a middle-class home and neighborhood, how can you not expect to achieve at least that level of lifestyle—maybe even wanting to strive for more? As you think about that, recall what the apostle Paul tells us in Romans

12:2: "Do not conform to the pattern of this world." So ... should the pattern that you grew up with or the pattern that you see around you, be your guideline on how God wants *you* to live? Think about that.

Question #3: Let's get at that issue from another angle—and this one may sting a bit. *How do the concepts of ambition and providing for the family reconcile with living "Godly" lives?*

What I mean is this: Obviously, when you are ambitious about something, whether pursuing a better education, your dream job, starting a business, or even chasing a certain girl or guy, that takes up both mental and physical time. And in "providing for the family" with its corresponding expectations set by your background ... or job ... or current environment—however you want to define them— that can also consume huge amounts of mental and physical time. So, to focus this question a bit: In your pursuing and providing, is it possible to get so focused on these things that you lose sight of the real reason you are here (recall Question #1)?

Question #4. To set the context for this question, you probably have read the latter part of John 10:10 before. Using several translations, note what Jesus offers us:

> (NIV) *I have come that they may have **life**, and have it to the **full**.*
>
> (ESV, NASB) *I came that they may have life and have it **abundantly**.*
>
> (NKJV) *I have come that they may have life, and that they may have it **more** abundantly.*

Isn't that what we all want, the abundant life? Isn't that what all those "get rich" advertorials on TV promise? Isn't that what a book about money is supposed to help you achieve?

I think if we are honest with ourselves, especially here in the U.S., we hope that the abundant life means some of this: A big house (or two!), a fancy car, nice clothes, the best education, a high-paying job, expensive vacations, a comfortable retirement and on and on. Am I right? I mean, this stuff is all around us, all the time; how can our thinking and desires not be impacted, especially when our neighbors have it, our co-workers are striving for it, and many in the Church either have it or are trying diligently to manage their money so they can get it.

Moreover, there is a type of popular theology out there that teaches that God *wants* to bless you materially. In fact, their message is that if God is not blessing you materially, there is something wrong with your life, or you have insufficient faith because material wealth and financial success is His will for you. Can you recall the name of this gospel? Yes, the *Prosperity Gospel* or *Name it and Claim it!*

Admittedly, it is a seductive message—who wouldn't want to believe that?

What does the "Abundant Life" Mean?

So, as you ponder that, here's **Question #4** (again, take a moment to really reflect on your answer): *Is the abundant life Jesus talks about in John 10:10 equivalent to material prosperity?*

> It's an important question to address at the beginning of a book of how God views money, don't you think?

To set your mind at ease a bit, we will examine the propriety of material things in our lives but at this point all we are trying to do is to step back a bit and clarify the whole context of the Bible and why we are here. If the Prosperity-gospel folks—or you—want to use John 10:10 to justify that we are here so God can give us material blessings, there is one little problem with this interpretation. To see it clearly, we need to read more of John 10 to determine the context of Jesus' words. First, verse 1:

> *Very truly I tell you Pharisees ...*

As this is the first of many encounters we will have with the Pharisees, a little background will be helpful. The Pharisees were part of the religious leadership of Israel, experts in the Mosaic Law, and extreme practitioners of external righteousness—we would say today that they made sure to "cross every 't' and dot every 'i.'" More importantly, they taught that the only way to God was by following every part of the Law—even the large body of traditions passed down from one generation to the next. So, Jesus is talking to these very legalistic law abiders. But they obviously didn't understand what He was trying to tell them because in verse 7 it says:

> *Therefore Jesus said **again**, "Very truly I tell you ..."*

And what was He trying to tell them? Let's read verses 7-11 and part of verse 14 to clarify the context of verse 10:

> *Therefore Jesus said again, "Very truly I tell you, I am the gate for the sheep. ⁸ All who have come before me are thieves and robbers, but the sheep have not listened to them. ⁹ I am the gate; whoever enters through me will be saved. They will come in and go out, and find pasture. ¹⁰ The thief comes only to steal and kill and destroy;* [here's our key verse:] *I have come that*

> *they may have life, and have it to the full. ¹¹ "I am the good shepherd. The good shepherd lays down his life for the sheep … ¹⁴ I know my sheep and my sheep know me …"*

Look at the passage carefully—can you see how verse 10 has been misinterpreted? Note that it has nothing to do with financial blessings or material prosperity—the context is dealing with *salvation*. In contrast to the thief whose only goal is to *steal* and *kill* and *destroy* the sheep—in essence, to keep you and me from knowing Jesus— He came to provide the way to be saved with its attendant ability to experience life "to the full," or literally … as He planned from the beginning! Can you see that? In fact, the whole sense of John 10 is to convey to the Jews and others listening how Jesus came and offered Himself so that we *could* obtain the life and fellowship with Him that was intended—the life lost through man's fall and the resulting gross distortion of relating to God presented by the Jewish teachers.

CAN THE ABUNDANT LIFE INCLUDE MATERIAL BLESSINGS?

Because John 10:10 has been so misinterpreted, here's what you might be thinking: "Well, can the phrase 'to the full' *include* material blessings?" Let me respond to that in two ways. First, if our lives are to be lives of leisure and material prosperity, don't you think that would have been exhibited and extolled by the pillars of our faith, the apostles, and Jesus Himself? Yet most of these died penniless martyrs' deaths. None preached or lived anything close to a "prosperity-type" gospel.

Second, listen to the alarming way Jesus Himself responds in Luke 12:15—especially the latter part of the verse—to someone in the crowd who has asked Him to tell his brother to split an inheritance with him:

> *Then he [Jesus] said to them, "Watch out! Be on your guard against all kinds of greed;* **life does not consist in an abundance of possessions.***"*

How much simpler could Jesus say it? "Watch out! Be on your guard!" Why? As the New Living Translation finishes the verse, "life is not measured by how much you own."

This is About Much More than Money!

Let's take a brief pause here and see where we are. As should be evident, this is not a book just about money. It is much more than that, as it is really about how God wants us to *live*. God has placed us here on His earth to be the light shining from the mountaintop. Whether you work as a dishwasher or as the CEO of some huge, multi-national company, all that will matter at the end of your life are two things. First, did you trust Jesus to be your Lord and Savior? Second, how did you use your life to impact others? Your title, your income, the size of your house, and on and on will be absolutely meaningless to God.

Yes, He expects us to work to provide for ourselves and our families. And yes, you may have a passion to do a certain type of work or start a certain type of business. But our driving ambition and motivation in life should be to use that work and passion to magnify *Him* from the particular mountaintop we are on. In other words, the kind of work we do is simply a tool in the process of magnifying Him, not an end in and of itself.

Finally, the overriding context of God's Word—and the "abundant life" He promises—is living and fulfilling the particular life God created you for. Identify *that* life and you will experience purpose, satisfaction, and contentment that nothing else can provide. If it is a place with fewer financial rewards, like a missionary in some far-off land, God will still take care of you. At the other extreme, it may be to use your skills and talents to start and grow a business that becomes wildly successful. Your business might end up not only providing a valuable service or product and employing hundreds or even thousands, but also providing a platform for you to share your faith with multitudes. It might even generate massive resources to help fund the operation of His church around the world.

The point is your goal in life, your primary ambition, should be to pursue His *will*, not financial wealth. Focusing solely on amassing wealth will result in your life mirroring our odd looking body builder:

A Warning

There is, however, an even worse potential outcome when the desire for wealth and things take precedence in one's life. Going back to Luke 12, Jesus follows up His "watch out!" warning with a knife-to-the-heart parable about a rich man who built more barns to store his abundance of goods so he could take life easy, eat, drink, and be merry. What does God say to him?

> *"You fool! This very night your life will be demanded from you. Then who will get what you have prepared for yourself?' "This is how it will be with whoever stores up things for themselves but is not rich toward God."*
> (Luke 12:20-21)

Have you ever been called a "fool" by someone? I have and it stings. Maybe the name-caller was right, maybe not. But how about being called a fool by the omniscient Creator of the universe? Here's a man who, likely through his own ingenuity and hard work, had set himself up for the rest of his life, without a financial care in the world—it kind of sounds like today's concept of retirement. What he didn't realize—and what made all of his efforts so foolish—was that all of that wealth could do absolutely nothing to protect his life … his soul.

In fact, in Matthew 16:26, Jesus lays it out as clearly as He can when He warned His disciples—and us today:

> *What good will it be for someone to gain the **whole world**, yet forfeit their soul? Or what can **anyone** give in **exchange** for their soul?*

Paraphrased bluntly, forgetting God and chasing after money and possessions can literally be deadly—for all eternity. That is why it is so critical to understand how the topic of money fits within the overall context of His Word.

Money in the Context of God's Word

And in simple terms, what is that context in God's Word? Very simply,

> Money is only a tool and a test, nothing more. Not a goal, not a measuring stick of success—but simply a tool and a test in the Christian life.

Alternatively, God's Word makes it crystal-clear that:

> Money will be either a tool or a god in your life; how you acquire it and how you handle it will be a clear reflection of which it is.

There is absolutely nothing inherently evil about money; in fact, we need it as a convenient medium of exchange. But there is something about it—or rather about us, our sin nature—that makes us want to crave it, to hoard it, to accumulate it, and to do crazy things to get more of it (like fighting over inheritances, money you never even earned yourself). God's Word speaks to each of these. In fact, King Solomon, the wisest person ever created, lays out in no uncertain terms the consequences of a life spent chasing after money. This is one of the all-time great verses to memorize, to put on your refrigerator, on your computer monitor, the dashboard of your car, maybe even your desk at work, but most of all, to etch on the walls of your heart:

> Ecclesiastes 5:10: *Whoever loves money **never** has enough; whoever loves wealth is **never** satisfied with their income. This too is meaningless.*

Let me rephrase what King Solomon is saying: How much money is enough? Just a little bit more! To see the truth of this statement we need only look at the lives of many multi-millionaires who continue striving endlessly to get more and more.

A Guiding Quote

As one final proof of the importance of context as far as understanding how God wants us to view money, let me share a quote from one of the most respected preachers in modern history, so pay close attention. This preacher stated:

> If a person gets their attitude toward money straight, it will help straighten out almost *every other area in their life.*[2]

Did you follow that? Our view of money is that important—get it wrong and our lives can get really messed up. And who said this? The late Billy Graham.

Importance of Money in God's Word

So, hopefully understanding the importance of context, let's get started on the road of getting our attitudes toward money straight. To begin, let me first share some Biblical "statistics" to provide an overview of just how much guidance *is* in God's Word. You don't need to remember any of the detail—just try to take away the big picture that God does have a lot to say to us about money and financial matters.

- There are about 32,000 verses in the entire Bible—think about all the important topics it covers: faith, prayer, sin, the end times, the history of Israel, the establishment of the early church, and on and on. Yet the number of verses dealing with money and financial issues far exceeds any of these. As just one example, I'm sure most readers would agree that prayer and faith are extremely important in their lives. Yet, there are over *four times* as many verses dealing with financial issues than prayer and faith combined.

- In total, about 2,200 verses—or seven percent of God's Word—deal with some aspect of wealth and finances—it is that important.
- Maybe more astounding, few realize that even in Jesus' teachings, the Biblical view of money was front and center:
    - Over seventy percent of His thirty major parables—two out of every three—utilize financial concepts to convey the point.
    - The whole point of twenty-five percent of them—or one in every four—*is* how to properly view or use money.

Again, no other topic even ... comes ... close. And sadly, so little of God's wisdom on this all-important topic is taught from the pulpit. In fact, for many people, the mere mention of money from the pulpit sends them scurrying towards the exits. No wonder we are in such a mess financially, both personally and corporately.

That is precisely why it has long been my passion to teach God's people what His Word says about how to correctly view and use this thing the Bible calls *mammon*. To paraphrase Billy Graham's words, view money right and you'll *live* right. Isn't that what we all want?

Foundational Concepts

Let me finish this introductory chapter with a broad overview of two absolutely foundational concepts which set the stage for the rest of what God's Word has to say about money and finances. Likely these are concepts you have read or heard before but never really thought much about. I can't emphasize strongly enough how critically important it is for you to not just nod your head but to really listen to and internalize these two concepts. If you do, here's my second guarantee: I guarantee that they will impact not only your views towards wealth and money but virtually *every other facet of your life*—they are that life-changing.

Concept #1

For this concept we'll look at two passages, one from the Old Testament and one from the New. As we go through them, try to conceptualize in your own mind the key thought. Look first at Psalm 24:1 where King David writes:

> *The earth is the Lord's and everything in it, the world, and all who live in it.*

What do you suppose the phrase "everything in it" means? Just to be sure, I did an exhaustive investigation to prove to myself that I had "everything" right and do you know what I found? It means ... everything! Or literally, "all it contains," which is the wording used in the NASB. King David even clarifies it for us, as the latter part says, "the world and what? *All ... who ... live ... in ... it.*" So "everything" even includes you and me.

For further confirmation, let's look at the New Testament passage—one of my favorites—Colossians 1:15-17. As you read it, notice how many "alls" there are:

> *The Son* [referring to Jesus] *is the image of the invisible God, the firstborn over* [#1] *all creation.* [16] *For in Him* [#2] *all things were created: things in heaven and on earth, visible and invisible, whether thrones or powers or rulers or authorities;* [#3] *all things have been created through Him and for Him.* [17] *He is before* [#4] *all things, and in Him* [#5] *all things hold* [or endure] *together.*

This is an absolutely amazing passage and is one of those "do you really believe God when He says" types of passages. It states that not only is:

> Jesus the visible *image* of God,

but that:

> He created what? *All* things—and Paul even lists a few of them.

> And, He holds them all together.

Wooden Blocks Illustration

Visualize, if you will, some wooden blocks with letters on them, like toddlers play with. While man may have fashioned the raw materials into the blocks, this passage says that not only did Christ create all the raw materials that went into making them, but He also holds all things together—visualize holding together five of the blocks spelling "w-o-r-l-d." If He doesn't continue holding them together, down to the floor they fall. In fact, during the end times this is exactly what happens as Satan is allowed to run amok, and unless Christ returns, the world will literally fall apart and destroy itself.

Recall that I encouraged you to conceptualize the critical first foundational issue yourself, as that makes it easier to internalize and remember it. It can be expressed in just four words and I'll even give you the first three:

> He owns it *what*? He owns it ... *all*.

He owns it all because He created it all—it's as simple as that. His Word even goes into the details. Take a short break and look at Psalm 50:10-12 and Haggai 2:8.

So, He ... owns ... it ... *all – everything:* Your house, your car, your clothes, your job, your 401-k, even your spouse and kids.

QUESTION TO THINK ABOUT

We'll pause here to ponder what will become a recurring question so think carefully about your answer: Do you believe, *really believe*, that He owns it all? Moreover, that as a consequence, He may choose—in His wisdom of what is best for you—to take it away, possibly to take it *all* away as He did with Job? Recall, God even took away Job's family members.

There is a beautiful worship song by Matt Redman, titled "Blessed Be Your Name," which captures this same thought when he sings:

> *You give and take away, you give and take away;*
>
> *My heart will choose to say Lord, blessed be Your name.*

He gives because He owns it all and He takes away because He owns it all—it's as simple as that. So ... *do you really believe this?* Will you be able to echo Job's words in the latter part of Job 2:10 when he responds to his wife, "shall we accept good from God and not trouble" when ... your house burns down ... or you lose it to foreclosure ... or you lose your job ... your 401k ... or your business? As tragic as any of these may be, God's Word clearly tells us that *it's not your stuff.* All of it ultimately belongs to Him.

This fundamental reality that God owns absolutely everything is part of that overall context of God's Word that is so important to understand before we look at its guidance on a specific hot-button topic like money. The more we accept and internalize into our daily lives the plain and simple fact that He really does own everything, the more it has to impact how we view money and "stuff" here on earth. Said another way, as we grow to know and experience His unending love and provision, we will also grow in our trust that He will take care of us—*no matter what*. Our trust and security will not be in money and things—which are so-o-o temporary—but instead in the One who provides us with those things and a life that lasts forever.

Do you remember radio personality Paul Harvey? He often uttered the classic line, "and now, the rest of the story." Note the astonishing thing that happened to Job after all of his trials. In the very last chapter, it says this in Job 42:10 and 12:

> *¹⁰After Job had prayed for his friends, the LORD restored his fortunes and gave him* [how much?] **twice** *as much as he had before … ¹²The Lord blessed the latter part of Job's life more than the first part …*

I'll leave it to you to read all the blessings listed in Job 42—even material ones—that God bestowed on Job.

Yes, the Lord does bless with material things—but we are never to forget that it is all *His* stuff.

Before moving on to foundational concept #2, I have to admit that getting our arms around the practical implications of that first concept can be a little difficult: Yes, He owns it all. But realistically, we are the ones that make all the decisions in choosing what to buy; we are the ones who take care of those things; and we are the ones who work and slave to pay for those things. So, it's very easy to view those things as "ours"—wouldn't you agree? How many times have you said, "*I* bought this," or "*we* own our home" or "I have finally paid off *my* car?"

Concept #2

If you really believe and live by this next concept, it will make a huge difference in your life—it just has to. Not only will it help you maintain the right attitude toward money and things, it will change what you *do* with the money and things you do have, and dramatically impact how you view life here on God's earth. In some senses, this second concept will be the ultimate "tool and test" of what you do with your money.

What is foundational concept #2? It sounds so simple and yet, as you'll learn, is really quite profound:

> We are only tenants and sojourners here on His earth ... just passing through.

We'll look at a couple of passages—one from the Old Testament and one from the New—for a crystal-clear picture of this concept. In a beautiful Old Testament passage reiterating God's ownership of everything, King David prays publicly to God in 1 Chronicles 29:11-15. We'll only read part of it but I encourage you to read all of it later:

> *"Yours, Lord, is the greatness and the power and the glory and the majesty and the splendor, for everything in heaven and earth is yours ...* [12]*Wealth and honor come from You; You are ruler of all things ...* [14]*But who am I and who are my people that we should be able to give as generously as this* [per verses 1-8, the offerings to build the temple]*? Everything comes from You, and we have given you only what comes from your hand.* [15] *We are foreigners and strangers in your sight, as were all our ancestors ..."*

Note that the latter part of verses 11 and 14 confirm our first foundational concept, that He owns everything. But the main issue in this passage is summarized in the last verse, verse 15. What does King David say is our true status in His creation?

Some Important Terms

The last verse calls the Hebrews "foreigners" and "strangers." The previous iteration of the NIV used "sojourners" and "tenants," and various translations use combinations of these four English words to convey the concept. To clearly explain what's being said here, I'll focus on the words "tenants" and "sojourners."

A "tenant" is one who occupies the property of another. So, as a tenant, you don't own the place. As a result, you also likely do not make any major improvements because "what's the point?" No new carpeting, no yard makeovers, no major remodeling—you just live there. Even better, if something does need to be repaired, that's the landlord's problem, not yours! And should you need or desire to move, if your lease period is over or you don't have a lease, all you have to do is give 30-days' notice. Yes, there are drawbacks to renting but the point here is that it is a pretty simple—and likely less expensive—way to live. Moreover—and remember this thought—there is less focus or concern about housing issues because … it is just a place to live.

Reinforcing this transient nature of a tenant is the word "sojourners." This term refers to "one who is a temporary resident and is just passing through." Or as the Living Bible puts it: "… we are here but for a moment." Combining these terms, King David was acknowledging that he and his people were simply temporary residents with no place to really call "home."

Interesting Twist in King David's Prayer

What's the big deal, you might be thinking? There is a fascinating twist to King David's statement. It is so easy to miss yet is critical to understanding *our* position and status here on earth.

When King David prayed these words, the people were *in* the land that God had promised to give them, His chosen people, *forever*. In essence, it *was* a place they could call home and fix up—in fact, they even built an elaborate temple there, with estimates in today's dollars of it costing billions.[3] So, why would King David view his people, now living in their Godly inheritance, as temporary residents?

Rope Illustration

To answer that, let me introduce another illustration from one of my former pastors. Visualize, if you will, a white rope that is miles and miles long, virtually unending. At the front end, there is an inch or so of red tape. That inch of the rope represents the time we spend here on earth and compared to the essentially unending length of the rope, it's unbelievably short, isn't it? Yet we fret and worry and labor over the dumbest things that occur during that red portion. They may seem important at the time, but when viewed from eternity's perspective, many of the things we do or things we strive to acquire, *just don't matter*. All that really matters are things that carry over to the white part of the rope.

In fact, Jesus deals with this very issue in Matthew 6:19-20, a passage you have likely read before:

> *"Do not store up for yourselves treasures on earth, where moths and vermin destroy, and where thieves break in and steal* [that's the red part of the rope].
> [20] *But store up for yourselves treasures in heaven* [the

white part], *where moths and vermin do not destroy, and where thieves do not break in and steal."*

To use an admittedly weak analogy—maybe one you have experienced—if you move to a town where you are fairly certain that you will remain for only a year or two, buying a house is almost out of the question—too many costs involved and too risky in being able to resell it. So, what do you do? You find a basic but satisfactory place to rent, and that's okay because you know that you are there only temporarily. You may even buy used furniture or go without a lot of things. Moreover, you save your resources for something more permanent in the future.

Can you see the application? When you have a lot of "stuff" or "treasure" during the red part of the rope, especially if it is really nice stuff, the more time and money you have to spend caring for and trying to protect it.

Be honest: If you have a nice house, it takes time, doesn't it? Cleaning, maintaining the yard, the taxes, keeping up with those mythical Jones. What about a nice new car? Just visit southern California some time to see what kind of money people lavish on their cars! This is the world and environment we live in and it is so easy to become part of it.

WHERE'S YOUR HEART?

But knowing us so well, Jesus says something else pretty heavy in Matthew 6. If you allow yourself to really think about it, it should bring tears to your eyes. Verse 21 is a white-hot laser beam that cuts to the very core of our being:

> *For where your treasure is, there your **heart** will be also.*

As human beings, our hearts are going to be somewhere. This verse is saying very clearly that the more stuff we have here, on the red part of the rope, the more our hearts will care about it. More importantly, as a consequence, the less our hearts will care about eternal things—and as believers, that should break our hearts. It's not that money and stuff are wrong in and of themselves; it's just that they can so easily capture our hearts. And the more anything captures our hearts, the less time there is for it to focus on other, potentially more important things that impact the white part of the rope.

Apostle Paul's Illustration

Paul deals with the practicalities of this reality when he contrasts being married vs. being single in 1 Corinthians 7:32-35:

> *I would like you to be free from concern. An unmarried man is concerned with the Lord's affairs—how he may please the Lord. But a married man is concerned about the affairs of this world—how he can please his wife—* ^{34} *and his interests are divided.* [A similar admonition for the women follows.]

So, Paul's point here is what? That marriage is a sin! Of course not! Whether married or not, the simpler and less cluttered and complicated our lives during the red part of the rope, the more we are able to respond to the Lord's leading—to make a real impact for the white part. Maybe you are feeling the urge to go to seminary or go on a missions trip or move where the Lord is leading you, or whatever. If you are living your life as a tenant, a sojourner, you can give your 30-days' notice, sell what little you have and be on your way. But if you have a house to sell, a nice car with many payments remaining, too much stuff to get rid of, and a high-paying job that pays for all of it—that little voice from God can so easily get lost in all the "concerns" of living everyday life. Again, I am not saying that any of these types of things are wrong, but as the apostle Paul advises in the next verse:

> *[35] I am saying this for your own good, not to restrict you, but so that you may live in a right way in undivided devotion to the Lord.*

And the simpler your life, the easier it is to live that right way.

To reinforce this concept of viewing your life as just being a tenant or sojourner, let's look at the second passage I alluded to earlier. You might be wondering, "won't this type of outlook mean that I may be 'missing out' on all the good stuff here?" Look at Hebrews 11:13-16, from the great chapter on faith. Speaking of some of these individuals of great faith, it tells us:

> *All these people were still living by faith when they died. They did not receive the things promised; they only saw them and welcomed them from a distance, admitting that they were* [here's the New Testament translation of our two terms] *foreigners and strangers on earth. [14] People who say such things show that they are looking for a country of their own. [15] If they had been thinking of the country they had left, they would have had opportunity to return. [16] Instead, they were longing for a better country—a heavenly one. Therefore God is not ashamed to be called their God, for he has prepared a city for them.*

Just so it's clear, many of these folks were quite rich: Noah, Abraham, Isaac, Jacob, etc. But what were they known for? People of great *faith*, living as foreigners and strangers here and … longing for a better place. That better place will be far beyond what our minds can ever imagine, be it Hearst Castle, the Palace of Versailles, or whatever. In fact, in many versions, John 14:2 says that there are many mansions waiting for us. So will it be compared to everything else here. It will be a Disney World we can't even visualize! And this city will be permanent—we will live there *forever*. No longer will we be just tenants, sojourners, foreigners or strangers, but we will live there for all eternity as sons and daughters of the King. The more we can get our hearts and minds around that future, which is guaranteed to us as believers by God Himself, the less we will worry and fret about what we have or don't have during the brief little red period on the rope.

So, concept #2—we truly are only tenants and sojourners here, just "passing through"—when properly understood and believed, has to have an immense impact on how we live our lives here. Due to our transient status, accumulating a lot of stuff is pretty pointless because it takes so much time and energy and money to care for it, to pay for it, to protect it. Moreover, in the end, what's left of it all stays here, or as Ecclesiastes 5:15 candidly puts it: "… as everyone comes, so they depart. **They take nothing from their toil that they can carry in their hands**." What really matters is what we do with it during our brief time here to "lay up treasure in heaven."

SUMMARY

God's Word still has much to share on the specific Biblical guidance for managing our finances, but that guidance is all motivated by the implications of these two foundational concepts:

1. God really *does* own it all … everything;
2. We *are* only tenants and sojourners here on His earth, just passing through.

To more fully ingrain these concepts into your heart and mind, let me ask you to answer three questions and, just to make your answers really clear, say them out loud:

> Question #1: How much of your stuff does God own? (Say it!) He owns it *all*!
>
> Question #2: What's your true status here on earth? (Say it, louder!) Tenant and sojourner!
>
> Question #3: Out of all the stuff you have right now, or ever will have, how much of it belongs to you? (Say it even louder!) None of it!

For some, that was *really* hard to do, wasn't it? But if you truly want to live by what God's Word teaches about money, you have just uttered the absolute *foundational* truths that are to guide our lives here. Billy Graham really did capture the essence of these truths in the quote that we read earlier:

> If a person gets their *attitude* toward money straight, it will help straighten out almost *every other area in their life*.

Before we start digging into the nitty-gritty of God's Word regarding financial issues, it is quite obvious that some have more money and "stuff"—maybe even a lot more. But as we'll learn, not only are there increased stewardship responsibilities with more money and stuff, those responsibilities increase exponentially the more we have. Furthermore, it becomes more difficult to handle those things Biblically, potentially leading us away from the very One who gave them to us in the first place.

Please don't move on to Chapter 2 yet. Take a brief pause and consider praying the following prayer:

> *Father God (or Papa or Dad, whatever you'd like): I love you so much and desire to serve you with everything I have—my time, my talents, even my money. Yet sometimes I get so caught up in trying to live life like everyone around me that I forget why I am even here—to honor You. I confess that I have often viewed all of what I have as mine. Moreover, I have spent so much of my precious time trying to build a safe and secure home here, forgetting that my real home is ultimately and eternally with You—a home that is far beyond what I can ever imagine here.*
>
> *Lord God, I know that this is a continual process, but here and now I acknowledge that everything I possess— my home, cars, investments, businesses, everything— belongs to You. Furthermore, I acknowledge that You have entrusted all of it to me as a tool and a test of using it for Your glory, not mine. In Your wisdom of what is best for me, You may choose to take some or all of it away ... or you may entrust me with more. Either way, I am to continue trusting You and using what I have to honor You. May I have a growing sense from You that my time here is temporary and that how I conduct my affairs here—how I lay up treasure in Heaven—will have eternal consequences. Amen*

MANAGING MAMMON

Planning is bringing the future into the present so that you can do something about it *now* – Alan Lakein

A goal without a plan is just a wish – Antoine de Saint-Exupery

Since my money is God's money, every spending decision I make is a spiritual decision - John Hagee

As we begin the process of digging into the specifics of what God's Word tells us about managing money and stuff, let me start by sharing an absolutely distressing statistic. Based on a recent survey by the world-wide employment site CareerBuilder.com,[4] seventy-eight percent—or *three out of every four people* in the U.S.—live paycheck to paycheck: no excess, no savings, no reserve for emergencies, just trying to make it to the next paycheck. In fact, according to Dave Ramsey in one of his books, the average family does not even have $1,000 in the bank. Maybe you have experienced the terrible stress that causes. Or maybe you are part of the twenty-two percent that have an excess yet at the end of the year, you look back and wonder where it all went.

Three Questions

So, regardless of which group you are in, consider your answer to three questions:

1. Irrespective of your current income, would you like to learn how to make it stretch further than you ever imagined possible?
2. Would you like to learn how to easily become debt-free—except for your mortgage—within a year or two?

And most importantly:

3. Would you like to be able to know—really know—that you *are* managing your (His!) resources not only efficiently, but in ways which also please and honor Him and, as a result, worry less about money?

By the end of this chapter you are going to have good, solid methods to do exactly that. To start us on this journey, recall that at the end of the last chapter, I reminded you of Billy Graham's statement—do you remember it?

> If a person gets their [what?] *attitude* toward money straight, it will help [what?] *straighten out almost every other area in their life.*

We've already seen that an essential part of getting our attitude straight is acknowledging sincerely and whole-heartedly that He really does own it all and that we are only tenants or sojourners here on His earth. What we are going to do now is get really practical and see how God wants us to implement those concepts on a daily basis, because that is where we live life every day, and where we'll see if money is a tool or a god in our lives.

Key Concept for Chapter

To pique your interest, let me share with you the end point—the overriding concept of this chapter—and it is a heavy one. The end point is captured in the last phrase in one of Jesus' parables in Luke 12. (Although this parable also deals with our managerial role here, there is an even more detailed parable dealing with that process which we will focus on in a bit so all we'll do here is read the relevant phrase.) This is the second parable in a section in the English Standard Version—one of the newer translations—appropriately titled "You must be ready."

In this parable, Jesus talks about a master who puts his manager in charge of feeding the servants before he goes away. If, upon his return, the manager is doing so, he will be put in charge of all the master's possessions. But, if that manager starts to believe that the master may not return and begins beating the servants, then when the master does return, that manager will be punished very severely, as you'll see if you read the entire parable.

But here's the verse which captures the essence and end point of this chapter. Look at the latter part of Luke 12:48:

From everyone who has been given much,

much will be demanded;

and from the one who has been entrusted with much,

much more will be asked.

Let these words sink in for a moment. You know which phrase scares me the most? The last one where Jesus says that of those who have been entrusted with much, "much more will be asked." Why is this scary? Because Jesus is referring not only to His first century audience but also to me, to you, to virtually everyone in the U.S., regardless of how much—or little—you have or earn. Just by living here, we have so much more than most of the world. Let me share some startling statistics—and just so you know, all of the data have been adjusted for what's called "purchasing power parity," which means we'll be comparing apples to apples.[5] Don't feel like you have to remember the details—just get the big picture:

- The median income per year in the U.S.—where half the population make more and half make less—is about $59,000[6]. That's a bit more than $160 per day to live on and is among the highest in the world.
- About sixty-five percent, or nearly two-thirds of all humanity—4.8 billion people or two out of every three people on earth—lives on $10 per day or less[7]—$10 bucks—although the numbers are improving somewhat due to increasing income levels in China. Here's what it looks like graphically:[8]

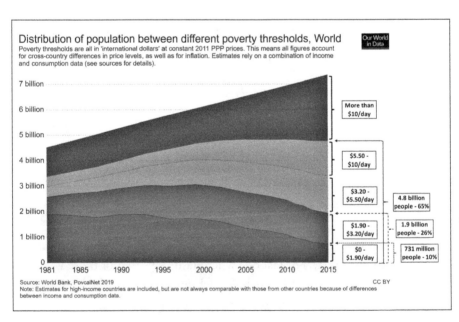

Looking at the graph, note:

- Twenty-six percent of all humanity—*almost two billion people*—live on $3.20 or less per day, the poverty level set by the World Bank. That's less than you might easily spend at Starbucks for a cup of coffee.
- Ten percent of all humanity—731 million, or about two and a half times the population in the U.S.—live on $1.90 or less per day, the extreme poverty level. That's about what a Redbox DVD rental costs.
- Let me make this a bit more shocking. Focusing on all the people making $10 per day or less, that means the average person in that group makes about $5 per day (midpoint between $0 and $10). What's $160 divided by $5? Thirty-two. So, compared to almost two-thirds of God's people on earth, the average person in the U.S.—and likely reading this book—makes over *thirty times more*: not two times or five times or ten times but *thirty times more*. Just think about that a bit.
- Let's take this one startling step further. The midpoint of the group making $3.20 per day or less is $1.60. $160 divided by $1.60 is 100. So, the average person in the U.S. makes *100 times more* than one-fourth of all the people on God's earth. And you can't wiggle out of this comparison because remember, all these numbers have been adjusted so that we *are* comparing apples to apples.
- Maybe one last way to look at this data. Using the $5 per day average for two-thirds of the world's population, that's $1,825 in earnings per year—about what the average person in the U.S. makes in just twelve days. So, while you are relaxing somewhere exotic during your annual vacation, your two-week vacation pay is almost equivalent to what two-thirds of the world makes in an entire year.

You Are ...

So, like it or not—and regardless of how you feel about your present financial position—you are *R-I-C-H*. On average, thirty times richer than two-thirds of the people on earth. You might not feel rich but that's likely because you are comparing yourself to your neighbor or your boss or Warren Buffett. But you know what? It's likely that you are not wondering where your next meal is coming from, that you don't have to walk miles simply to obtain drinking water, that you won't go to sleep wondering if you will live through the night. Just by God choosing for you to live in the U.S., you already have so much more than most of the world.

Not only are we rich income-wise, we are rich opportunity-wise: education, shopping, traveling, eating out, you name it. Compared to most of the world, we have so much: nice cars, big houses, closets full of clothes, full refrigerators, water at the twist of a knob—and yet, we want more and more stuff. And you know what's crazy? We have so much stuff, some of us have to rent self-storage units because it won't all fit in our houses! That sure sounds eerily similar to the rich fool in this same chapter of Luke who had to build bigger barns saying, "there I will store all my grain and my goods," doesn't it?

But what does Jesus say? "... from the one who has been entrusted with much, much more will be asked." That sounds pretty scary, doesn't it? It's an application of the "tool and a test" axiom, it's Billy Graham's "get your attitude toward money straight" quote, and it's the reason we need to learn how to properly view and manage mammon.

Our Role

Note that I have already used the word "manage" several times. That's because the Greek word used in the Luke 12 parable to describe the servant's role—*our* role—is the exact same word that will be used in the more detailed parable that we will look at in a moment. That word is *oikonómos* (*oy-kon-om'-os*). It is used in the very first verse of the parable where Jesus asks:

> Luke 12:42: *"Who then is the faithful and wise oikonómos ...?"*

In some versions, the word is translated "steward" rather than "manager." Both words capture the essence of our role here: We are simply managers or stewards of all that God allows to pass through our hands. Similar to the "tenant" concept in Chapter 1, we own nothing here.

But, as *oikonómos*, we *are* responsible for what we *do* with our money and stuff because we have been entrusted with it by the Creator of the universe. The Greek word used literally means "to deposit" or "entrust" in a legal sense of leaving a valuable object in another's keeping, with strict penalties for embezzlement or misuse. Recall again Jesus' admonition in Luke 12:48 about being entrusted with more—read it from several versions:

> (NIV) ... *much **more** will be asked.*

> (NASB) ... *of him they will ask **all the more**.*

> (NRSV) ... *even **more** will be demanded.*

And *that* is the increased responsibility shouldered by those entrusted with more money and stuff mentioned at the end of Chapter 1. Put simply:

> More money and stuff means more expectations

Remember: It's not me saying this but Jesus Himself. While you may at times, feel overwhelmed by what it costs to live here in the U.S., let me be a little blunt with you: Yes, houses can be really expensive in some parts of the U.S.; and yes, private schools or universities for your kids are expensive; and yes, your job might require you to outwardly live a certain lifestyle, but listen carefully—these are all *choices*. Do you know that Warren Buffet still lives in the same house in Omaha he bought in 1958 for $31,500? And that he drives a Cadillac he bought almost a decade ago? Sure, a job with Apple or Google sounds glamourous but with the high housing costs surrounding their headquarters, are you willing to live with the potential of a lifetime of both spouses having to work simply to make the house payments? Just so you know, the median home value in Apple's home town of Cupertino, California is about $2.2 *million*. And of course, with a job like that, you can't drive a clunker. Some choose to live far away from work to find affordable housing but then pay the price in one- to two-hour commutes each way. Is that worth it? I can't answer that question for you. What I am simply saying is that these are all ... choices.

Is Having "Stuff" OK?

Before continuing, let me reinforce something from Chapter 1. There is nothing inherently sinful about having stuff like cars or boats or houses or whatever. But there's a deeper issue which applies even to those who truly *can* afford lots of stuff: How often do we look "horizontally"—in essence, at the environment around us—to justify our lifestyle rather than "vertically," and His desires for us? And even if we can "afford" our stuff, does that automatically mean having it is His will for us? As an extreme example, maybe you can "afford" to go to Las Vegas and lose $10,000—does that mean you should? New cars, new houses—or new whatevers—are nice, but look at what Jesus says one more time:

> ... *from the one who has been **entrusted** with much, **much more** will be asked.*

You may not have given the "stewardship" concept much serious thought before but this concept is front and center in how He wants us to live here. To see it in more detail, let's look at the other parable I alluded to earlier.

THE CONCEPT OF TRUST ... AND MONEY

This parable is in Luke 16:1-15. On the surface, it sounds crazy, yet when you see Jesus' point, His message hits to the very heart of why we are here. Look first at Luke 16:1-2:

> *Jesus told his disciples: "There was a rich man whose manager—oikonómos—was accused of wasting his possessions. ²So he called him in and asked him, 'What is this I hear about you? Give an account of your management because you cannot be manager— oikonómos—any longer.'"*

In essence, the rich man fired his manager, and the rest of the parable talks about what this fired *oikonómos* did to "grease the wheels" of finding a new job. Unbelievably, he colluded with the master's creditors and wrote off twenty to fifty percent of the receivables, wasting even more of the rich man's resources!

Now, here's where the parable gets crazy. Because of the manager's ingenuity, the master, who has been ripped off twice by this guy, actually praises his inventiveness! Has the master lost his marbles? Let's get to the heart of Jesus' message in this parable—and it's really pretty simple but also pretty profound.

As it says in verse 2, managers *will be* asked to give an account of their management and in verses 10-12, Jesus tells us *why* we will be evaluated—and note that a very important word appears five times:

> *Whoever can be **trusted** with very little can also be **trusted** with much, and whoever is dishonest with very little will also be dishonest with much. [11]So if you have not been **trustworthy** in handling worldly wealth, who will **trust** you with true riches? [12]And if you have not been **trustworthy** with someone else's property, who will give you property of your own?*

This is actually part of the context of God's Word discussed in Chapter 1. Our brief time here on God's earth—the red part of the rope—is just a test, a time of training; the real deal comes in eternity. That's when we get to handle some really valuable stuff. According to God's Word, however, it all depends on how we have managed what He has entrusted to us here and now: If we are wasteful here, we will be wasteful there; if we have exhibited excellent management skills here, He knows that we will continue to do so in the future to come. In simple terms, trust begets more trust. In the workplace, for example, when your employer finds you more and more trustworthy and capable, up the ladder you go.

In the specific area of finances, however, Jesus puts it even more bluntly. Note what He says next in verse 13—you have probably read or heard this before:

> *"No servant **can** serve two masters. Either he will hate the one and love the other, or he will be devoted to the one and despise the other. **You cannot serve both God and Money.**"*

This is a hard verse to accept, isn't it? Jesus is laying out a stark contrast here and I don't think we really want to believe this. We want to think that we *can* handle money impassively and love God. Moreover, it is so easy for us to compare ourselves to others and say, "well, at least I'm not chasing the dollar as much as that person!"

But Jesus says, it is one or the other—you either love Me or you love Money. No sliding scale, no gray areas, just one or the other.

AN EXAMPLE OF WEALTH VS. GOD

As an extreme but very convicting example, you may remember the story of the rich young ruler, in Mark 10:17-31,[9] who fell on his knees and asked Jesus what he needed to do to inherit eternal life. Jesus actually "toys" with the man a bit as He responds that he should keep the commandments: don't murder, don't commit adultery, don't steal, honor your father and mother, etc. The man doesn't really catch on to Jesus' implied test of the impossibility of keeping *all* the commandments *all* the time because he responds, "all these I have kept since I was a boy." I just love what Mark writes next: *"Jesus looked at him and loved him."* Why? Here's a man who earnestly wants to know how to have assurance of eternal life and yet doesn't have the faintest idea that he is going about it all wrong. Note how Jesus responds to him. He doesn't correct the man, He simply gives him another "to do" in verse 21:

> *"One thing you lack,"* he [Jesus] *said. "Go, sell everything you have and give to the poor, and you will have treasure in heaven. Then come, follow me."*

There it is, in black and white. Sell it all—the house, the car, the boat, everything—and follow Me. Now, whether Jesus was asking the man to actually go and sell everything or just looking for the willingness to do so, what was the man's response? Verse 22:

> *At this the man's face fell. He went away sad* [literally grieved to the point of distress], *because **he had great wealth**.*

And standing before the Creator of the universe, before the very One who entrusted all that wealth to the rich young ruler in the first place, what was this man's choice between God and money? Taking a little liberty here, it was as if in one hand, he held all his wealth and in the other, the opportunity to follow Jesus and live life forever. Back and forth his head went looking at each hand intently: do I choose wealth or Jesus? He went away sad, grieved to the point of distress, because *he loved his wealth too much.*

Money or wealth—especially a lot of it—seems to have the ability to do weird things to people. It can have such a hold on us that it can cause us to reject the very One who gave it to us in the first place. It's that old saying: "money can be a tool or a god—which is it in your life?" Jesus is saying—and I would suggest *pleading* with us—don't be like this man. If we go back to the shrewd manager parable in Luke 16, we'll see Jesus puts it even more strongly. Just after He says, "You cannot serve both God and Money," it says in verses 14-15:

> *The Pharisees, who loved money, heard all this and were sneering at Jesus. ¹⁵He said to them, "You are the ones who justify yourselves in the eyes of others* [that's the horizontal view], *but God knows your hearts. What people value highly is detestable in God's sight.*

Jesus says a love of money is *detestable* in God's sight. Other translations of this harsh Greek word are *abomination* and *abhorrent.* That's why it is so important for us to understand our role as managers or stewards of His resources. Managing God's stuff is serious business. The Pharisees were obviously blinded by their love of money, as the passage says that they heard all this and were doing what? Sneering at Jesus! Can you imagine that, sneering into the very face of God—money does weird things to people. That's why for a Christ-follower, we must get our heads "screwed on right"—or as Billy Graham said, get our *attitudes* right—towards this thing called money. Are you starting to grasp the gravity of your role as *oikonómos*?

ANOTHER EXAMPLE

To reinforce this concept let's look briefly at part of another parable, one that we will deal with in more depth in Chapter 5. Coming in a group of parables which deal with being ready for the Son of Man's return, in Matthew 25:14-30 Jesus presents the parable of what the NIV titles the "bags of gold"—which most other translations call the parable of the talents. Back then, a talent was not a skill but rather the largest measurement of money, worth upwards of $30,000 each, a humongous sum in those days. Put in different terms, one talent represented about twenty years'-worth of a day laborer's wages.[10] Today, assuming a day laborer's average income is half the median family income of $59,000 documented previously—let's just use $30,000—each talent would represent about $600,000 ($30,000 x twenty years). One servant was given *five* talents—$3 million or one hundred *years'* wages—obviously a lot of money!

As you may recall in the parable, the master was leaving on a long trip and entrusted the talents to each of three servants, who were to invest them while the master was away. Each was given a different amount "according to his ability" (verse 15)—just like He does with us today. Two servants invested successfully while the third buried his, supposedly for "safekeeping." When the master returned, he "settled accounts" with each servant, or as the version in Luke says, "find out what they had gained with it." The two successful servants, who, remember, were given different amounts to invest, received the exact same reward. Note how happy the master is:

> (Matthew 25: 21 *and* 23) *'Well done, good and faithful servant! You have been faithful with a few*

> *things; I will put you in charge of many things. Come and share your master's happiness!'*

But to the third servant, who did nothing but hide the talent in the ground, not even earning interest, the master replied in verses 26 and 30:

> *'You **wicked, lazy** servant! ... ^{30} throw that worthless servant outside, into the darkness, where there will be weeping and gnashing of teeth.'*

Again, God *is* quite serious about how we manage His resources. Moreover, note this: the two successful servants never considered the money to be their own. They were simply stewards or managers taking care of the master's wealth—just as we are to do today.

The Recurring Question

We are just about ready to get into some "good and faithful servant" tools of managing His resources. Before we do, let me pause here and ask my recurring question again. Applying this parable to your life today, do you believe, really believe that God *is* going to "settle accounts" with you? If not, the rest of this book will be pointless because without a belief in an "end-of-life evaluation," we don't really have any motivation to watch what we do with what we will likely view as "our" money and stuff. Recall Jesus' stern warning in Luke 12:15 when He responds to someone in the crowd asking Him to tell his brother to divide an inheritance:

> *Watch out! Be on your guard against all kinds of greed; **life does not consist in the abundance of possessions.***

Moreover, just after this, Jesus tells the parable of the rich fool who had finished building bigger barns to store his surplus. What does Jesus say to him? This is one time when the *Living Bible* puts it more succinctly than all the other translations—pay attention to this!

> Luke 12:20-21: *'Fool! Tonight you die. Then who will get it all?'* "Yes, every man is a fool who gets rich on earth but not in heaven."

But if you do embrace the lessons from the parable of the talents in Matthew 25, surely you want to hear that magical evaluation from Him, don't you? What did the master say? "Well done, good and faithful servant! You **have** been faithful with a few things; I will put you in charge of many things." So, let's get started on just how to do that.

Do you remember the three questions I asked at the beginning of this chapter?

1. Irrespective of your current income, would you like to learn how to make it stretch further than you ever imagined possible?
2. Would you like to learn how to easily become debt free—except for your mortgage—within a year or two?

And most importantly:

3. Would you like to be able to know—really know—that you are managing your (His!) resources not only efficiently, but in ways which also please and honor Him and, as a result, worry less about money?

EXCELLING AS AN *OIKONOMOS*

Implementing the process I am going to share with you will result in a resounding "yes" to all three questions. The steps are presented by *priority*—for two critical reasons. First, right from the get-go, I want you to be able to acknowledge in a tangible way that you really do believe in Him and His Word. Second, I want it to be crystal-clear what you are to start working on *tomorrow*. To help you remember them, I will also give you a silly acronym!

STEP #1: HONOR GOD BY GIVING BACK A PORTION TO HIM

This first step may be completely unexpected, especially for those who are just living paycheck to paycheck. There is a verse in 1 Samuel 2 that comes in the midst of a prophecy against the house of Eli—he was the High Priest but his sons had completely apostatized and used their priestly office for their own gain and licentious pursuits—even sleeping with the women at the gate (2:22). Although God says in this prophecy that He will essentially wipe out the priestly line of Eli, He inserts this remarkable and hope-inspiring declaration in verse 30:

> *Those who honor me I will honor.*

As you'll learn in Chapter 3, one of the best ways to honor Him is to give back to Him some of those precious resources He has entrusted to you. Why? Because it forces you to trust Him even more, as you will now have *fewer* resources than you did before. But here's the amazing thing about that kind of honor: He is far more concerned with your *attitude* when you give than the amount, because remember, whose is it in the first place?

As a brief introduction to God's motivation for giving, read what the apostle Paul writes to the Corinthian believers in 2 Corinthians, chapters 8 and 9. These are the two most important chapters on giving in all of God's Word as they encapsulate the entire Biblical message on not only *how* we should give but how *much* we should give. For now, we'll read only the two pivotal verses—and may these be forever burned into your heart and mind when you give:

> (2 Corinthians 9:7) *Each of you should give what you have decided in your heart to give, not reluctantly or under compulsion, for God loves a cheerful giver.* (8:12) *For if the willingness is there, the gift is acceptable according to what one has, not according to what one does not have.*

Look closely ... *how* are we to give? Not reluctantly, not under compulsion, but willingly, even cheerfully. Is an *amount* specified? Lest you think I have taken these verses out of context, I will deal with the whole tithing concept in the next chapter. As a head's up, the Biblical message may not be what you think or what you may have been taught—so, for the moment, trust me.

No matter your current financial position, if you are going to church this weekend, put in an offering, whether large or small—the widow's offering in Mark 12 was only a fraction of a penny. What is important is your *attitude*, that you are giving to honor *Him*, to acknowledge that not only is it really His anyway, but—*and read this carefully*—He promises to take care of you *no matter what*. So, when you put your money in the offering, do so with a cheerful, willing, and expectant heart, okay?

If you are not going to church this weekend, stop right now, put an offering—either cash or a check—into an envelope and have it ready for when you do go.

So, step #1—and "H" for the acronym—is to recognize Him as Lord of your life and of everything you have, and *honor* Him by giving back a portion of it to Him.

STEP #2: LIVE ONLY ON CASH

You might not like this one, so let me motivate it with another alarming statistic put in question form: How much more, percentage-wise, do you think the average person spends when they don't pay with cash, the green stuff? Study after study has shown that the average person will spend somewhere between *fifty and seventy percent* more—and this even includes using a debit card. Are you surprised by that? This is exactly why casinos use chips, cruise lines use an ID card for spending and Walt Disney World uses "Disney Dollars." When you don't have to pull the cash out of your wallet or purse, you just … spend … more. This has been proven by Arby's, by McDonalds, by car dealers, and many others.

To bring this troublesome reality home, you need to experience it for yourself, so here's Step #2: For just one short month, pay cash for *everything*, whether for groceries, for eating out, for clothing, you name it, everything that you can practically pay cash for. You may even be able to pay cash for your utilities and your cable or satellite bill by going to the local office. Excluded from this would be your housing and car payment. This is what I call the "living on cash" test as you are not to use your credit or debit cards for *anything*. You won't believe what a tightwad you'll become when you physically see the green stuff leaving your hands. I can't explain it, but this reality scares me more and more as we move towards a cashless society because I guarantee you, that statistic—the fifty to seventy percent more—will not change, and maybe that is exactly why so many businesses are pushing for this.

To bring this point home, let me ask you: Would you have been able to buy the car you are currently driving if you had had to pay cash up front? Living on the cash basis conveys one critical reality:

> If you ain't got the cash, you ain't gettin' the goods.

So, live only on cash—and "L" for "live" for our acronym—for just one month and let me know how it goes; you've got my email address at the back of the book. And as we'll talk about in Chapter 4, if you want to save really big bucks, actually do consider paying cash for your next car.

STEP #3: THE LITTLE SPIRAL NOTEBOOK

This next step is not very glamourous, but if you stick with it, it also comes with a guarantee. Later today or no later than Monday, go to an office products store and buy one of these - a little three- by five-inch spiral notebook:

Maybe you already have one around your house. It may seem pretty innocuous, but you are going to see that this is one of the most powerful tools in becoming a good steward—maybe even a little magical. I am dead serious about this, because this little notebook can grab a hold of your expenditures and help you start whacking away at them.

Here's what you do. In tandem with Step 2, every time you spend money, either using good old cash or if you must, your debit card, simply write it down in the little notebook. Use the K-I-S-S principle—**k**eep **i**t **s**imple, **s**illy—and round to the nearest dollar, using categories of your choice. That's all you have to do ... write it down, every time. Remember Adam Sandler's classic words on the golf course in the movie *Happy Gilmore*? "Just tap it in, just tap it in ..." So ... "just write it down."

Why do you need to this? When you write it down, you become more *aware* of what you're spending—and in some cases, more *alarmed* by it. You look at it and say to yourself, I'm spending $50 per week on ... coffee?[11] I'm spending $150 per week on ... gas? Even the amount you spend on groceries or snacks can blow you away. Here's where the magic comes in: consciously or unconsciously, you will begin looking for ways to reduce—maybe even eliminate—some expenditures. And if you reduce your expenditures, what starts happening? Your money starts stretching farther!

So, just the process of writing your expenditures down will alter your spending habits. If you don't believe me, here's the guarantee: Do this for only one month. If one of two things doesn't happen, I'll gladly refund the price you paid for the book:

1. You'll conveniently start "forgetting" to write things down because inwardly you are embarrassed about how you are spending your (God's?) money; or
2. You are diligent in writing things down and as a result of what you have learned, you *do* change your spending habits.

And, you will likely feel compelled to continue "just writing things down."

That's it. As your personal financial trainer, I am telling you that this is the third thing you must do as a good *oikonómos* to begin getting into good financial shape. And you only have to do this for one month. If you don't see any results, you can fire me! So, Step 3 is use a little spiral notebook—and "S" for spiral—and write down your daily expenditures.

Step #4: Establish your "Oh Thank God" fund

Because of their importance, you should start Steps 1-3 *tomorrow*— or Monday at the latest. Because I am so sure of the impact Steps 2 and 3 will have on your psyche, I urge to start Step #4 next week also. In my humanness, I wanted to put this one first—a lot of non-faith-based financial planners will do just that—but honoring God with your finances is absolutely foundational to viewing money correctly. I didn't make this step #2 or #3 because those steps are actually going to help you put this one into action—it is an important one in allowing you to worry less about money.

Do you remember that statistic on the percentage of people living paycheck to paycheck? An astounding seventy-eight percent, or three out of every four. Maybe you are one of those three. If so, you know the stress that is created by always wondering if you'll make it to the next paycheck. And should something unexpected pop up—car repairs, airfares to attend a funeral, or whatever—the stress levels can skyrocket. And, you know that unexpected things *are* going to happen.

Yet, this stress is so easy to avoid. Here's a simple analogy: when you go shopping for groceries, do you shop for just that day? No way!

You buy more than you need and store it in your cabinets so food is there when you need it. Do the same with your money!

Step #4 goes by various names—"emergency fund" is very common—but I really like the Christianized version: the "Oh Thank God!" fund, and "T" for "thank" for the acronym. If you have one, emergencies are no longer emergencies. You can now say "oh thank God" because an unexpected financial event is now simply an additional item that can be funded from the money you have "stored away." Instead of stress, you have peace.

How much money is reasonable to have in your "oh thank God" fund? If you don't currently have a fund, start out with $1,000—and I know some are immediately shaking their heads thinking, "yeah, right, where am I going to get $1,000?" If necessary, go through all your stuff and start selling some—nearly everyone has stuff they don't use anymore. Or, because you've been following Steps 2 and 3 and only buying things with cash and always writing those expenditures down, money may have magically appeared due to you consciously or subconsciously reducing your spending. So, it can be done. The great thing is that $1,000 dollars will give you some "breathing room." Over time, grow your fund to one month's net pay—that can pay for a lot of unplanned stuff. Then, grow it into a three-month—maybe even six-month—reserve that could be there for such major events as losing your job. But the first goal—so essential for daily well-being that I will state it as an order—is to get $1,000 set aside, untouchable except for emergencies. Exercise some of the "d" word—discipline—to reduce the stress by turning the unexpected into the expected.

STEP #5: ELIMINATE DEBT USING THE "SNOWBALL" METHOD

Step 2, the month-long "living on cash" test, specified that you are not to use your credit cards. Current statistics indicate that over seventy percent of Americans have at least one credit card, with the average being almost four—and Chapter 4 discusses more about the use and misuse of credit. For now, we'll focus on those with lots of credit card debt—the two-thirds of credit card users which statistics reveal are only paying the minimum amount each month—although this step works for anybody. This step should be started after you have established your $1,000 "Oh Thank God" fund.

Originated, I think, by the late Larry Burkett in the 1970s, the "snowball" method of debt elimination is designed to motivate you more and more as you pay off your debts. In simple terms,

1. List all your debts—excluding your mortgage payment—in terms of amount owed, smallest to largest, *not* in terms of interest rate.
2. Pay the minimum due on all accounts except for the smallest one—on that one, do all you can to pay it off as quickly as possible. This could be accomplished by using funds saved in Steps 2 and 3—only using cash and always writing it down—or step 6, which is covered below. You could also consider getting some type of temporary second job but as I'll also cover in Step 6, that comes with some troubling risks.
3. After that smallest debt is paid off, do two things: First, you give yourself a massive pat on the back—you have paid off one of your debts! Second, add the payment you were making on that first account to the payment on the next smallest balance owed until that one is paid off.
4. Keep going, growing in excitement as you watch the payment "snowball" grow larger and larger, rolling over and vanquishing debts faster and faster.

Can you sense the inspiring incentives with this method? Rather than working on all your debts at the same time, and rarely seeing much progress, with this process *you get quicker gratification* because you see your debts getting paid off faster and faster—and *that* is what keeps you going. Just like in the gym, where keeping at it is the main key to goal achievement, seeing debt rapidly melt away is the motivating success factor in the snowball process—far more important than obsessing over the highest interest rate debt. Many people who stick with this plan become debt free—except for their mortgage—in anywhere from one to two years. Wouldn't that be fantastic? So, Step 5 is to **e**liminate debt—and "E" for our acronym—using the snowball method and the answer to question #2 posed at the beginning of the chapter of how to easily pay off most of your debt within a year or two.

STEP #6: DEVELOP A PERSONAL FINANCIAL <u>R</u>OADMAP

This last step takes the most time to implement but other than Step 1, is by far the most important step in the stewardship process because it creates a rock-solid foundation upon which you can build just about anything you'd like. To motivate you for this all-important step, let me ask you this: have you ever gone on a long driving trip, maybe on a family vacation, to someplace you've never been before? Are you old enough to remember "TripTiks" that the AAA would give you when they planned a route for you? Maybe you have used an old-fashioned paper road map? Or maybe, in this day and age, you simply use Google Maps? No matter which you use, what's its purpose? To figure where you are going, and how to get there. Sure, you can just take off and wing it and you'll likely get there eventually, but after how much wasted time and money? And wasted time and money—especially with your finances—can be crippling. Let me show you why—and may this illustration be forever burned into your brain.

There is a saying that goes like this: *Spending is consumptive whereas saving is creative*. What this means is that when you spend money—say on a car, or groceries, or clothing—it is gone forever. There may be enjoyment of the item for a while, but eventually it is used up. Money saved, however, not only sticks around, it can grow and grow fantastically due to what I call "mathematical magic." Let me show you an example that is used in one form or another by many financial advisors.

- Could you reduce your spending, either singly or as a family unit, by a measly five dollars per day? Could you? Sure you can—that's maybe the difference between eating out for lunch verses packing a nice sack lunch, or skipping Starbucks, or whatever.
- Let's say you deposited that five dollars every day in some type of savings instrument that earns ten percent per year, with interest compounded daily. Ten percent may seem unrealistic, but just trust me for the moment.
- If you did this every day for forty years, you would have deposited $73,000, admittedly a sizable sum.
- Now, close your eyes for moment and think about this: Do you have any idea how much that $73,000 would have grown to? Unbelievably, almost a million dollars ($977,888)! Take a look at this graph. The bottom line represents your deposits and the top line how much they have grown. What does this graph tell you? Becoming a millionaire is easy—it costs only five dollars a day! What if you could really stretch and set aside ten dollars a day?

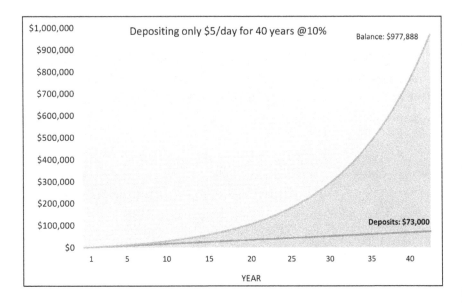

Now, I can imagine some of you thinking: I don't want to go to the bank every day. All right, how about once a month? You might even be able to have the money taken directly out of your paycheck and invested for you. But because you're investing less frequently, it doesn't grow quite as much. At the end of forty years, you'll have "only" $961,766. Others of you might be thinking, "make ten percent on my money?—Impossible!" Any idea of the long-run average return from the stock market? Ten percent.

That is the mathematical magic of interest compounding. No less a luminary than Albert Einstein was stirred by this concept—read the amazing things he said about it:

- Compound interest is the greatest mathematical discovery of all time.
- Compound interest is the eighth wonder of the world. He who understands it, earns it; he who doesn't, pays it.

And although he likely didn't know the Creator of the universe, he also said this:

- Compound interest is the most powerful force in the universe.

Perhaps most importantly, God's Word, written thousands of years ago, also describes this very process—let this be the best incentive to help prod you along. Look at the latter part of Proverbs 13:11, written by the wisest man ever created, King Solomon, and stated as simply as can be:

> ... *whoever gathers money* **little by little** *makes it grow.*

So, don't try to wimp out thinking that you just can't seem to save anything—we're only talking five bucks a day. Any hesitation you feel is likely due to wanting to enjoy *spending* now, *enjoying* now, not worrying about some far-off time. But having such a cavalier "I don't care" attitude can so jeopardize your financial future that you will look back some day lamenting, "what in the world happened?" or "where did all my money go?" What did I say earlier?

> Spending is *consumptive*—the money is gone *forever*—whereas saving is creative.

Remember, you are God's *oikonómos*, managing *HIS* stuff. Frittering away even five dollars a day on stuff that is gone in a moment is ... can I be blunt? D-U-M-B, irresponsible, irrational, foolish, reckless, stupid, negligent. Do you remember the convicting verses you read earlier?

> ... *from the one who has been entrusted with much, much more will be asked.* (Luke 12:48)

Whoever can be trusted with very little can also be trusted with much. ¹¹So if you have not been trustworthy in handling worldly wealth, who will trust you with true riches? ¹²And if you have not been trustworthy with someone else's property, who will give you property of your own? (Luke 16:10-12)

THE COST OF DELAY

Some of you may be thinking, "well, maybe I'll start doing that *down the road*." Want to know what that costs you?

- Delaying five years—just $1,825—maybe the cost of an upgraded sound system for your new car, or super plush carpeting vs. regular plush for your home, or whatever: you'll have $585,986, or almost *$400,000* less.
- Delaying ten years—frittering away just $3,650: you'll have only $348,256, almost *$630,000* less (nearly *two-thirds* less than you could have had).

So, never forget: Spending ... is ... consumptive; the money is gone forever.

Your money is going to go somewhere. It's kind of like the old saying, "if you aim at nothing, you'll surely hit it." Instead of looking back and wondering where it all went, wouldn't it be better to spend just a little time thinking and dreaming about where you'd like it to go, put together a reasonable plan—a target—on how to get there, and start working on it? Isn't this the same thing you do when planning to buy a car, or a house, or a new job, or whatever is important to you?

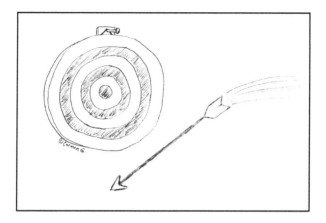

verses

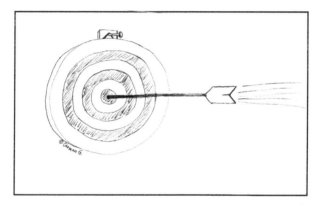

And you know what? The concept of planning is *Biblical,* as even God uses plans! Did you realize that? Look at these references:

- Genesis 6:14 - 7:5: God had very specific plans for Noah on how the Ark was to be built. Given its ultimate purpose and the amazing fact that nothing like it had ever been built before, having plans was probably pretty important, don't you think?

- Exodus 26:30: God told Moses to set up the tabernacle according to the *plan* shown to him on the mountain.
- Ephesians 1:11: The apostle Paul talks about how we were predestined according to the "*plan* of Him who works out everything in conformity with the purpose of His will." That also sounds pretty important, don't you think?

So, God Himself—the Creator of the universe and the creator of y-o-u—uses plans to accomplish His will. So, doesn't that at least imply that as His *oikonómos,* you should also?

In fact, look at two more amazing verses:

- Proverbs 13:16: *All who are prudent act with knowledge, but fools expose their folly.*
- Psalms 25:12: *Who, then, are those who fear the LORD? He will instruct them in the ways they should c-h-o-o-s-e.*

Observe that Psalm 25:12 says God has a "way"—literally a "path or direction or journey that has ultimate and eternal significance"—for each of us.[12]

What Makes This All Work

Note, however, one little—but very important—word in Psalm 25:12: It says that He (God) will "instruct" us in the way. In order to be "instructed" by God, we need to both know Him and His voice, and be listening! That's why the first verse, Proverbs 13:16, says that all who are prudent—literally 'shrewd' in a good sense—act out of "knowledge." Guess where that prudent person gets their knowledge? From God's instruction manual, His Holy Word! That is exactly what I am trying to do here. So, my question to you is: Are you paying attention? Planning is not just good financial sense, it makes great Biblical sense because it was invented and utilized by God Himself!

For some of you, there may be an even more fundamental question: do you even know Him? We'll talk about that critical question at the end of the chapter. For now, just know that having a personal, life-motivating relationship with Him is far more important at this point than simply planning your finances.

Step #6 goes by many different names, but here's what I call it: develop a personal financial *roadmap*—and "R" for the acronym. I call it that because combined with Step 3—writing down your cash expenditures—I guarantee that implemented and followed, two rewards will follow: the answers to questions #1 and #3 posed at the beginning of the chapter:

- Your money stretches further than you ever thought possible;
- You have confidence that you are managing His resources efficiently, in ways that please and honor Him, and without worry.

The roadmap is simply a reasoned outline of what you would like your financial future to look like and how to get there. It takes a couple of weeks of thinking and organizing to get the basics of your route planned and then another two months or so fleshing it out so that it becomes a solid line leading to your destination. But, once you start on your journey, you'll be amazed at the results. Not only will you be spending less and saving more, your money will seem to magically go farther than ever before. Because of that, you will worry less and less about money, knowing that you are being a wise *oikonómos*, just waiting to hear those delightful words from your loving Father, "*well done, good and faithful servant …*"

The Personal Financial Roadmap Process

There are four steps or procedures in developing your roadmap. The basics are covered here with more detailed, step-by-step instructions, including sample forms, presented in Appendix #2a—Developing Your Personal Financial Roadmap. For those of you that are married, likely one of you will be more inclined/motivated/talented in the area of finances. Whether married or not, however, never forget that this is *God's* money we're dealing with, not yours!

Step or Procedure #1—Where are You NOW?

Using Form #1—Actual/Desired Amounts per Month (found in Appendix 2a), you will summarize where your money has been going. To obtain the actual amounts, you will need to review your checkbook or debit slips for the past couple of months. Those items that you pay cash for should be getting nicely summarized in the little spiral notebook you've been using. Because some expenditures are "lumpy," meaning they don't occur regularly (for example, subscriptions or many types of insurance), Form #2—Lumpy Items—is used to get monthly amounts for these. And Form #3—List of Debts—is used to get a summary monthly amount for any credit card or other debt you may have. (Note: If your monthly income is highly variable, then you can either do all of this on an annual basis or compile your expenditures for three or six months and divide by the appropriate number of months to obtain a monthly average.)

After you have filled in everything on Form #1, total all your expenditures. If you are one of the many living paycheck-to-paycheck, don't be surprised if there is nothing in the box for "SAVINGS/INVESTMENT."

At this point, you now have a general idea of where your money has been going. So, let me ask you a question: Could it be that your spending *exceeds* your income? Is that even possible? Oh, yes. With today's credit-saturated society, you are almost not considered normal if you don't spend more than you make! Whether by using credit cards, home equity loans, even borrowing against or cashing out retirement funds, this "go for the gusto" country we live in says "I ... want ... it ... now!" Obviously, that kind of lifestyle cannot continue indefinitely. If you are currently in that situation, read on—we'll deal with it in a bit. But I'll give you a hint now: It's ... not ... going ... to ... be ... easy ... or quick.

I also need to warn you, that if you just keep on spending, then neither I nor anyone else can help you. To use an analogy, if you want to lose weight, you can't keep eating, eating, eating. You may want to be able to spend, spend, spend but if you don't really have the resources to do that, it has to come back and bite you at some point. I have known folks making $100,000, even $200,000 a year, who run out of money! Even multi-millionaires can go bankrupt. It is not a matter of how much you earn—it is a matter of how you *spend* it.

STEP OR PROCEDURE #2 – WHERE SHOULD YOU BE?

What you'll do next is use Form #4—Percentage Guide—and compare your list of actual expenditures on Form #1 with some well-documented guidelines on how much spending should occur in each category for your current income level. In essence, where are you compared to where you should be?

Not everybody has to live the same way—that's why I call this a *personal* financial roadmap—but to be able to save anything, you need to be fairly close to the guidelines. As your income changes, the applicable percentages will change a bit. But—and this is a big and magical "but"—as your income *in*creases, you should have more and more left over because, for example, if your income doubled, your food expenditures, your mortgage, your car payment don't automatically double. Where do those leftover amounts go? Into that all-important box, SAVINGS/INVESTMENT. Form #1 puts that item before all your expenditures so that you can keep the saving/investing process at the forefront of your thinking ... and planning ... and directing because if you're not careful, then the following pithy saying will likely be your experience:

> Spending is like a gas. Just as a gas expands to fill a given volume, so will our spending expand to use up our available income.

Here's a personal example. Back in 1969, during the summer between my senior year in high school and my freshman year in college, I drove a gasoline truck at the local airport, fueling small aircraft. Part of my pay was based on how many gallons I pumped. That summer, there were lots of forest fires nearby and all the Forest Service aircraft came to my airport for refueling. It was quite an unexpected bonanza of fuel sales and summer earnings for me—over $2,000, which was a lot of money back then. Yet by the end of the summer, all of those first-year college dollars had evaporated—I had nothing left. To this day, I still don't know where all the money went. But I learned the costly, life-changing lesson of the need for a personal financial roadmap.

Thus far, we've figured out where your money has been going and compared it to some well-developed guidelines. Now comes the fun part: You're ready to put together your personal roadmap. Step back for a moment, take a deep breath, and ask yourself, "Where do I want to go?" In the short run, you may not be able to increase your monthly income by much, but you have virtually unlimited control over your expenditures. You might feel like you are locked into some of them—like housing and car payments—but those can be sold and cheaper alternatives acquired. Think of people who lose their jobs or have their hours reduced. Do they have to cut back? Absolutely! Is it easy? Rarely. But given enough incentive, anybody—and I mean anybody—*can* cut their spending by twenty, twenty-five, even thirty percent.

The real question is: are you willing? Are you willing to exercise the "d" word—discipline—in order to spend less, pay off more, save more and even be able to give more? If you want proof that it can be done, read an amazing little book titled *"The Power of Half,"* written by father-daughter team Kevin and Hannah Salwen, who reduced their family spending lifestyle, not by twenty percent ... or thirty percent, but by *fifty* percent, so they *could* live on less and give more. It can be done—you just have to want to do it.

STEP OR PROCEDURE #3—WHERE DO YOU WANT TO GO?

This is where you mark the route on your personal financial roadmap. Using a blank Form #1, you'll note that there are highlighted or bolded categories. For the moment, these represent your "fixed" or unchangeable items, both income and expenditures, so fill them in with the amounts from your original Form #1.

There are two italicized boxes on Form #1, one for GIVING and one for SAVINGS/INVESTMENT. Before doing anything else with this form, enter how much you would like the amounts for these two items to be. If you want your giving to be ten percent of your income, write it down. If you can save that measly $5 per day, put down $150 per month. Remember, this is only a plan or roadmap—but you have to start somewhere.

Now, here is where I differ from virtually every other financial advisor out there, Christian or non-Christian. On Form #1, both "GIVING" and "SAVINGS/INVESTMENT" come *before* all your expenditures, for two critical reasons. First, as we have already talked about, it is important to honor God with a portion of the income He has blessed you with (I will elaborate on this in the next chapter). Second, I need to state something that is obvious to many but which often takes years for others to finally "get it:" in order for you to be able to save anything, *your spending must be less than your income*! Sure, you can borrow and set some aside but the interest rate on borrowing is always higher than the interest rate for saving. So, over time, you are actually spending, not saving.

By subtracting your planned "giving" and "savings/investing" funds from your income, it forces you to live on the remainder. Just like you live without the taxes and other items that are deducted from your paycheck by your employer, when you construct your personal financial roadmap this way, you view your giving and your saving/investing as coming off the top *before anything else*. Here's another way to look at this: view these two items as absolute priorities—basically non-negotiable. And depending on your employer's policies, you may be able to have them automatically deducted from your check. What's the old saying? Out of sight, out of mind.

Finally, fill the rest of Form #1 with your planned monthly expenditures, taking into consideration the guideline amounts from Form #4. This is where you get to have a little fun with yourself or have some back-and-forth banter with your spouse, because all these items together cannot exceed what's left of your income after specifying your giving and saving/investment amounts. If they are excessive on your first pass—which is not at all uncommon—you're going to have to do some massaging or negotiating:

- Cable/satellite costs too high? Get rid of some of the premium channels you rarely or never watch.
- Auto insurance costs too high? Change your coverage or deductibles—or maybe even the insurance company.

- Food costs too high? I know folks who through better planning and intelligent use of coupons, cut their grocery bill by $50 or more per week.
- Housing costs or car payments too high? Just like the Salwen family did in the example cited previously, these can be reduced if the need or desire is great enough.

Category by category, you find ways to bring your expenditures in line with that remainder amount. Companies do this all the time and it is amazing how much slack or waste they find. And if your expenditures go down, what goes up even if your income does not change? That all-important category of savings/investment.

Here's some encouragement. I have found that most families—regardless of income level—*can* reduce their spending, with virtually zero change in lifestyle, by $300-$500 per month ... imagine that. Yes, this takes a bit of work, but approached from a light-hearted "how-do-we-do-this" mindset, you'll be amazed how easily you can get on the road of not only living within your income but being able to give more and save more—all without increasing your income. And should the Lord bless you with more income—which He often does—you have all the more opportunity to be a faithful and wise *oikonómos* managing that increase in resources.

So, have I have convinced you that this whole roadmap planning process is not only Biblical, but also the most sensible way to reach the financial goals you have carefully and prayerfully mapped out?

While you may be nodding your head up and down, I need to make you aware of a dismaying disconnect in this process: Study after study has shown that *sixty to ninety percent* of us don't implement even this most basic—and Biblical—financial planning process. How can that be good stewardship? Put another way, it's really the choice we all have of viewing our resources as His ... or ours. Remember what Reverend Graham said?

> When a person gets their attitude toward money straight, it will do what? It will help straighten out *almost every other area of their life*.

Some readers might have already put together their personal financial roadmap and be well on their way to reaching their financial goals. Others may now be energized to begin that process, and I would be glad to hear from you from time to time. There may be some of you, however, who—after perusing this chapter and sensing some difficult decisions might have to be made about your current lifestyle and spending habits—may be tempted to simply try to increase your income (perhaps by getting a second job or having your spouse go to work). While it might help, here's the most common reality in the form of a Japanese proverb:

> Getting money is like digging with a needle; spending it is like water soaking into sand.

The potential problem with both extra income-generating choices is that there will be increased taxes, more meals out, maybe babysitting costs, and for a spouse going to work, appropriate clothing to be purchased. When all is said and done, the marginal extra income may not be all that much. Additionally, now that one or both of you are working more, the temptation is to "reward" yourself and spend more, just like the Japanese proverb above indicates. Finally, there may be significantly less quality time for family life. So, evaluate this approach very carefully; it can be net beneficial overall, especially if you use the added funds in the debt snowball process, but don't use it simply to avoid the responsibility of being a wise *oikonómos* and taking that critical look at your expenditures.

One additional comment and a bit of encouragement is appropriate here. In the beginning stages of traveling your roadmap, you may not be able to give or save much but the key is to *start* giving if you are not doing so regularly, and to start saving—no matter what. An old proverb goes like this: A journey of a thousand miles begins with a single step. Recall the example of how your savings can grow magically over time with only $5 per day. Once giving and saving become a habitual way of living, most find that the desire to increase both over time just comes naturally. And if you want to make it *really* easy, as I said before, if possible, have the amounts for both taken directly out of your paycheck for you, just like your taxes. Doing so *forces* you to live on the rest. Moreover, as you become more "efficient" in your spending—actually living the "spending is consumptive, saving is creative" maxim—eliminating waste becomes a gratifying game. It also allows you to enjoy your spending because you are now consciously directing where and how you want your hard-earned dollars spent. Even more important, you also know that you can truly "afford" it!

That's the process of creating your personal financial roadmap. Yes, it takes some work. For those of you who are married, you *do* know the number one cause of relational difficulties and eventually divorce, don't you? Yes, financial stress. Managing your finances is something you need to do *together* so that you can both be on the same page and working towards the same goals. If you don't—married or not—do you know what will likely happen ... and maybe this is already your experience?

> You will run out of money before you run out of month.

It's as simple as that. So, heed the Biblical advice:

Proverbs 13:16: *All who are **prudent** act with **knowledge**,*

and

Psalms 25:12: *Who, then, are those who fear the LORD? Let Him instruct **you** in the ways **you** should choose.*

STEP OR PROCEDURE #4—ARE ... YOU ... GETTING ... THERE?

This last step or procedure in the personal financial roadmap process is by far the most important one. However, it is likely to cause some of you the most angst so let me motivate it with a couple of questions: Do you ever check the oil level in your car? Why? Those of you who have been on diets before, did you ever get on the scale or use the tape measure to see how you are doing?

By the same reasoning, you need to look at your roadmap occasionally to see if you are still on your planned route! Put another way, you must monitor your expenditures and growth in savings compared to your roadmap—you must walk the talk. To bring in the "d" word again, following your roadmap takes discipline and this is where many folks fail. They determine where their money is going, they create the roadmap and then ... into the drawer it goes. It's like joining a gym, going there, getting a workout plan and then, like most new members, what happens? They rarely or never go again.

So, you can't know how you are doing unless you know how you are doing! Once a month, use Form #5—Desired to Actual Monthly Comparison—to check the oil, get on the scales, and do a periodic financial check-up. Alternatively, you can use one of the many online budgeting sites such as Mint.com or YouNeedABudget.com. Whatever you use, not everything will automatically be within your desired amount guidelines, so you may need to do some massaging or shifting. Just remember the overriding goal is that the resources under your management, under your stewardship, are used in the ways you and your Master planned. Put another way, control your money or … it will control you.

Let me step on your toes again by being very blunt. If you are not willing to do this, not willing to "walk the talk," not willing to use the most basic stewardship tools, what you are really saying is that "it's my money and I'll do whatever I want with it." If that's what you really believe, then, I can't help you—in fact, nobody can. And you likely will never hear those magical "well done" words from your Lord and Savior.

Monitoring your expenditures is the last step in the process in generating and successfully navigating your personal financial *r*oadmap, and "R" for the acronym. It takes about three months to get the roadmap really humming but once it is, you'll find that not only does your money go farther, you *are* saving more and able to give more! This is all because as a prudent manager or steward, you are being more careful and deliberate—in essence, what the parable in Matthew 25 means when it says that the wise servants "went at once and put their money *to work*." So, stop fidgeting, stop procrastinating, and start working on your plan. If you are married, this is one of those critical moments in your marriage where you need to turn to your spouse and say, "honey, can we sit down soon—maybe even tomorrow—and start working on this *together*?"

SUMMARY OF THE PROCESS

You've now learned the six absolutely essential steps to begin the process of getting your financial house on a firm Biblical foundation and in line with the timeless guidance in God's Word:

Step #1: **H**—Start *h*onoring Him by giving *now*!

Step #2: **L**—Take the "*l*iving on cash" test

Step #3: **S**—Use a little *s*piral notebook and write down your expenditures

Step #4: **T**—Get $1,000 set aside in your "oh *t*hank God" fund

Step #5: **E**—Debt *e*limination using the snowball process

Step #6: **R**—Develop your own personal financial *r*oadmap

H-L-S-T-E-R—or HoLSTER. Just as a holster holds a gun than can provide a sense of safety and security for its owner, so does God's "holster"—His Word—contain truths that can profoundly transform our lives. In the area of managing mammon, following the timeless guidance in His Word gives us confidence that we are being a wise *oikonómos*. It's not rocket science how to do any of this—it is mostly time and discipline to stick with the process—but the rest of God's guidance on successfully managing His resources depends on having this essential foundation in place. It should be clear, however, that if you do follow this 6-step HoLSTER process, you will have affirmatively answered the three questions posed at the beginning of this chapter:

- Irrespective of your current income, you have learned how to make it stretch further than you ever imagined possible.
- You have learned how to easily become debt-free—except for your mortgage—within a year or two.

And most importantly:

- You now know how to manage your (His!) resources efficiently and in ways that please and honor Him. As a result, you will worry less about money.

Moreover, whatever amount He decides to entrust into your care, you will have no fear of the upcoming evaluation of Luke 12:48 because as a wise *oikonómos*, you'll actually be looking forward to hearing those magical words from Him, "well done, good and faithful servant."

One last thing before moving on to the next chapter. I mentioned earlier that for some readers, there is an even more important step than learning how to manage money Biblically. In order to become that good and faithful *oikonómos*, you must first know the Master Himself. That relationship is not one of master and slave but one between a loving Father—some even call Him Papa—and His son or daughter. This is the most important relationship you can ever develop. Appendix 2b for this chapter shows you how to do that. I implore you to read that appendix before continuing.

Appendix 2a – Developing Your Personal Financial Roadmap

As discussed in the chapter, there are four steps or procedures in developing your own personal financial roadmap. This appendix will take you through the "nuts and bolts" of how to do that, with forms following the explanation of the process. Should you have questions, don't hesitate to contact me. My website, BibleBasedFinances.com, also has downloadable blank forms, as well as a step-by-step PowerPoint presentation of the entire process.

STEP OR PROCEDURE #1 – WHERE ARE YOU NOW?

Using Form #1—Actual/Desired Amounts per Month—fill in the appropriate boxes. Note that many categories have boxes on the left, which are used for detail, and boxes on the right, which are used for totals. To get the actual amounts, you will need to review your checkbook or debit slips for the past couple of months. Those items for which you pay cash should be nicely summarized in your little spiral notebook.

For your "lumpy" expenditures, those which don't occur regularly, like subscriptions or most types of insurance, use Form #2—Lumpy Expenditures—to get a monthly amount for these. Use Form #3—List of Debts—to get a summary monthly amount for any credit card or other debt you may have.

Once everything is filled in, put the grand total in box 18. Don't be surprised if at this stage there is nothing in box 6, "SAVINGS/INVESTMENT." If your monthly income is really variable, then either you will have to do all of this on an annual basis or compile your expenditures for three or six months and divide by the appropriate number of months for an average.

*STEP OR PROCEDURE #2 – WHERE **SHOULD** YOU BE?*

Using Form #4—Percentage Guidelines:

1. Enter your amounts from Form #1 in the first "Actual" column. Then calculate the percentage of your NSI (net spendable income) for each item (savings, housing, food, etc.) by dividing it by your NSI.
2. Find the guideline percentages for the guideline NSI closest to your actual NSI and enter those percentages in the farthest right column. Multiply those percentages times your NSI—not the guideline NSI—to get the guideline amount for each category.
3. Compare your actual to the guideline for each category. Example: Your net spendable income per month is $4,000 and your food costs are $575 per month. Dividing $575 by $4,000 yields .144 or 14.4%. This is the actual percentage of your NSI for Food/Grocery. Using the closest guideline NSI monthly amount—in this case $4,166—your amount should be 13% or $520. At your current spending rate, you exceed the guideline by $55, or a bit more than 1%.

STEP OR PROCEDURE #3 – WHERE DO YOU WANT TO GO?

Using a blank Form #1—Actual/Desired Amounts per Month—note that some boxes on the form are **bolded**—for the moment, these represent your "fixed" or unchangeable items such as your income, house and car payments (remember, however, virtually any expenditure can be changed with enough motivation). Fill in these boxes with the amounts from your original Form #1.

Next, there are two *italicized* boxes: #2—GIVING and #6—SAVINGS/INVESTMENT. These represent "prioritized" expenditures—amounts to be set aside or funded first, before all your other expenditures. Enter your desired amounts for these in the appropriate boxes; if you want your giving to be ten percent of your income, put it down. If you can save $5 per day, put down $150 per month. Remember, this is only a *plan* or *roadmap*—whatever amounts you enter, the goal is to fund or live on what is left. At this point, you can also determine the amounts for boxes #5—NSI and #7—REMAINDER.

Now, fill in the rest of the boxes. But when you total these up (#8–#17), the amount in box #18—TOTAL EXPENDITURES—can't *exceed* the REMAINDER amount in box #7; you may have to go back, compare your amounts to the guideline amounts on Form #4, and "massage" things as discussed in the chapter. For example:

- Cable/satellite costs: get rid of some of the premium channels you rarely or never watch.
- Auto insurance costs: change your coverage or deductibles—maybe even the insurance company.
- Food costs: through better planning and intelligent use of coupons, grocery bills can be cut by $50 or more per week.
- Housing costs or car payments: just like the Salwen family did in the example cited in the chapter, these costs can also be reduced if the need or desire is great enough.

After several iterations of massaging the numbers—and if you are married, after some frank, loving and prayerful discussions with your spouse—you will have generated a workable personal financial roadmap.

STEP OR PROCEDURE #4 – ARE YOU GETTING THERE?

Creation of your personal financial roadmap does not signal the end of this process, just as printing out a Google roadmap does not get you to your desired destination. Just as unmarked intersections may put you on the wrong road, unexpected events could cause your financial roadmap to differ from the plan. Using Form #5—Desired to Actual Monthly Comparison, periodically compare your actual expenditures to your financial roadmap. Not everything will automatically be within your desired amounts, so you may need to do some massaging or shifting because in the short run, you likely can't increase your income. Remember, your roadmap is just a plan—it should never be used to bludgeon yourself or your spouse when spending exceeds desired amounts. Instead, it should act as a flashing yellow light, causing you to be more careful so that at the end of the month, you haven't spent more money than you have.

As the weeks and months roll by—following your roadmap and continuing to write down your daily cash expenditures in the little spiral notebook—you will be increasingly amazed as you watch your expenses decrease and the amounts available for giving and saving/investing grow ever larger. And should your Father increase your financial resources, it will be a joy to use Form #1 again to create a revised roadmap, carefully and prayerfully determining how to allocate that increase.

Dr. Michael Davis

Form #1: Actual/Desired Amounts per Month (xerox as needed)

	Detail	Totals		Detail	Totals
1. INCOME PER MONTH			11. INSURANCE (not part of		
Salary (Annual/12)			payroll deducts)		
Interest (Annual/12			**Life**		
Dividends			**Medical**		
Notes Receivable			Other		
Rental Income					
Alimony			12. DEBT PAYMENTS**		
Social Security			Credit card		
Other:			Loans & Notes		
			Other		
			13. ENTERTAINMENT +		
Less:			RECREATION		
2. Giving		−	Vacation/Trips*		
			Eating out		
3. Taxes (Fed, State, Local, FICA)		−	Babysitters		
			Other activities		
4. Other Paycheck deductions:		−	Other		
5. NET SPENDABLE INCOME			14. CLOTHING*		
[1-(2+3+4)]:		=			
			15. MEDICAL (unreimbursable)*		
6. SAVINGS/INVESTMENT*		−	Doctor		
			Dentist		
7. REMAINDER (5-6)		=	Vision		
			Prescriptions		
8. HOUSING:			Other		
Mortgage/Rent					
Homeowners Ins.*					
Property taxes*			16. SCHOOL/CHILDCARE		
Utilities:			Tuition*		
Electricity			Books/Materials*		
Gas			Activities*		
Water/Sewer			Childcare		
Trash					
Telephone			17. MISCELLANEOUS		
Cable/Satellite			Beauty/Barber		
Housing maintenance*			Dry cleaning		
Other			Subscriptions*		
			Allowances		
9. FOOD/GROCERY STORE			Lunches		
Food			Gifts (incl. Christmas)*		
Toiletry/Cosmetics			Other:		
Laundry					
Pets			18. TOTAL EXPENDITURES		
			(Sum of #8 - #17)		
10. AUTOS/TRANSPORTATION					
Payments			INCOME VS. EXPENDITURES:		
Gas + Oil			Remainder (#7 above)		
Insurance*			− Total Expendures (#18 above)		−
License/Taxes*			= Excess or (Deficiency)		=
Maint, Repairs*					
Replacmt fund					
Tolls/Subway,Bus Fare					

Bolded items generally represent fixed or "hard to change" items
* See Form # 2: Lumpy Expenditures Worksheet
** From Form #3: List of Debts Worksheet

Form #2: "Lumpy" Items Worksheet			
	Annual Amount		Monthly Amount
6. Savings/Investments		÷ 12	
8. Housing:			
Homeowners Ins		÷ 12	
Property taxes		÷ 12	
Housing maintenance		÷ 12	
10. Autos:			
Insurance		÷ 12	
License/Taxes		÷ 12	
Maint/Repairs		÷ 12	
13. Vacation/Trips		÷ 12	
14. Clothing		÷ 12	
15. Medical (unreimbursable):			
Doctors		÷ 12	
Dentists		÷ 12	
Vision		÷ 12	
Other		÷ 12	
16. Schooling:			
Tuition		÷ 12	
Books/Materials		÷ 12	
Activities		÷ 12	
17. Miscellaneous			
Subscriptions		÷ 12	
Gifts (incl. Christmas)		÷ 12	

Note: The monthly amounts are entered into the appropriate box on Form #1.

Form #3: List of Debts (exclude mortgage/rent + auto payments)				
Owed to	Total Amount	Monthly Payment	Est. # of Payments	Interest Rate
Credit Card Cos:				
Total CC Amounts:[1]				
Other "Loans & Notes:"				
Total Other "Loans & Notes:" [2]				
Grand Total (Item #1+#2)				

[1] Transfer "Monthly Payment" total to appropriate box on Form #1 under item #12 - Debt Payments

[2] Transfer "Monthly Payment" total to appropriate box on Form #1 under item #12 - Debt Payments

Form #4: Percentage Guidelines (these are ROUGH estimates)[1]
(Note: Categories match Form #1)

							Your Numbers: Actual		Guideline	
							Amount	%	Amount	%
5. Net Spendable Income (NSI)	$2,500	$3,333	$4,166	$6,250	$8,333	$12,500	[2]	100%	[5]	100%
(NSI on annual basis)	$30,000	$40,000	$50,000	$75,000	$100,000	$150,000				
6. Savings/Investment	2%	5%	8%	9%	11%	15%	[2]	%[3]	[7]	%[6]
8. Housing	38%	34%	31%	30%	29%	25%	[2]	%[3]	[7]	%[6]
9. Food/Grocery	15%	14%	13%	12%	11%	10%	[2]	%[3]	[7]	%[6]
10. Autos/Transportaion	15%	14%	13%	12%	11%	10%	[2]	%[3]	[7]	%[6]
11. Insurance	4%	5%	5%	5%	5%	5%	[2]	%[3]	[7]	%[6]
12. Debt Payments	5%	5%	5%	5%	5%	5%	[2]	%[3]	[7]	%[6]
13. Entertainment/Recreation	3%	4%	5%	7%	8%	10%	[2]	%[3]	[7]	%[6]
14. Clothing	4%	5%	5%	5%	5%	5%	[2]	%[3]	[7]	%[6]
15. Medical (unreimbursable)	5%	5%	5%	5%	5%	5%	[2]	%[3]	[7]	%[6]
16. School/Childcare	6%	5%	5%	5%	5%	5%	[2]	%[3]	[7]	%[6]
17. Miscellaneous	3%	4%	5%	5%	5%	5%	[2]	%[3]	[7]	%[6]
Total	100%	100%	100%	100%	100%	100%		%[4]		100%

[1] This percentage guide is based upon a married couple with two children. Percentages can be flexed a bit if you are single, have roommates or if you are a single parent. The main thing is that the percentages MUST add up to 100%. When schooling/childcare is no longer needed, spread those amounts to other categories, especially Savings/Investment.
[2] Actual dollar amounts come from Form #1: Actual/Desired Amounts per Month
[3] To obtain percentage, divide amount by your Net Spendable Income
[4] If you are OVER spending, this may add up to more than 100%
[5] Enter the NSI from the left side that most closely matches your actual NSI.
[6] Enter applicable percentages under NSI on left side for NSI put in the Guideline amount in box #5
[7] Multiply guideline percentages times your **ACTUAL** NSI (not Guideline NSI) to get guideline amounts for your actual income level

Dr. Michael Davis

	Form #5: Desired to Actual Monthly Comparison: Month: _____					Difference for:	
	(xerox as needed)					Month	Year to Date
	Desired[1]		Actual for Month[2]			$ Ahead/	$ Ahead/
	Amount	%	Amount	%		(Behind)	(Behind)
5. Net Spendable Income (**NSI**)		100%		100%			
6. Savings/Investment		%		%			
7. Housing		%		%			
8. Food/Grocery		%		%			
9. Autos/Transportaion		%		%			
10. Insurance		%		%			
11. Debt Payments		%		%			
12. Entertainment/Recreation		%		%			
13. Clothing		%		%			
14. Medical (unreimbursable)		%		%			
15. School/Childcare		%		%			
16. Miscellaneous		%		%			
Total Items #6 to #16; MUST = #5		100%		%			

[1] From Form #2: Percentage Guide. Unless your income or circumstances change significantly, these amounts should stay constant.
[2] The amounts come from Form #1 for your current month's expenditures

Appendix 2b - How to Become a Christ-Follower

Yes, learning how to manage money Biblically is an important element of a believer's life, as that provides assurance we are on the path to eventually hearing those magical words from God, "Well done good and faithful servant." But to be able to ultimately hear those words, a person must know God Himself.

Regardless of your background—religious or not, having lived a "good" life or not—know that God wants to have a personal relationship with *you*. You may have thought that He is unknowable, or that you don't "measure up" to His standards, or even that He's not a loving God. What you may not know, however, is that He loves you so much and wants to have a one-on-one relationship with you so badly, He sent His one and only Son to earth to make that possible.

Why did He have to send His Son? You may view God as a stern and righteous judge, and in a sense, you are correct: He has His law and His righteousness demands that there be a penalty for failing to live up to that law. It's no different than laws set up here on earth: If you are caught going over the speed limit, there is a fine to pay; if you are caught stealing, there is restitution to make; if you are convicted of murder, your life may be taken in return. And although we may differ in degree, all of us fail man's laws at some point ... and we all fail God's. The Bible calls this failure *sin*. Romans 3:20 and 23 say this:

> *Therefore no one will be declared righteous in God's sight by the works of the law; rather, through the law we become conscious of our sin ... for all have sinned and fall short of the glory of God.*

As harsh as it may seem, the penalty for failing to live by His law is death. Look at Romans 6:23:

> ... *for the wages of sin is death.*

But here's where God differs from man. Knowing that His law—and its punishments—had to be satisfied, He sent His only Son to pay the penalty ... for *our* sin, for *our* failures. Although Jesus lived a sinless life, His love was so great for each and every one of us, that He freely chose to go to the Cross, bearing the penalty for our sins, not His, and dying in our place. Romans 5:8 says this:

> *But God demonstrates his own love for us in this: While we were still sinners, Christ died for us.*

Thankfully, His love doesn't stop there. Dying is one thing ... living is another. Just three days later, in one of the most well-documented facts in history, Christ rose from the dead—just read Matthew chapter 28. Moreover, Jesus Himself says in John 14:6:

> *I am the way and the truth and the life. No one comes to the Father except through me.*

And the apostle Paul puts it as bluntly as possible in 1 Timothy 2:5:

> *For there is one God and one mediator between God and mankind, the man Christ Jesus.*

We can have that personal, one-on-one relationship with the creator of the universe, only by acknowledging and embracing that sacrifice of His son through faith in Him. Look carefully at Romans 3:22 and 24-25:

> *This righteousness is given **through faith in Jesus Christ** to all who believe ... all are justified freely by*

> his grace through the redemption that came by Christ Jesus. God presented Christ as a sacrifice of atonement, through the shedding of his blood—**to be received by faith**.

And if we do that, two marvelous and miraculous changes occur in our lives. First, while we are still on earth, Hebrews 10:10 declares that:

> ... we have been made holy through the sacrifice of the body of Jesus Christ once for all.

Regardless of your past, when you accept the sacrifice that Christ made for your sins by dying on the cross, amazingly, God now views you as *holy*. Another way to put it is that He views you *just as if you had never sinned*. Sound too good to be true? This is not cheap grace ... this was God's very own sinless and righteous Son paying the penalty for *your* sins—past, present and even future ones—once for all.

It gets even better than that. Note what fabulous gift God gives you when you accept that sacrifice. The latter part of Romans 6:23 says:

> ... the gift of God is eternal life in Christ Jesus our Lord.

Eternal life ... that is life that even mature believers have a hard time comprehending. There will be no sin, no war, no disease, but an unending time of life with God as He truly intended from the beginning. And it is available to those who will simply humble themselves, acknowledge their sin, and accept what Christ has done for them.

There is a great verse that we will deal with in more detail in Chapter 5. It comes in the midst of a passage where Jesus is dealing with people in a church in which they think they have done everything necessary, including good deeds, to be accepted by God. Jesus tells them, convincingly, they are instead "wretched, pitiful, poor, blind and naked," and need to repent. Then He invites them—and anyone else who will listen—into the Kingdom by declaring in Revelation 3:20:

> *Here I am! I stand at the door and knock. If anyone hears my voice and opens the door, I will come in and eat with that person, and they with me.*

How about you? Are you ready to acknowledge your sin—your falling far short of His standards—and accept His payment for that sin by inviting Him into your life? Are you willing to follow Him wherever He may lead you, confident it will be the most fulfilling life you can ever imagine? If so, here's a suggested prayer that you can pray—feel free to modify it to better fit your circumstances:

> Dear God, I come to you acknowledging that I have sinned and fallen far short of Your law, Your standards. You have every right to punish me for those failures; yet I acknowledge and accept the payment for those sins which Your Son Jesus accomplished when He died on the Cross and rose from the grave. I invite Jesus into my life and my heart, and ask that You begin guiding and leading me into that marvelous life You have planned for me. In Jesus name I pray, Amen.

If you prayed that prayer, congratulations! You are now a new creature in Christ and are viewed as holy as God is holy, ready to begin a new life in Him. Yet, this is just the start of your journey. Like beginning a new job, there is so much to learn and the best way to do that as a new Christ-follower is to get involved with a local church, a local group of believers. Ask Him to help you to do that, to look for a local body that comes together to study His Word and grow.

Finally, if you did pray that prayer, would you let me know? As I indicated in the chapter, although getting your finances on a firm Biblical foundation is a critical step in Christian growth, even more important is taking that first step and becoming a believer, letting Him guide you day-by-day along the path He has chosen for you. My contact information is at the back of the book.

3

THE SERMON ON THE AMOUNT

> Only by giving are you able to receive more than you already have - Jim Rohn
>
> Think of giving not as a duty but as a privilege - John D. Rockefeller Jr.

With the critical importance of developing your personal financial roadmap established, this chapter digs deeper into Step #1 of that process—giving. On the surface, this issue seems so simple, and many churches present it that way. But recall that in Chapter 1 we talked about the importance of *context*. To be frank, giving is an area where much of the church has misunderstood God's intent. Instead of teaching the clear message that began early in the Old Testament and continued unchanged into the New, many church leaders and Christian organizations have presented an erroneous requirement for Christ-followers—one that not only has been taken out of context but also misrepresented as to the applicable amount.

In order to clearly see God's intent for true, heartfelt giving, this chapter provides an in-depth—and educational—examination of numerous passages in both Testaments that have been cited as guidance for New Testament believers. The end result will be that you see for yourself what God's real guidance is—and what it is not.

Understanding the pivotal role that true, heartfelt giving plays in our lives as Christians—*why*, *how*, and *how much* we should give—is *the most important step* in getting our attitudes towards money straight. While you may be anxious to get into what God's Word has to teach us about investing, or retirement, or estate planning, His Word is quite clear that you can't have your mind straight on the reasons for making money until you have your heart straight on the reasons for giving it away.

To be honest, *giving* is a topic that troubled me for much of my Christian life. Ever since I became a believer, I knew that I should give. I also acknowledged—at least mentally—that everything I had was His. Yet, it still seemed so hard at times to give some of those precious, hard-earned resources away, given all the alternative uses—and needs—I had for my money. Have you ever felt the same?

On top of that, for the longest time, I never really felt comfortable with how *much* I was giving. Sure, I was familiar with the concept of tithing—giving ten percent—but there was that nagging issue of: should it be on my gross income or my net? Even more troubling was, given all my other commitments, there often just wasn't ten percent left to give. So, whenever I heard a message on giving, the guilt trip would start again.

But the more I studied His Word and read about the freedom, joy, and eager willingness exhibited by those who freely gave to God regardless of their financial condition, the more I realized that maybe I was doing it all wrong. Perhaps the admittedly easy-to-understand concept of the tithe did not even come close to capturing God's real intent on why He asks us to give back to Him. So as part of my decades-long process of educating myself on what His Word really teaches about money, I spent long hours delving into the history and background of numerous Biblical passages dealing with giving—both Old and New Testaments. What amazed me most about that study was how consistent and clear His guidance is and yet how rarely it is taught in the Church.

Because of the importance of getting this essential aspect of our daily Christian life properly and firmly ingrained in our hearts and minds, the goal of this chapter is two-fold. First, we will clear up any confusion about the role and purposes of the tithe—there are actually three—by examining every important passage that mentions the concept. In doing so, the erroneous requirement mentioned earlier will be exposed. Then, going all the way back to the book of Exodus, we will trace the timeless guidance of how God desires for us to freely and willingly participate in honoring Him when we give today—a "blueprint" that you can come back to should you ever get confused about this issue again. I must warn you, however, that there is a potentially uncomfortable consequence of giving in the way He truly desires. To be able to fully grasp the nature of that consequence, we need to first understand the origin and intent of the tithe.

History and Purpose of the Tithe

The Hebrew word used in the Old Testament is *ma'ăśēr* (ma-as-ayr'), literally, a tenth part. In Greek, it's *děkatē* (dek-at'-ay)—the tenth—and is the same root from which the word "decathlon" or "ten events" comes.

Ma'ăśēr wasn't a religious word, but a mathematical one—it only had to do with a percentage. It's origin? We know from ancient sources that man has always used ten as the basic number for counting systems, no doubt because he had ten fingers and ten toes. Throughout man's history ten has been used both as a basis of measurement and a symbol of completeness. Even today we use the phrase "a perfect 10!"

The exact time of the origin of this concept is not known, but we do know that the tenth was a common pagan offering well before, during and after Abraham's time. For example, the Phoenicians and Carthaginians[13] (circa 1550 BC) sent a tithe annually to the Tyrian leader Hercules. The Lydians (circa 700 BC) offered a tithe of their booty[14] taken in battle. And, as you may know, the Egyptians were required to give a fifth part—or twenty percent—of their crops to Pharaoh.[15]

First Biblical Use

The first Biblical mention of *ma'ăśēr* is in the very first book, Genesis, chapter 14. Abraham (or Abram, his pre-Abrahamic covenant name used here) has just returned from conquering Chedorlaomer and other kings in the valley of Shaveh and has a tremendous amount of spoil and treasure. Two kings come out to meet him, the King of Sodom and the King of Salem (the ancient name for Jerusalem)— who was an interesting character named Melchizedek. In verses 18-20 of chapter 14 it says:

> ... *Melchizedek king of Salem brought out bread and wine. He was priest of God Most High, and he blessed Abram, saying,*
>
> *"Blessed be Abram by God Most High, Creator of heaven and earth. And praise be to God Most High, who delivered your enemies into your hand."*

Then Abram gave him a tenth (ma'ăśēr) of everything.

We don't know a lot about Melchizedek, but it says here that he was a priest of "God most high." And he blesses Abram. What does Abram do in return? He gives Melchizedek a tenth. Of tenth of what? Of everything. Seems pretty obvious, doesn't it? And in many printed documents that discuss tithing as the requirement for New Testament believers, this is their first justification for it.

Take a closer look at the passage:

- Is there any indication that Abram was commanded or ordered to give a tenth? Remember that this is pre-Law. Could it be that this was simply giving of the common pagan amount back then?
- There's a bigger issue here. Regardless of whether this was strictly voluntary or if there was some unspoken or undocumented requirement, did Abram really give a tenth of *everything*? Or does "everything" mean something else? As a simple analogy, when someone asks you "how are you doing" and you respond, "I feel like *everything* in my life is messed up," it doesn't really mean that every part of your life is messed up, does it?

An Interesting Twist

To answer the "everything" question, we need to look at the New Testament book of Hebrews, chapter 7, where the author recalls this event in their effort to show how much greater the Melchizedek priesthood is to the Aaronic priesthood. In doing so, the writer provides an interpretation of exactly what "everything" means. Look at verse 4 of chapter 7, where it says:

> *Just think how great he* [Melchizedek] *was: Even the patriarch Abraham gave him a tenth of the plunder* ["spoils" in the KJV]*!*

What's the big deal, you may be wondering? This is what makes proper study of God's Word so important, otherwise you can easily come to the wrong conclusions. Remember that we are reading a translation from the Greek and not all translations get everything completely correct. The Greek word used for "plunder" or "spoils" is used only here in the New Testament and is a fascinating one: *akrŏthiniŏn* (ak-roth-in'-ee-on).

It's meaning? It's actually a combination of two Greek words: *akro,* which means the "top-most" or "uttermost point" and *thin,* which means "a heap." So, what Abraham gave Melchizedek was a tenth part of the *top-most* or *uttermost point* of the pile or heap. *Strong's Concordance* states it as a tenth of "the best of the booty." Do you see the difference? Abraham did not give a tenth of *all* the spoils but only a tenth of the *best* of the spoils. Or said another way, he gave "the best of the best." That could easily have been only one percent of the total!

The "Heap" or "Pile"
Hebrews 7:4

Tenth of "topmost" part

"Topmost" part

Look at how other translations put it:

> ... a tenth out of the *chief* spoils (ASV)

> ... gave a tenth out of the best plunder (World English Bible)

> ... a tenth of the *choicest* spoils (NASB)

> ... gave tithes of the *best* things (Wycliffe)

> ... a tenth ... out of the *best* of the spoils (Young's Literal Translation)

Can you see that Abraham didn't give a tithe—or tenth—from *all* the spoils but only a tithe of the best of the spoils? Look at it this way: no doubt at the end of the battle, there were many broken spears, shields, saddles, probably even some half-dead captured warriors and horses. If Melchizedek was as great as both Genesis and Hebrews say he was, there's no way Abraham would have included a tenth of all the useless broken stuff—he would have offered a portion only of the best stuff. Moreover, there is no record that he ever did this again.

One last thing. According to both Genesis 13:2 and 24:35, Abraham was "very rich in livestock, in silver and in gold," amongst other things. We have no evidence that Abraham ever gave a tithe of these things. Taken together, then, using the Genesis 14:18-20 passage as conclusive evidence that Abraham gave a tithe of "everything"—or that it was required—seems a bit absurd, doesn't it?

Then Comes Jacob

The next mention of the tithe is in Genesis 28, involving Jacob and his amazing dream at Bethel. In the dream he sees a stairway reaching up to heaven, with angels going up and down. Above the stairway is the Lord, and He tells Jacob how his descendants will be like the dust of the earth and will spread out to the west and the east and the north and the south. Jacob hears the Lord say that all peoples will be blessed through him and his offspring. The Lord also tells him that He will watch over him wherever he goes and will not leave him until He has done what He has promised. When he awoke, Jacob said "how awesome is this place! This is none other than the house of God; this is the gate of heaven." To use twenty-first century vernacular, he was blown away by the dream, as I think all of us would have been!

Jacob then makes an interesting vow. See if you can pick out the essence of what he promised in verses 20-22:

> *"If God will be with me and will watch over me on this journey I am taking and will give me food to eat and clothes to wear [21] so that I return safely to my father's household, then the Lord will be my God [22] and this stone that I have set up as a pillar will be God's house, and of all that you give me I will give you a tenth."*

Did you catch it? Remember that this is still pre-Law. Yes, Jacob promises to give a tenth ... but does he really? Notice two important words in the passage—and these are the same words in virtually every translation: ***If*** *God ...* ***then*** *the Lord will be my God ... and of all that you give me I will give you a tenth.* Jacob has this tremendous dream, calling the place literally the gate of heaven and what does he do? He makes a *conditional* promise: *If* you, God, provide me food ... and clothing ... and safety, *then* you will be my God and I will do this and that, including giving you a tenth. Can you see how ridiculous that is? Jacob is trying to run the show here, vowing that the Lord will not even be his God unless He essentially proves Himself to him by meeting his demands. And if He does, then and only then will he give a tenth.

Not a very convincing model for tithing, is it? It would be like the church today saying "don't give now; lay out all your demands to Him to prove Himself and wait to see if He satisfies them." Not much faith in that, is there?

One other thing. Did Jacob ever satisfy his vow? We don't know. But not surprisingly, this passage is often not mentioned when tithing is presented as the requirement for today.

FIRST TITHE UNDER THE LAW

Let's move forward to the next mention of the tithe—called the Levitical tithe as it was given to the Levitical priests—and the second passage most often used to support the concept of tithing as a requirement. This comes from the Mosaic Law, so we had better make sure we get it right! Look at Leviticus 27:30 and 32-33 where God is speaking to Moses, telling him:

> *A tithe of everything from the land, whether grain from the soil or fruit from the trees, belongs to the LORD; it is holy to the LORD ...* [32] *Every tithe of the herd and flock—every tenth animal that passes under the shepherd's rod—will be holy to the LORD.* [33] *No one may pick out the good from the bad or make any substitution. If anyone does make a substitution, both the animal and its substitute become holy and cannot be redeemed.*

That seems pretty clear and non-disputable, doesn't it? In this passage, "everything" and "every" really do seem to mean *everything*, since the Israelites were an agrarian society at this point and the latter part of verse 32 says that it even includes every tenth animal that passes under the shepherd's rod.

There are, however, three interesting twists to this passage. First, you may have noticed that I conveniently "skipped over" verse 31—which I did on purpose. Here's why.

The whole twenty-seventh chapter of Leviticus deals with physical things promised to the Lord, such as a house, or an animal, or a field. Provisions were made, however, for the owner to "redeem"—or keep—the item and give money instead. For example, in Leviticus 27:14 and 15 it says:

> *If anyone dedicates their house as something holy to the Lord, the priest will judge its quality as good or bad. Whatever value the priest then sets, so it will remain.* ¹⁵ *If the one who dedicates their house wishes to* **redeem** *it ….*

But here's the kicker in the remainder of verse 15. If money was to be given in place of the actual offering:

> *they must add a **fifth** to its value, and the house will again become theirs.*

In other words, twenty percent of the item's value had to be added to the cash amount to be given in its place. If the item was worth, say $100, twenty percent or $20, had to be added, making it a $120 cash offering. If we now go back to the tithe of the grain, etc., in verses 30 and 32-33, here's what it says in verse 31, the one I conveniently skipped over:

> *A tithe of everything from the land, whether grain from the soil or fruit from the trees, belongs to the LORD; it is holy to the LORD.* ³¹ ***Whoever would redeem any of their tithe must add a <u>fifth</u> of the value to it.*** ³² *Every tithe of the herd and flock—every*

> tenth animal that passes under the shepherd's rod—will be holy to the LORD. *33* No one may pick out the good from the bad or make any substitution. If anyone does make a substitution, both the animal and its substitute become holy and cannot be redeemed.

So, if the landowner wanted to use money for their tithe of everything from the land, it was how much? Twelve percent, not ten percent. I would be willing to guess that most of you have never heard that from the pulpit!

Second, although verse 33 indicates that the tithe of the herd and flock could not be redeemed, this tithe was actually not ten percent! Look at the verse closely, as the rules governing this process were very specific: "every tenth animal that *passes under the shepherd's rod.*" If a shepherd owned nine or fewer animals, no tithe was required! Or, if the shepherd owned, say, nineteen animals, only one animal—the tenth one—was taken for sacrifice, making the tithe about five percent!

Finally—and this will likely come as a shock to many readers—there was a large segment of Israelites who paid *no* tithes! Remember that we are dealing with specific requirements spelled out in the Mosaic Law so read this carefully: *The only individuals subject to the Levitical tithe were the landowners and shepherds who owned animals.* Excluded from this requirement would be all the other types of workers, such as hired hands working for the landowners or shepherds, those earning an income from weaving, or handicrafts, or fishing, or any form of manufacturing or merchandising. And, as Israel's economy grew, there were bankers, lawyers, accountants, doctors, construction firm owners and workers, and on and on. *There was no law that required a tenth of one's salary from these types of jobs*; only the crops and animals of those who owned them were subject to the tithe.

Let's pause here and summarize what we have learned from this passage so that it can sink in. First, landowners were required to give a tenth of all that their land produced each year. However, if they wanted to keep some or all of it and pay cash instead, they had to add twenty percent to the cash value of the grain or fruit from the vines kept back, making their tithe twelve percent. Second, shepherds—those who owned animals—gave a tithe only of every tenth animal; if they owned less than ten, no tithe was required; if they owned more, only the tenth out of every ten that passed under the shepherd's rod was tithed. Finally—and maybe most importantly—these were the only individuals subject to these requirements. All other workers and business owners were exempt.

Pretty enlightening, isn't it? This is the erroneous interpretation mentioned at the start of the chapter: not only was this tithe not really ten percent if 1) cash was used (tithe from the soil) or 2) animals were counted (tithe of the herd and flock), it didn't apply to much of the Hebrew population. Using this passage, then, as justification for us in New Testament times, to tithe seems pretty ridiculous, don't you think? Taking this one step further, if a minister today wanted the members of his church to abide by this portion of the Law, those members with gardens would need to be paying a tenth of their produce—or twelve percent if they chose to give cash instead—those with chickens giving a tenth of their eggs, and so on. But they couldn't be required to give ten percent from their earnings as accountants, or construction workers, or whatever they did for a living. So, the only "support" the church would have would be from the members' gardens and chicken coops! This illustrates the danger of referring to the Law for guidance today: the Law requires adherence to very specific requirements—no exceptions, no modifications and *no extending it to excluded situations*. Again, pretty ridiculous to use this as guidance for us today.

Two More Tithes Under the Law

But wait—there's *more* (just like those TV infomercials)! In addition to this annual requirement, there were two other well-defined required tithes under the Law—and these are rarely acknowledged when tithing is presented as the requirement for us today.

First, Deuteronomy 14:22-23 requires a tithe that was to be *eaten*. Called the "Festival" tithe, God says:

> *Be sure to set aside a tenth of all that your fields produce each year.* ^{23} **Eat** *the tithe of your grain, new wine and oil, and the firstborn of your herds and flocks in the presence of the LORD your God at the place he will choose as a dwelling for his Name, so that you may learn to revere the LORD your God always.*

This was basically to be a huge, nationwide "potluck" celebration every year! And if the celebration venue was too distant to bring the physical tithe, it could be exchanged for silver and used to buy what was needed upon arrival. It is unclear, however, whether the extra one-fifth redemption rule applied to this tithe.

Second, there is the "Welfare" tithe recorded five verses later in Deuteronomy 14:28-29:

> *At the end of every three years, bring all the tithes of that year's produce and store it in your towns,* ^{29} *so that the Levites (who have no allotment or inheritance of their own) and the aliens, the fatherless and the widows who live in your towns may come and eat and be satisfied, and so that the LORD your God may bless you in all the work of your hands.*

There is uncertainty whether this third tithe was the second one put to special use or a separate tithe every third year. In any event, it was still a *required* tithe. Assuming, conservatively, that this third tithe was the second one put to special use, then how much was *required* each year? Ten percent plus ten percent equals twenty percent. And if cash was used by the landowners for the first one, it would be twelve percent plus ten percent—or twenty-two percent.

In summary, if someone wants to disregard the context of the first tithe in Leviticus 27—that it was directed only towards landowners and shepherds—and suggest it applies to us today, then the other two—the Festival and Welfare tithes—must also be followed, because all three are specified and required under the Law. To be blunt, you can't preach one and leave out the other two. And, if cash is to be used for the first tithe from the soil, it has to be twelve percent—there is just no other way to read it, unless, of course, you want to argue with God's Law.

WHAT WERE THESE TITHES, REALLY?

There is one mitigating factor in all of this. Israel was a theocracy, or government by God. Because these tithes basically funded operation of the government of Israel (the priests and taking care of the poor) and they were required, most scholars view these tithes as *taxation*. Even so, God did promise fabulous blessings for following this portion of the Law. In this same chapter of Deuteronomy, just after the third tithe, God says in verse 29:

> *so that the LORD your God may* **bless** *you in* **all the work of your hands**.

With that hanging in the air—and before moving on to the last major Old Testament passage dealing with the tithe—let me pose a question for you to ponder: If these three required tithes really are to be viewed as taxation in Israel's economy, then how can they possibly be used as guidance for *giving*, whether in the Old Testament or New? As you mull that over, be aware that the Old Testament contains separate guidance on true freewill giving, to be covered later in the chapter.

The "Test Me" Tithe in Malachi

Did the Israelites follow these requirements? If we jump forward to the last book in the Old Testament, Malachi, we'll see that it was unlikely. The passage in Malachi is the last major mention of the tithe in the Old Testament and the third one normally used by proponents of the tithe. This is another passage where we have to be very careful of context in determining the proper interpretation.

Let's first talk about the book of Malachi as a whole. The Israelites had recently been allowed to return from exile and rebuild the temple. Chapter 4, verse 4 makes it very clear that they were still subject to the Mosaic Law:

> *Remember the law of my servant Moses, the decrees and laws I gave him at Horeb for all Israel.*

The very first verse of the book, however, begins with the word "oracle"—the Hebrew word literally means *burden*—giving the hearers and readers of the prophet's message an immediate sense of anxiety and foreboding. And rightfully so, as both the priests and the people had been violating the stipulations of the Law regarding sacrifices, tithes, and offerings. Moreover, the people were intermarrying with pagans, as well as practicing divorce. Malachi 3:7 provides proof of their failings:

> *Ever since the time of your ancestors you have turned away from my decrees and have not kept them. Return to me, and I will return to you," says the Lord Almighty.*

There is also evidence that life had not been easy for them: they were under the political domination of Persia and harvests had been poor, subject to locust damage. As a result, they were discouraged in a lot of ways, especially that God had not yet returned to the temple to display His majesty and power and exalt His kingdom in sight of the nations (3:1).

With that as the context, let's now read the passage about tithing in Malachi 3:8-11:

> *"Will a mere mortal rob God? Yet you rob me.*
>
> *"But you ask, 'How are we robbing you?'*
>
> *"In tithes and offerings. [9] You are under a curse—your whole nation—because you are robbing me. [10] Bring the whole tithe into the storehouse, that there may be food in my house. Test me in this," says the Lord Almighty, "and see if I will not throw open the floodgates of heaven and pour out so much blessing that there will not be room enough to store it. [11] I will prevent pests from devouring your crops, and the vines in your fields will not drop their fruit before it is ripe," says the Lord Almighty*

An amazing passage, don't you think? Here's God telling Israel straight out that they are robbing Him. Like other instances in the book, they respond with a sarcastic question: "How are we robbing you?" Their question is reminiscent of a classic confrontation between Jack Nicholson and Tom Cruise in the movie "A Few Good Men"—if you've seen the movie, you likely remember it:

> Nicholson: You want answers?
>
> Cruise: I want the truth!
>
> Nicholson: You can't handle the truth!

In Malachi, God gives the truth to the Israelites, whether they can handle it or not. First, He tells them that they are not following His Law by bringing the required tithes and offerings—and the answer to my earlier question. Since some of these offerings went to support the priests, and they were part of the temple system, and the temple was God's house, failure to bring in what the law required was equivalent to robbing God Himself.

Second, He tells them that, as a result, the whole nation is under a curse—the very curse specified in the Mosaic Law in Deuteronomy 28:38-40:

> *You will sow much seed in the field but you will harvest little, because locusts will devour it. [39] You will plant vineyards and cultivate them but you will not drink the wine or gather the grapes, because worms will eat them. [40] You will have olive trees throughout your country but you will not use the oil, because the olives will drop off.*

Then an amazing thing happens. After sternly telling the Israelites how they have failed and received the righteous judgment they deserved, God then demonstrates His unending and ever-forgiving love for them by making the same offer to them as He does to anyone truly seeking to return to Him, saying in verses 7 and 10-11 (paraphrased):

> "Return to Me ... honor Me by doing what I ask ... even test Me in this ... and see that I will not only reverse the curse but bless you mightily again."

Did the Israelites rise up to God's challenge of "test me in this" and return to following Him? We don't know, for soon thereafter the 400-year silence between the Old and New Testaments begins. But given their history, what do you think?

And ponder this: This is the only occasion in the entire Bible where God says, "test me in this." Coming from God Himself, it is, admittedly, a powerful statement—and many use it as part of their justification for tithing today. But remember the critical importance of *context*. Not only is the overall context of Malachi ominous, recall the specific condemning accusations God makes against the Israelites in the chapter 3 passage:

> 3:7: *Ever since the time of your ancestors you have turned away from my decrees and have not kept them.*

> 3:8: *Yet you rob me.*

> 3:9: *You are under a curse—your whole nation.*

But then, He softens and lovingly offers these stubborn and disobedient Israelites the way back, the actions they need to take to receive the blessings He promised them all along:

> 3:10: *Bring the whole tithe into the storehouse ... Test me in this ... and see if I will not throw open the*

floodgates of heaven and pour out so much blessing that there will not be room enough to store it.

So ... does it seem appropriate to use a passage aimed at Israel's numerous failures under the Law—and how they can get back into "Law abiding" fellowship with Him—and apply it to New Testament believers? In other words, is there any indication in this passage that God's disappointment with the Israelite's failure to follow the Law regarding tithing—whether it is ten percent, twenty-percent, or whatever—is also directed to us in New Testament times? Realize that some churches will even go so far as to suggest that not following the tithe requirements in Malachi 3 will result in the believer being under a curse.

As you think about that, let me mention something else before we consider another facet of this issue: When you refer back to the Old Testament for guidance during New Testament times—especially when referring to the Mosaic Law—you cannot "pick and choose" what you want to follow. If you are going to draw things from the Law, you must then follow the *whole* Law: Temple worship, the sacrificial system, circumcision—in essence, all that is laid out in the book of Deuteronomy. Are you willing to do that? Have you even ever heard that resultant obligation mentioned from the pulpit?

THE OFTEN OVERLOOKED WORD IN THE MALACHI PASSAGE

Regarding the second facet of this issue, alluded to above, reread Malachi 3:8 a little more carefully:

> "But you ask, 'How are we robbing you?' 'In tithes and **offerings**.'"

Beyond the three tithes we read about, there was also a whole host of *offerings* specified under the Law, many required and some completely freewill. Per the table below, all of the required tithes and offerings added up to somewhere between thirty and forty-five percent of their income. Add to that all the freewill offerings and ... well, I think you get the picture. If someone wants to suggest that tithing is the requirement for us today, then we need to be giving a lot more than simply ten percent!

TYPE	AMOUNT	FREQUENCY
1. Levitical Tithe – Lev. 27:30, 32	10% (12% if paid cash)	Annual
2. Festival Tithe—Deut. 14:22-23	10%	Annual
3. Welfare Tithe—Deut. 14:28-29	3 1/3%?	Every 3rd year
4. Gleanings—Lev. 19:9	?	Every harvest
5. Temple Tax—Matt. 17:24	1%	Annual
6. Land Sabbath Rest—Lev. 25:4	14%*	Every 7th year
7. Debts set aside—Deut. 15:1	?	Every 7th year
Total	30-45%	

* 1 year out of 7 = 14% for landowners

THE TITHE IN THE NEW TESTAMENT

A fair question at this point would be: "Doesn't the *New* Testament talk about tithing?" Yes, it does. Let's cover that base so that we can come to a sensible conclusion as to whether God's Word teaches that New Testament believers should tithe.

Other than the passage in Hebrews 7:4 (which we looked at), there are only three other mentions of the tithe in the New Testament: Matthew 23:23 and its parallel in Luke 11:42, where Jesus is dealing with the Pharisees again, and Luke 18:9-14, which is the parable of the self-righteous Pharisee and the lowly tax collector. Let's take a brief look at them.

Matthew 23:23 says this:

> *"Woe to you, teachers of the law and Pharisees, you hypocrites! You give a **tenth** of your spices—mint, dill and cumin. But you have neglected the more important matters of the law—justice, mercy and faithfulness. You should have practiced the latter, without neglecting the former."*

Follow closely here because you are going to see some real "stretching" of the context. Proponents of a current-day requirement to tithe refer to this verse, and even though it is dealing specifically with the teachers of the law and the Pharisees, they focus solely on two words in the passage:

> *You **should have** practiced the latter* [giving a tenth of their spices], *without neglecting the former.*

Here's how their thinking goes: Because this is in the *New* Testament and it says, "should have," it implies that giving a tenth is a given, no matter what, and therefore, applies to us. That seems a bit far-fetched, don't you think? As proof, let me share with you the problem with that interpretation—and then we'll read the rest of the story for confirmation. If you want to use this verse as guidance, you have to use the *whole* verse—there is no picking and choosing allowed! Not only should you not neglect the more important matters of the Law—justice, mercy and faithfulness—you had better give a tithe of *everything*, down even to the spices in your cupboard!

But, again, this is where proper study of God's Word—especially the context—is so important to being able to yield the correct interpretation. Matthew 23:13-39 is titled "Seven Woes," as it describes seven denunciations of the teachers of the Law and the Pharisees—denouncing false religion as utterly abhorrent to God and worthy of … eternal damnation. So, we must be very careful about what we draw from this single verse. To get a sense of the context, read verses 1-3 of chapter 23:

> *Then Jesus said to the crowds and to his disciples:* ² *"The teachers of the law and the Pharisees sit in Moses' seat.* ³ *So you must be careful to do everything they tell you. But do not do what they do, for they do not practice what they preach.*

Admittedly, this passage is a bit difficult to interpret but is well worth the effort. Note that the passage says the listeners must "do" everything the teachers of the law and Pharisees "tell" them but then it seems to contradict that by saying "do *not* do what they do …" I consulted a lot of sources to make sure I got it right. Virtually every one of them says this: Since they—the teachers of the Law and the Pharisees—"sit in Moses' seat," they *are* the authorized successors of Moses as teachers of the Law and their *authority* was to be recognized. But their *practice* of the Law, being hypocritical, should not be followed. In other words, they don't "walk the talk." Look at how some other translations put verse 3:

> *Do not, however,* **imitate** *their actions, because they don't practice what they preach* (Good News Translation)

> *But you must not* **imitate** *their lives! For they preach but do not practise.* (Phillips)

> *But do not do according to their* **works***; for they say, and do not do.* (NKJV)

> *But don't follow their* **example***. For they don't practice what they teach.* (New Living Translation)

Even the Complete Jewish Bible says:

> *But don't do what they **do**, because they talk but don't act!*

Listed below are some of Jesus' denunciations of these teachers—remember, this is to help in identifying the context of verse 23:

> Vs. 13b: *You **shut the door** of the **kingdom of heaven** in people's faces. You yourselves **do not enter**, nor will you let those enter who are trying to.*
>
> Vs. 15b: *You make them* [a new convert] ***twice as much as a child of hell as you are...*** [ouch!]
>
> Vs. 25b: *You clean the outside of the cup and dish, but inside they are **full of greed and self-indulgence**.*
>
> Vs. 27b: *You are like **whitewashed tombs**, which look beautiful on the outside but on the inside are **full of the bones of the dead and everything unclean**.*

Going back to verse 23, what *is* the proper interpretation? Is it a command, either direct or indirect, for *us* to tithe? Look at it again:

> *...you **hypocrites**. You give a tenth of your spices—mint, dill and cummin. But you have **neglected** the more **important** matters of the law—justice, mercy and faithfulness. You should have practiced the latter, without neglecting the former.*

In the context of this passage, Jesus is talking to two groups, 1) the crowds and His disciples, and 2) the teachers of the Law and the Pharisees. He is illustrating to the crowds and His disciples the complete hypocrisy and the ultimate destiny of these teachers. Jesus also lectures these teachers on all the ways they are failing to live by the very same Law they teach. His last words to them in verse 33 are the most telling:

> *"You snakes! You brood of vipers! How will you escape being condemned to hell?"*

As God's Word makes perfectly clear, if you want to come to God by following the Law, you must live by the whole Law *perfectly*—with not one single mis-step. The teachers of the Law and the Pharisees failed miserably—and so will you if you try. If someone wants to use Matthew 23:23 to support tithing for New Testament believers, they had better require two things: tithing down to every last item in your cupboards, as well as requiring adherence to all of the Law—again, no picking and choosing allowed. To use another phrase, Biblical hop-scotch is not Biblical.

THE PHARISEE VS. THE TAX GATHERER

The other mention of tithing in the New Testament, Luke 18:9-14, puts the concept in a completely different light. This is the parable of the self-righteous Pharisee—yes, them again!—and the lowly Jewish tax collector. To help in interpreting this parable, realize that tax collectors were hated and ostracized by other Jews because they basically extorted the tax from them. Pay attention when reading this passage so you don't miss the two critical lessons Jesus is trying to convey. In brief, the two men go to pray. The Pharisee stands and prays about how great he is in verses 11-12:

> 'God, I thank you that I am not like other people—robbers, evildoers, adulterers—or even like this tax collector. I fast twice a week and give a tenth of all I get.'

The tax collector, however, could not even look up, but beats his breast and confesses in verse 13:

> "God, have mercy on me, a sinner."

Jesus then says in verse 14:

> "I tell you that this man [the tax gatherer], rather than the other, went home justified before God. For all those who exalt themselves will be humbled, and those who humble themselves will be exalted."

Did you catch Jesus' two lessons? The first one is embedded in His use of the word "justified." Justification is one of the key foundational blessings when someone accepts Jesus into his or her life, as the word literally means "to be viewed as righteous as God is righteous." Don't gloss over this. In essence, this is the Gospel in a single word: no matter your past, God now views you *just as if you had never sinned*. In humbling yourself before Him, you are acknowledging that you do *nothing* ... He does everything to bring you to Himself. So, this hated and despised tax gatherer, who depended solely on God's mercy, "... *went home **justified before God**,*" completely accepted by the Creator of the universe.

The second lesson is unspoken but nearly as important. Note that the tax collector says nothing about tithing. But being ostracized and hated by his own people, he likely gave nothing away. He is the one, however, that God exalts into His kingdom, not the self-righteous Pharisee, who, by the way, tithed.

It should be apparent that there's no real support for tithing by true believers here either—just another mention of a legalistic act by someone under the Law trying to exalt themselves whom Jesus says will eventually be humbled. And that is the extent of the New Testament's input on tithing.

Summary of Tithing in God's Word

What do I hope you take away from this review? First, an understanding that the concept of offering or requiring a tenth was a common pagan practice before, during and after Abraham's life. There is no evidence that it was instituted by God but was instead a simple representation of completeness or of giving your all. And with Abraham's offering in Genesis 14, it was only a tenth of the best—not a tenth of all the spoils from the battle—and there is no evidence that he ever did this again or that he tithed on his substantial wealth.

Second, when the tenth—or tithe—is incorporated into the Mosaic Law, there is not one tithe but three, and they only applied to landowners and shepherds that owned animals. Moreover, with the first tithe, the requirement for landowners was actually twelve percent if cash was given in place of the physical offering, and the tithe for shepherds was not ten percent in most cases. Many Old Testament scholars however, viewed these three tithes as taxation, not as giving. On top of this, there was other required giving so that the amount totaled somewhere between an average of thirty to forty-five percent per year. As heavy as a burden this was, God still promised amazing blessings for obedience. Recall the outcome if the Israelites would only return to God and follow His decrees in Malachi 3:10:

> *Test me in this ... and see if I will not **throw open the floodgates of heaven** and **pour out so much blessing** that there will not be room enough to store it.*

Sadly, however, we have no evidence that the Israelites ever had the faith to experience those blessings.

Finally, when we examined the New Testament references to the tithe, we saw that they were simply additional examples of people living under the Law and not following all its requirements. Most significantly, we saw in the Luke 18 parable of the Pharisee and the tax collector that tithing really has nothing to do with being completely accepted by God.

IF NOT THE TITHE, THEN WHAT?

At this point, you might be wondering: If tithing is not the requirement for New Testament believers, then what is the guidance for giving? As we'll learn, this is yet another beautiful illustration of how God's Word is completely consistent from Old Testament to New. His guidance on giving—not legalistic requirements but real, heart-felt giving—started all the way back in the second book of the Bible, Exodus.

Besides the concept of tithing in the Old Testament, there is also the concept of *freewill* offerings, of which there were basically two types: first fruits and truly freewill. As you read the following passages, notice one critical element embedded in the freewill offerings—this element will be the guiding principle that carries forward into the New Testament:

> Exodus 25:1, 2: *The Lord said to Moses, ² "Tell the Israelites to bring me an offering. You are to receive the offering for me from everyone **whose heart prompts them to give.***
>
> Exodus 35:4-5: *Moses said to the whole Israelite community, "This is what the Lord has commanded:*

> *From what you have, take an offering for the Lord.* ***Everyone who is willing*** *is to bring to the Lord an offering of gold, silver . . .*
>
> In 1 Chronicles 29:17, regarding giving for the Temple, King David prays: *I know, my God, that you test the heart and are pleased with integrity. All these things* ***have I given willingly and with honest intent****. And now I have seen with joy* ***how willingly your people who are here have given to you****.*

What is that all important thread, so crucial to true freewill giving that it even keeps weaving its way through the New Testament? It can be stated in just three words: They gave *willingly*.

To highlight the importance of this concept, read a few more passages, focusing on the bolded portion. You'll also see examples of how much they gave:

> Exodus 35:21: *...and everyone* ***who was willing and whose heart moved them*** *came and brought an offering ...*
>
> Exodus 36:3, 6: *And the people continued to bring* ***freewill offerings*** *morning after morning* **...** ***the people were*** (listen to this!) ***restrained from bringing more ...***
>
> Here's the first one that also talks about the amount: Deuteronomy 16:10, 17: *Then celebrate the Festival of Weeks to the Lord your God by giving a* ***freewill offering*** [here's the amount] ***in proportion to the blessings the Lord your God has given you*** *...*

*Each of you must bring a gift **in proportion to the way the Lord your God has blessed you.***

Ezra 1:6: *All their neighbors assisted them* [in rebuilding the temple] *with articles of silver and gold, with goods and livestock, and with valuable gifts, in addition to all the **freewill offerings.***

Here's another one that also talks about the amount: Ezra 2:68-69: *When they arrived at the house of the Lord in Jerusalem, some of the heads of the families gave **freewill offerings** toward the rebuilding of the house of God on its site. **According to their ability** they gave to the treasury for this work...*

Is that thread clear now? They gave willingly or freely ... and how much? In proportion to the Lord's blessing or according to their ability. What was important was the *attitude* of the giver, not the specific amount, but amazingly, the amount was usually huge! And note the blessing God promises for this type of giving—remembering that we are still in the Old Testament. In Proverbs 11:24-25, King Solomon writes:

*One person gives freely, **yet gains even more;** another withholds unduly, but comes to poverty. **A generous person will prosper;** whoever refreshes others will be refreshed.*

What are the implications of Solomon's words? Read this carefully because it really is true: The more you give, the *more you will gain*; you refresh others and you yourself will be refreshed. And as you'll learn, that refreshing is often something far more important than mere financial blessings.

Summarized then, the Old Testament clearly teaches:

1. The Israelites were to give freely or willingly; and
2. They were to give in proportion to how the Lord had blessed them or according to their ability. No percentages, no minimums, no maximums—it's all His anyway.

THE NEW TESTAMENT: GET READY TO FEEL UNCOMFORTABLE

What about the guidance for us in New Testament times? Not only does the New Testament confirm the guidance given in the Old Testament, it actually contains more detail, as it also provides guidelines on *who* we should give to and *why* we should give, including many promised blessings.

Before we look at those passages, let me clarify the "uncomfortable" aspect of true Biblical giving mentioned in the beginning of the chapter—an uncomfortableness you might already be sensing. As frustrating as it may seem, *there is no set percentage or amount* with freewill giving … there is no "bright line" standard. If that sounds or feels uncomfortable, it is. The biggest problem with a bright line amount is that you can be tempted to think, well, ten percent belongs to Him so ninety belongs to me! Nothing could be further from the truth. We've already learned that it all belongs to Him. But more importantly, our giving—and in fact our entire lives of faith—are not to be a legalistic application of rules and procedures, of "checking boxes" as a way of determining that we are "doing good" in His eyes. Rather, we are to follow His leading, wherever and however He leads. Taking it one step further, should the Lord request, we should be willing—like the apostles—to give everything up to follow Him. And, should He so lead, He absolutely promises to provide our every need.

Please don't start getting crazy nervous because in most cases, He doesn't ask us to give it all up. But, because we have learned that we are only stewards of all we have and that we will be evaluated on that stewardship, if His Word tells us we should be giving some of it away, we should be doing so, right? Moreover, if God's Word contains clear guidance on how to do that giving, it makes pretty good sense to have a good understanding of that guidance, don't you think?

I think it's easy to nod our heads—and hearts—in agreement. Yet I think it's also fair to acknowledge that, in our humanness, it can be difficult to give away that which we worked so hard to obtain—and which we could easily spend providing for ourselves and our families. Moreover, I think there is something even more fundamental impacting our giving habits. Deep down, I think most of us don't really believe that anything *will* happen to us when we give. What else could explain why most of us give so little—or nothing at all? If we really believed that God *will* bless us when we give, like the Israelites in Exodus 36 (cited above), we would have to be *"restrained from bringing more."* Instead, as demonstrated by giving habits across denominations, we give as little as possible, likely because we believe that not only is there no real tangible blessing but once given, the money is gone forever.[16]

To see if that really is the case, we'll do two things with the remainder of the chapter. First, we'll look at a few verses to illustrate that the Old Testament giving model *is* the same in the New Testament. Second, we'll examine what God says *will* happen when we give.

THE GUIDANCE IS THE SAME

To see that the thread of the Old Testament model weaves into the New, we need only look at one verse. However, we'll read a second one because it is so graphic. Both come from the most concentrated teaching on giving in the New Testament, 2 Corinthians 8 and 9— the chapters mentioned in Chapter 2. The primary verse is one we read, chapter 8, verse 12, where the apostle Paul writes:

> *For if the **willingness** is there, the gift is acceptable **according to what one has**, not according to what he does not have.*

That's the exact same guidance we saw in the Old Testament. This guidance comes in the midst of Paul's plea for the offering being collected for the poor believers in Jerusalem, and it crystalizes again *how* and *how much* we are to give. The previous two verses, verses 10 and 11, provide the context:

> *Last year you were the first not only to give but also to have the **desire** to do so. ¹¹Now finish the work, so that your **eager willingness** to do it may be matched by your completion of it, **according to your means**.*

Note that not only is Paul asking the Corinthians to complete the offering they had apparently promised, but he mentions their "eager willingness." Isn't that amazing? Have you ever experienced giving that way? This same "eager willingness" is also mentioned in verses 2–3 of chapter 8, where Paul is recounting the giving by the Macedonians:

> *And now, brothers and sisters, we want you to know about the grace that God has given the Macedonian churches. ²In the midst of a very severe trial, their overflowing joy and their extreme poverty welled up in rich generosity. ³For I testify that they gave as much as they were able, and even beyond their ability.*

This is an incredible passage—don't miss what it says: Overflowing joy ... rich generosity ... they gave as much as they were able ... and ... beyond ... even though they were in extreme poverty and experiencing a severe trial. Verse 4 even says that they urgently "pleaded" with the apostles to be able to participate! If ever there was an ideal setting in all of God's Word to stipulate the tithe as being the required amount, this is it. Instead, what does it say? "And now ... we want you to know about the *grace* that God has given the Macedonian churches." Grace—that single act of Christ dying on the Cross so that we could once more experience the incredible life He desired for us all along. The more we comprehend and appreciate all that His grace has accomplished, the more we will *want* to honor Him. Read how *The Message* translates this passage and captures the amazing impact that a proper understanding of God's grace can have on our giving:

> *Now, friends, I want to report on the surprising and generous ways in which God is working in the churches in Macedonia province. Fierce troubles came down on the people of those churches, pushing them to the very limit. The trial exposed their true colors: They were incredibly happy, though desperately poor. The pressure triggered something totally unexpected: an outpouring of pure and generous gifts. I was there and saw it for myself. They gave offerings of whatever they could— far more than they could afford!—pleading for the privilege of helping out in the relief of poor Christians.*

That is true, grace-motivated giving. And that's why Paul tells the Corinthians in verse 7:

> *... see that you also excel in this grace of giving.*

But wait ... there's more! Look at the second supporting verse, 2 Corinthians 9:7—we also read this one in Chapter 2. To help clearly convey the point, I've added literal meaning to some of the words:

> *Each of you should give what you have* **decided in your heart to give** [made up your *mind* to give;

as your *heart* tells you], **not reluctantly or under compulsion** [not with *pain* or *constraint*; there should be no *reluctance*, no sense of *compulsion*; not out of a *troubled* or *annoyed* heart; not out of *necessity*], *for God loves a* **cheerful** [hilarious, merry, joyful, glad to give; ready] *giver.*

That is how true Biblical giving is to be done. Although this would have been another perfect place to say it, nothing is said about the tithe—or any specific amount for that matter—simply give what you have *decided in your heart.* Not under guilt … or requirement … or obligation, but cheerful, hilarious giving, no matter what financial position you are in. How often does that kind of giving happen? How often does the Church even present giving this way? I must confess how easy it has been for my giving at times to become rote, emotionless, obligatory and even purely tax-motivated, especially near the end of the year. Have you ever felt that way?

But if we really understand 2 Corinthians 9:7, that's obviously not what God desires. Taking all these passages together, His Word is quite clear that He wants:

- The "desire" to give,
- "Eager willingness,"
- "Overflowing joy,"
- Not "reluctantly" but "cheerfully."

And the amount?

- "According to your *means*" or out of "what you *have*,"
- "Rich generosity" and even "beyond your ability,"

because it is what you have:

- "Decided in your *heart* to give," even though you might be in the "midst of a very severe trial" or "extreme poverty."

APPLYING THIS OPEN-ENDED GUIDANCE

Do you want *your* giving experience to match that? Before I share a couple of surprising Biblical admonitions that have really helped me in this area, I need to ask you to take a moment and seriously ponder your answer to my oft-asked question, as that answer will be one of the truest tests of your faith: Do you believe, *really believe* God and His Word here, that this *is* the model of how He wants us to give? No percentages, no minimum or maximum amounts; instead, give cheerfully, eagerly, joyfully, maybe even beyond what you think you can afford because that is what you have decided in your heart.

An honest answer is incredibly important because I would venture to say that for virtually every reader, it would be easy for the daily requirements of life to soak up every dollar of income they have. For those with an excess of resources, it is easy to become overwhelmed by the amounts needed to pay for your children's education, or set aside for retirement, or take care of elderly parents. And for those living paycheck to paycheck, all of that is but a distant dream. Whichever group you are in, the idea of giving your precious and hard-earned dollars away makes paying for or funding all of these items that much harder. Here's the first admonition ... and where the rubber meets the road.

First, we must believe – *really believe*—that giving away results in *more*, not less. As contrary as it might seem, that is the Biblical message in verse after verse. While financial blessings are never guaranteed when we give, here's what God's Word does say, both Old and New Testaments. Be alert to who's talking in these passages:

Luke 6:38, **Jesus** says: *"Give, and it **will be** given to you. A good measure, pressed down, shaken together and running over, will be poured into your lap. For with the measure you use, it will be measured to you."*

2 Corinthians 9:6, 8, 10–11, the apostle **Paul** provides some unbelievable promises: *Remember this: Whoever sows sparingly will also reap sparingly, and whoever sows generously will also reap generously … ⁸ And God is able to bless you **abundantly**, so that in **all** things at **all** times, having all that you need, you will **abound** in every good work … ¹⁰ Now he who supplies seed to the sower and bread for food will also supply and **increase** your store of seed and will **enlarge** the harvest of your righteousness. ¹¹ You will be **enriched in every way** so that you can be generous on every occasion, and through us your generosity will result in thanksgiving to God.*

Even with the legalistic tithes in Malachi 3, recall the tremendous physical blessings **God** promised for obedience in verse 10: *Bring the whole tithe into the storehouse, that there may be food in my house. Test me in this," says the LORD Almighty, "and see if I will not throw open the floodgates of heaven and pour out **so much blessing that there will not be room enough to store it**.*

Proverbs 3: 9–10, **King Solomon** says: *Honor the LORD with your wealth, with the firstfruits of all your crops; ¹⁰ then your barns will be **filled to overflowing*** [Did you get that? Not just filled but filled to *overflowing*!], *and your vats will **brim over** with new wine.*

> Deuteronomy 15:10, **God** says: *Give generously to them* [your poor brothers] *and do so without a grudging heart; then because of this the LORD your God will bless you* [listen to this!] ***in <u>all</u> your work and in <u>everything</u> you put your hand to.***

Note that there is always a blessing, sometimes a material one—as in Proverbs 3:9-10 and Malachi 3:10—while other times, the blessing is something far more important: in 2 Corinthians 9:10 it says "harvest of your righteousness" and "enriched in every way" and in Deuteronomy 15:10, "everything you put your hand to."

Believers who like to give ten percent of their income have a saying that goes like this: *You can live better on 90% than on 100%!* As crazy as that sounds, that is exactly the Biblical message. When we give as He leads—whatever the amount—He absolutely promises to bless us in some way. As the apostle Paul writes in Philippians 4:19:

> *And my God will meet **all** your needs according to the riches of his glory in Christ Jesus.*

For Paul, that "meeting all your needs" was not living a life of leisure and material prosperity but instead, living day-by-day in dependence on Him, whether well fed or hungry, in plenty and in want ... so that the Lord could use him to change the world.

So, here again is my recurring question: Do ... you ... believe ... that? Do you believe, really believe that when you give you will end up with more, not less? It's the kind of question that really tests your faith, doesn't it? It's not the false doctrine of "giving to get," but rather giving to God *knowing* that He *will* bless you in some amazing way so that you, like the Macedonians, will yearn or plead to give even more in the future. You may have to grow in this belief, but I would suggest that it is the only way you will be able to give cheerfully, without compulsion and so on, fully trusting that He *will* meet your needs, whatever He determines them to be.

SOME EXAMPLES

Here are a couple of modern-day examples. In a book titled *Joyful Giving*, author Don Sisk tells the following story about a Mrs. Barron, who became widowed during the Depression while living in Chicago.

> Although her two boys attended Sunday School, she had to work as a nurse on Sundays. Coming home one Sunday, they were excited about an upcoming "Mission Sunday" where offerings for missions were going to be received, and they were excited about bringing an offering. Mrs. Barron explained that they wouldn't be able to do so because of a need to use the only savings she had—$200—to repair the roof for the upcoming winter. The boys understood. She went to bed that night and in her own words told Brother Sisk: "I lay there thinking about the $200 and the missions offering. God began to speak to my heart and say, 'I want you to give the $200 to missions.'" Mrs. Barron went on the say, "I learned a long time ago not to argue with God; and thus, before I went to sleep that night, I said 'God, we'll take the $200 next week and give that to missions.'" They did this.
>
> The following Monday, one of the boys came home from school and asked Mrs. Barron, "Do you know who Pikes Peak is named after?" She answered that she did not know; but she promised that they would look it up in a reference book and find out who

> Pike's Peak was named after. As they consulted the reference book, they found out that Pike's Peak was named after Zebulon Pike. After dinner that evening as they were reading, the phone rang. The voice on the other end asked, "Is this Mrs. Mabel Barron?" She answered that she was. The voice then said, "This is your quiz master from WMAQ. We have chosen your name at random from the phone book." Then he said, "Our question this week is, 'we would like to know if you know who Pikes Peak is named after?'" Mrs. Barron said, "Oh, yes, I know. Pikes Peak was named after Zebulon Pike." The man said, "Congratulations! You have just won $200!"

An amazing story ... but it gets better. That event so impacted Mrs. Barron that she told author Sisk, "since that time, I have given over half my income to the work of God for worldwide evangelization." And Sisk's reply? Proper giving does perpetuate God's provision.

Here's another example from *The Grace of Giving*, by Stephen Olford:

> I think of the late Robert A. Laidlaw, well-known businessman of Auckland, New Zealand and author of *The Reason Why*. As a young man of eighteen and a half, he made a covenant with God that he would give a tenth of all his earnings. Later, at the age of twenty-five, he decided to change that amount to fifty percent of all his earnings. God continued to multiply his resources until he was giving even more to the work of the Lord. Later, writing at the age of seventy, he could say, "I want to bear testimony that, in spiritual communion and material things, God has blessed me one hundredfold, and has

graciously entrusted to me a stewardship far beyond my expectations, when as a lad of eighteen, I gave God a definite portion of my wages."

REMEMBER THIS

As miraculous as those testimonies are, there is another, even more powerful motivator. It is a corollary to the first foundational concept presented in Chapter 1—do you remember it? He owns it *ALL*! Because few believers acknowledge the reality of this corollary, it is presented as an admonition—or gentle reproof: *He doesn't need … your … money*—it's already His! Let that sink in for a moment … and try to deduce the motivating aspect.

There are a couple of facets to the reality that He doesn't need the money. First, the whole process of giving back to Him must then be primarily for *our* benefit. In other words, by not doing it, we lose out on something, and by doing it, we gain something. To illustrate, let me go back to the five dollar per day investing example I presented in Chapter 2. If you save a measly five dollars per day for forty years—or $73,000—investing it in something that provides a ten percent return, how much will you have? Almost a million bucks. Now, by sharing that illustration with you, do I get any benefit out of it? I wish! What I do get, however, is the satisfaction of demonstrating something so beneficial to you that maybe, just maybe, you will do it and benefit by winding up with nearly a million dollars. If you don't, at the end of those forty years, what will you have to show for that $73,000 frittered away? Likely nothing. So … that choice of either setting aside only five dollars per day and winding up with a million bucks or doing nothing and winding up with nothing was solely for *your* benefit.

So … application time. God, the creator of the universe and the creator of y-o-u, is not sitting on His throne, hoping beyond hope and praying mightily that you will help Him out by tossing a few of your loose coins into His heavenly paper bag so that you can feel good about helping someone in need. No, that is not the purpose of giving at all. It is, instead, like the president of the U.S. walking up to *you*, pausing, looking you in the eye, and saying, "would you like to join me in helping to change the world?"

When we give, God is giving us the opportunity, the privilege, to participate in building His kingdom. And this is no nebulous "pie in the sky" dream. As the writer of Hebrews says in chapter 11, verse 15 about the "hall of fame people of faith"—Abel, Enoch, Noah, Abraham and others:

> "… they were longing for a **better** country—a **heavenly** one. Therefore God is not ashamed to be called their God, for he [listen to this]—**has prepared a city for them**."

Remember the first question I asked you in Chapter 1: Why are you here? And remember the rope illustration from Session #2: Our lives here are simply the little, unbelievably short red portion of the rope. Our purpose here is to use our lives to serve Him in whatever way He has for us, using our time, talents and resources to, as it says in Matt 6:20,

> "*store up treasure in* **Heaven**."

Because if we do, do you remember Jesus's reassuring words in verse 21?

> *For where your treasure is, there your* **heart** *will be also.*

Do you need any more powerful motivation than that? He doesn't need your money because what He really wants is *you* … investing yourself in His Kingdom, looking forward to all the treasure that will be waiting for you there. The more you can grasp this certainty, the better you will understand *how* we are to give: not reluctantly or under compulsion, but willingly, as you have decided in your heart.

The other facet of the reality that He doesn't need the money leads to the second freewill giving guideline, *who* we are to give to.

THE "WHO" OF FREEWILL GIVING

Although we normally give to specific entities or individuals, our hearts have a better chance of being cheerful when we remind ourselves that we are giving first and foremost *to the Lord* for use in such and such organization or individual. As we read above in Matthew 6:20, the ultimate benefit is in the *heavenly* realm. Two Old Testament passages make this a little clearer. In both Exodus 25:1-2 and 1 Chronicles 29:9, note carefully what it says:

> Exodus 25:1-2: *The Lord said to Moses, "Tell the Israelites to bring **me** an offering.*

> 1 Chronicles 29:9: *The people rejoiced at the willing response of their leaders, for they had given freely and wholeheartedly **to the Lord**.*

In both passages, note that there were physical things given for a specific purpose, but that the attitude of the giver was to give first to the Lord, and secondarily, for the purpose indicated.

Do you know why God wants it this way? I think that it's to keep our egos out of the process. Remember when we talked about how everything is God's and we are just giving back to Him what He has given us (1 Chronicles 29:16)? Yet, isn't it possible that we can forget that and start thinking that *we* are giving to the organization or individual?

Another one of my former pastors provides a convicting example of this potential risk. He tells the story about a close friend, congregant, and occasional counselee of his who had asked him to come look at a car he had recently purchased–a beautifully restored 1960s-era muscle car. After admiring it, the pastor asked him which of his sons he was giving it to and the man replied, "oh, I didn't buy it for them, I bought it for you–get in and let's take a drive." Admittedly flabbergasted, the pastor drove it a bit and then stopped, realizing the enormity of the gift. He turned to his friend and told him that he could not accept the car unless he was willing to "first give it to the Lord and let me take care of it." The man paused a bit and then said, "hmmm, I see what you mean," and then bowed his head praying, "Lord, I give this to You." By giving the car to the Lord, there were no strings on the pastor. He could drive the car freely, with his conscience never being troubled whenever he interacted with the man by a nagging reminder of "that's the person who gave me the car."

So, we are to give first and foremost *to the Lord*. That is to be our attitude. Then we can seek His guidance on specifically who to give His resources to, knowing that we are just a conduit and not the source. Of course, due diligence is appropriate to try to make sure that our offerings are used wisely because, after all, it is His money.

The "Why" of Freewill Giving

Finally, I want to leave you with the greatest motivation possible— the *why* to give as the Lord has prospered you. God guarantees that not only *will* He bless you when you give, you get far more back than what you gave! Read these verses very carefully.

Do you remember 2 Corinthians 9:8, which follows the "giving cheerfully" verse?

> *And God is able to make all grace abound to you, so that* [what?] *in* **all things** *at* **all times**, *having* **all that you need**, *you will* **abound** *in every good work.*

And verse 11 says:

> *You will be made rich in* [what?] **every way** *so that you can be generous on* [what?] **every occasion** ...

But **Jesus** says it even better in Luke 6:38:

> *Give, and it will be given to you. A good measure, pressed down, shaken together* **and running over**, *will be poured into your lap. For with the measure you use, it will be measured to you.*

This is just a basic earthly and heavenly principle: you sow a little, you get a little; you sow a lot and you get a lot. But note that Jesus says "give, and it **will be** given to you ... **running over** ..." Although you may not know the form of how God will bless you in return, you will receive the greater blessing.

Now What?

So ... how to wrap up an admittedly controversial chapter? For some of you—whether pastor, non-profit leader, or layperson—the clear giving principles specified in His Word may be radically different from what you have been taught. My hope is that you have seen for yourself how God truly wants New Testament believers to give. To put it bluntly, it really comes down to this: Do you believe everything you've read in this chapter? Are you convinced that this really *is* God's message and method for true, heartfelt giving? If so:

- And you are a layperson, His Word clearly says that when you give as He leads, He is waiting to bless you abundantly. Not only will you have all you need, you will abound in every good work, desiring to give even more in the future.
- And you are a church or non-profit organization leader involved in teaching God's people via the written or spoken word, you can have confident faith knowing that:

    - When your readers or hearers give as you have taught them about God's desires for true, heartfelt giving—the how, the who to give to, the why we should give—God will bless them abundantly so that they will have all they need and abound in every good work,

and

    - Your organization will have all it needs to fund the operation and projects that are truly God-inspired and directed.

If, as an individual, you choose to disregard this clear guidance in His Word, your giving will likely remain rote and legalistic, done reluctantly and under compulsion. Moreover, you will likely never experience the overflowing joy of giving *simply because you want to ... giving simply because you want to honor Him* and participate in building His eternal Kingdom. For organizations, presenting a method and motivation for giving contrary to His clear guidance will result in recurrent struggles to fund your operations as well as contributors who must be continually compelled and cajoled into giving up some of their precious and hard-earned dollars. Is that what you want?

Concluding Thoughts for Christ-Followers

Recall what I said at the beginning: You can't have your mind straight on the reasons for making money until you have your heart straight on the reasons for giving it away. Whether you have little or much, whether you are in tremendous times of blessing or in the midst of severe trials, God wants you to acknowledge Him not only as owner of it all but as owner of *you*, as Lord of your life. While He doesn't need your money, His Word is quite clear that He desires that we give—literally investing in His Kingdom and storing up treasure in Heaven—as He leads, whether to help the poor and needy, to help spread His message around the world, or to help fund operation of the local church body. And when you give, He absolutely guarantees that He *will* bless you in some way. If you can't believe that, then it will be virtually impossible for you to understand the guidance He provides on the practical areas of living here on His earth: debt, investing, retirement and estate planning. Before moving on to the next chapter, let me encourage you to ponder and pray about the following:

1. Give to the Lord as He *leads* you, not because I say so, but because His *Word* says so. Pray about it and do it. Give as the Lord has prospered you, as you purpose in your heart. If you're not giving now, sit down tonight, or no later than tomorrow, and plan to do some giving. Initially, the attitude, the willingness to give, is what's important, not the amount.

2. As for guidelines for the actual amount, let me put it bluntly: *there is no set amount*—God's Word simply says to give generously, sacrificially, and according to your ability, or in proportion to the Lord's blessings. For some of you, in your present financial position, that may only mean one or two percent—or even less. For others, it may mean ten, twenty, thirty percent or more—it's between you and God. But as we talked about in the previous chapter and the

six-step personal financial roadmap, do it *first* before paying any other bill; do it first because … He comes first. You will be amazed at how far the rest will "stretch" when you acknowledge up front that it is all His to begin with. If you don't do it first, it will likely be "crowded out" by all your other spending with little or nothing left to give except a token amount that is—in the words of the apostle Paul—given reluctantly and/or under compulsion.

3. What this issue really comes down to can, quite honestly, be put in question form:

> Knowing what you know now about Godly giving and how He *will* bless you in the process, how much do you want to honor *Him*?

2 Corinthians 8:9 says that Jesus, although He was rich, for our sakes become poor so that we, through His poverty, might become rich. Part of being "rich" is the privilege of being invited to help build His kingdom here on earth and in the process, storing up treasure—true treasure—in Heaven. How much of a part do you want in that?

4. What if you still feel you need a number to hang your hat on? I don't really like stating a bright line here because it is not in God's Word for true, heartfelt giving. But I do know that some people just work better with guidelines. Here's what I suggest: since a tenth has historically been symbolic of giving your all, of acknowledging that He not only owns it all, but gave it to you in the first place, it is a worthy *first* goal. I will say that it was my first goal when I put my finances in His hands. I now give a higher percentage and desire to continue increasing that percentage as the Lord

blesses. But never forget, what is foremost with true freewill giving is the *attitude*—the heart—not the amount. Give as He leads and watch ... Him ... bless for honoring Him!

To put a capstone on this chapter, here's a great verse to memorize that captures the essence of Christian giving, Old and New Testament:

2 Corinthians 9:7:

Each of you

should give what you have decided in your heart to give,

not reluctantly

or under compulsion,

for God loves a [what?] *cheerful giver.*

APPENDIX 3: Additional Comments on Giving

Possible questions:

1. **Should my giving be based on gross or net pay?** Some have replied to that question with another question, asking, "Do you want to be blessed net or gross?" I would reply that if God *is* first in your life, giving to Him should come *before* all other expenditures. As an aside, remember that He is ultimately in charge of the governmental authorities. You can acknowledge this reality by giving to Him based on your pay before taxes are withheld. In addition, the amount of your giving can directly impact how much income tax *should be* deducted from your paycheck. If you have a reasonable estimate of how much charitable giving you will do in a given year, you can use that amount to determine how many exemptions to claim on your annual W-4—Employee's Withholding Allowance Certificate (use the "Personal Allowances Worksheet" that comes with the form). This is the form that your employer uses to calculate how much income tax to withhold from your check. In other words, let your giving determine your withholding, and therefore, your net pay, instead of your net pay determining your giving.

2. **Should all my giving go to the local church?** There are three considerations to my answer. First, many who teach that the tithe is the requirement for us today also teach that it should be given to the local church, citing the Old Testament practice in Deuteronomy 14:28 and Malachi 3:10 of bringing the tithes to the local "storehouse;" giving over that amount can then be directed elsewhere. The problem with this interpretation is that 1) it neglects the fact that the Old Testament tithes were of bulky, physical things (animals, grains, etc.), and especially with the animals, the

dead meat would not last very long, so that storing them locally would be the most practical; 2) today, when we give, we usually give money, and that is very easy to send anywhere; and 3) as you have learned, the Malachi 3:8-11 passage only applied to those under the Old Testament Mosaic Law. Saying that the local church is equivalent to the Old Testament concept of the "storehouse" would be a gross disregard for the context of the passage. Furthermore, the storehouse concept is never used in the New Testament. Second, looking at two passages in Acts that deal with giving to the needy, it appears that it can be done either directly or indirectly through the local body:

> Acts 2:44-45, giving directly: *All the believers were together and had everything in common. They sold property and possessions **to give to anyone** who had need.*

> Acts 4:34-35, giving through the local body: *For from time to time those who owned land or houses sold them, brought the money from the sales and **put it at the apostles' feet, and it was distributed to anyone who had need** ...*

Third, during New Testament times, local bodies were all that existed—it would have been natural for funds to flow to and through them. However, today, there are many parachurch ministries that are not connected to any one body. They are missions in the truest sense of the word, meeting people's needs, and many have come to the Lord through them.

So, my opinion is this: 1 Timothy 5:17-18 is clear that the leaders of the local body are worthy of their wages, so if you are a member of a local body, you have a responsibility to "pay your laborers." But today we also have national and international bodies that minister in ways that the local body cannot (i.e., unified campus ministries, famine relief, etc.) and these are also important. Finally, we are under grace, not law. Taken together, support of the local body deserves priority, but giving to other groups, under God's leading, can be just as fruitful and provide many blessings to both the giver and receiver.

3. **What if a church has historically taught tithing as the requirement for giving?** As discussed in the chapter, tithing is such an easy concept to present that many churches have stated it as the expectation or requirement. But "ease" does not justify taking a Mosaic Law requirement for taxation, misrepresenting it as "giving"—both in terms of intent and amount—and then teaching that it represents God's model for New Testament believers. Not only is this bad theology, it is an erroneous representation of how God wants His people to honor Him. And to be frank, it doesn't work—legalism never does. While there may be some short-term compliance, no matter how hard church leaders try, they can't get the average giving to be more than about three percent. Yes, some may give more—maybe even more than a tenth—but many give far less. Why? Because legalistic tithing does not *motivate* people to truly give freely, without obligation, without being under compulsion. Wrong methods—especially when wrong Biblically—produce wrong results.

For churches in this situation, like a sinner seeking salvation, the church and its leaders must acknowledge their sin—its failure to "hit the mark"—seek His forgiveness and begin teaching the truth as it does with the rest of God's Word. Should there be concern that teaching God's real message on how giving should be done will result in the church not being able to pay its bills? This is like asking, "should we teach what His Word says or should we teach what we want it to say?" Either His Word is true or it's not. If God's people—His bride—are teaching and living by that truth, He absolutely promises to take care of them. Moreover, when Christians are motivated to give in a godly manner and for a godly purpose, not only will their giving be done cheerfully, not reluctantly or under compulsion, His Word is clear that there will be an *abundance* of resources, not a shortage—review Exodus 36:3,6, 1 Chronicles 29: 9 and 16-17, and all of 2 Corinthians 8 and 9, but especially 8:2-4, 9:1-2 and 9:7-8.

4

IS DEBT A DIRTY FOUR-LETTER WORD?

Never spend your money before you have it - Thomas Jefferson

Every time you borrow money, you're robbing
your future self - Nathan W. Morris

Some debts are fun when you are acquiring them, but none
are fun when you set about retiring them - Ogden Nash

As you start this chapter, it should be obvious that giving money away is so elemental in getting our attitudes straight on how to properly view money that we had to deal with that issue first in order to set the stage for understanding His guidance on spending. With those concepts firmly etched into your heart and mind, we are now ready to switch gears and get into some real practical Biblical guidance regarding what to do—and not to do—with the resources that we don't give away. In preparation for dealing with the Biblical guidance, let me briefly review the world we live in.

Amazingly, over seventy percent of our annual GDP (Gross Domestic Product) here in the U.S.—the sum of all the finished goods and services produced in a year—is powered by personal consumption expenditures, and much of that is fueled by credit. If we slow down or stop spending, especially on credit, the economy goes rapidly into the toilet. And since it seems that just about everyone uses some form of credit—whether to buy a house, finance an education, buy a car, or even to buy groceries, it is reasonable as a wise *oikonómos* to step back a bit and examine the costs of a debt-fueled lifestyle. You will be amazed by what it actually does cost.

Along the way, we'll talk about those innocuous looking but magical little two-inch by three-inch pieces of plastic almost all of us over the age eighteen carry in our wallet—credit cards. How important are they? I think this cartoon captures it completely!

"You're a lucky man. One inch farther to the right, and it would have hit your credit cards."

And, since its younger brother, the debit card, is becoming so prevalent, we will also deal with those. They must be munching on steroids because debit card charges now exceed credit card charges, even though debit cards are only about half as old.

How Much Do You Know About Debt?

Let's start by taking a fun little test. The answers are shown at the end.

1. Including mortgages, credit cards, student loans, and auto loans, what is the *average amount of debt per household*?

    A. $50,000
    B. $75,000
    C. $100,000
    D. $135,000
    E. $160,000
    F. $200,000

2. What percentage of American households have at least *one credit card*?

    A. 20%
    B. 40%
    C. 60%
    D. 70%
    E. 95%
    F. 100%

3. *How many* credit cards does the average American have?

    A. 1
    B. 2
    C. 4
    D. 5

E. 10
F. 20

4. According to information gathered by the Census Bureau in 2017 (the latest year available), there were approximately 189 million credit card holders in the U.S. Approximately how many do *not* pay off their bill *in full* each month?

    A. about 60%
    B. about 40%
    C. about 25%
    D. about 10%

5. Let's get a little more specific. Approximately what percentage of Americans pay *only the minimum payment* required each month?

    A. 50%
    B. 35%
    C. 30%
    D. 10%

6. Approximately how much credit card debt does the average American family carry?

    A. $2,500
    B. $5,000
    C. $10,000
    D. $15,000
    E. $25,000
    F. $50,000

7. Although there have been changes to credit card laws recently, there was no required change in minimum payments and many credit card companies still use the old rules: the interest charges

and 1% of the balance owed. Using our average family owing $10,000 on their cards—who can only pay the minimum balance every month, has an interest rate of 18% (the most common) and never charges another penny—how long will it take to pay off the balance?

A. 4 years
B. 8 years
C. 13 years
D. 18 years
E. 23 years
F. 28 years
G. 50 years

8. What is the highest interest rate credit card companies can charge?

A. 18%
B. 19.99%
C. 24%
D. 36%
E. 79.9%
F. No limit

9. What percentage of credit card users *do not know* the interest rate on the credit card they use most often?

A. 5%
B. 10%
C. 15%
D. 25%
E. 35%
F. 50%
G. 90%

And one more —for those of you who have become avid users of *debit* cards:

10. Debit cards are hugely popular—more transactions now occur using these now than for credit cards. But like credit cards they can be lost or stolen. What maximum loss are you liable for if your card is lost or stolen?

    A. Similar to a credit card: $50 as long as you inform the card issuer when you get your statement
    B. $50 if you report the card missing after two business days of unauthorized charges occurring
    C. $500 if you report the card missing after two business days have passed
    D. Unlimited if you fail to report the card lost or stolen within sixty days of receiving the bank statement
    E. Always responsible for the loss—the card is just like money
    F. b, c and d

Answers:

1. C – $135,000; actually a little more than $137,000 per the Federal Reserve, November 2017.
2. D - 70% [www.creditcards.com/credit-card-news/ownership-statistics.php]
3. C – 4: actually 3.7 [www.fool.com/credit-cards/2017/08/13/how-many-credit-cards-does-the-average-person-have.aspx]
4. A – 60%: actually 58% [www.creditdonkey.com/credit-card-debt-statistics.html; 189 million cardholders per www.creditcards.com/credit-card-news/ownership-statistics.php]
5. C – 30% [www.creditdonkey.com/credit-card-debt-statistics.html]
6. D – $15,000: actually $15,482 [www.nerdwallet.com/blog/average-credit-card-debt-household]
7. F – 28 years; actually, about 28 ½ years.
8. F – no limit: Federal law sets NO limit. While many states regulate rates, they only apply to banks based in that state and don't protect consumers who borrow from out-of-state lenders. Delaware and South Dakota have no limits; as a result, many credit card companies are based in those two states.
9. F – 50%: actually 48% or almost one out of every two users; yet, this is among *the most expensive borrowing* you can do.
10. F – b, c and d are correct; note that if the thief drains all the money out of your checking account, it can take the bank a while to investigate. In the meantime, you could bounce checks to your landlord, your mortgage company, your credit card company, and so on [www.consumer.ftc.gov/articles/0213-lost-or-stolen-credit-atm-and-debit-cards]

So, how did you do? Did you learn anything? And, per the correct answer to question #2 of how many have at least one credit card, it is obvious that credit card usage is the norm here in the U.S. Like getting your driver's license, getting your first credit card has become one of those ceremonial "rites of passage" in life. Yet, unbelievably, it has not always been the case. In fact, credit card usage is just a bit over sixty years old, and the explosive and ubiquitous use is only about thirty years old. But, oh what marketers they are. See if you can finish these jingles:

- Master Card: There's some things money can't buy … *(for everything else, there's Mastercard)*
- VISA: It's everywhere … *(you want to be)*
- American Express: Don't leave home … *(without it!)*

Speaking of American Express, here's a startling bit of trivia for you: Back in 1958, when the first American Express cards were issued, they were touted as the *new money*—boy, how right they were. But here's the critical question: Is that little piece of plastic really money? Or could it be something so dangerous—so potentially ruinous to your financial health—that you should at least consider whether you should be using it at all? Maybe it's a radical question but as your financial physician, it will be my job during this chapter to help you answer that question by clearly explaining both the risks and the potential costs of using credit.

What You'll Learn

Let me tell you upfront, the three main purposes for this chapter. In terms of a picture, they form a "hamburger," because there's a bun on top, a bun on the bottom and a whole lot of meat in the middle. So, loosen your belts and get ready to digest some pretty heavy stuff.

Main point #1—the top bun—is composed of the Biblical input. Summarized in question form: Is it wrong to eat this hamburger? In other words, does the Bible say that borrowing or debt is a sin? Think about your answer for a moment and the support for your answer.

Main point #2—the meat of this chapter: Understand the cost. Borrowing to buy just about anything on credit is *ex-pen-sive*. That's because there are actually *two* costs to debt, not just one. You're likely pretty familiar with the first cost, interest, and as you learned with our little quiz, those rates can be enormous on credit cards. But the second cost—and one that is rarely acknowledged—is actually far larger than the first—and the digestive problems of that lead us to main point #3.

Main point #3—the bottom bun: Recommendations. Admittedly, this is going to sound pretty radical. Due to the painful side-effects of main point #2, stop eating this nasty hamburger! In other words, stop taking on more debt. Instead, work on getting rid of all the debt in your life. Just as you feel better when you eat right, you are going to live better—far better—when you jettison all that resource-draining debt that sinks you deeper into the pit of never-ending payments.

Main point #1: Is borrowing a sin? There's not a lot of direct Biblical guidance but I can say unequivocally that nowhere in God's Word does it say that borrowing is a sin or that debt is prohibited. In fact, many passages simply acknowledge it as a common practice.[17] For example, Psalm 112:5 speaks very positively to a generous lender:

> *Good will come to those who are generous and lend freely, who conduct their affairs with justice.*

And none other than our Lord Jesus says this in Matthew 5:42:[18]

> *Give to the one who asks you, and do not turn away from the one who wants to **borrow** from you.*

Now, obviously, since there is a lender, there must also be a borrower. From God's point of view, however, there are two types of borrowers and the rules are different for each group. The guidance for the first type of borrower, the poor and needy, comes from the Pentateuch, the first five books of the Old Testament that contain the Law, and form what I term the "laws of lending to the poor." There are three primary passages that also provide a Biblical meaning of "poor" and "needy:"

> Exodus 22:25: *If you lend money to one of my people among you who is needy, do not treat it like a business deal; charge no interest.*

> Leviticus 25:35-37: *If any of your fellow Israelites become poor and are unable to support themselves among you, help them as you would a foreigner and stranger, so they can continue to live among you. [36] Do not take interest or any profit from them, but fear your God, so that they may continue to live among you. [37] You must not lend them money at interest or sell them food at a profit.*

> Deuteronomy 15:7-8: *If anyone is poor among your fellow Israelites in any of the towns of the land the LORD your God is giving you, do not be hardhearted or tightfisted toward them. [8] Rather, be openhanded and freely lend them whatever they need.*

The Hebrew words used in these passages for "poor" and "needy" literally mean "destitute" or "impoverished" or a "beggar." Moreover, realize that the poor and needy in Biblical times did not have access to all the forms of credit that we have today so they likely got into their predicament either by losing their jobs, being robbed, or having some sort of serious medical condition. As a result, their borrowing was to provide the absolute basic necessities of life. So, God said to lend them *whatever* they need, including selling them food at cost and lending them money interest-free. Highlighting the dire straits these borrowers were in, lenders were even provided with a beautiful word-picture on how to lend in these situations: *Rather be **openhanded**.* Many other translations put it this way: *open your hand **wide** to them.* So, although repayment was expected, the spirit of these passages was for the lenders to help in any way they could and worry about repayment later, as the goal was for the borrowers to be able to "continue to live among you." Recall the amazing reward for such benevolence just two verses later in the Deuteronomy 15 passage, verse 10, that we read in Chapter 3:

> *… then because of this the Lord your God will bless you in **all** your work and in **everything** you put your hand to.*

So, think about this question: how much—if any—of our borrowing today fits these circumstances? In other words, how much of our borrowing is because we are destitute, impoverished and forced to beg? While there are the truly poor and needy among us today, likely 99.9% of our borrowing fits the second Biblical category, which is referred to cryptically in the Exodus passage above, and what I term *voluntary* or *non-need* borrowing. Note that Exodus 22:25 says regarding lending to the needy: "do not treat it like a business deal." So, by implication, when lending to everyone else, it should be done in the "ordinary way of charging interest."

That "ordinary way," which, again, is simply presented as common practice, is primarily what we encounter today: not "openhanded," not interest-free, but rather the result of a structured, agreed-upon transaction between a willing lender and a willing borrower. Three main passages in God's Word provide guidance on these more common, everyday types of borrowing situations. The first deals with our *position*, the second with our *responsibility*, and the third with what should be our *goal*.

1. Our *position*: Nod you head if the following verse captures your experience:

   > Proverbs 22:7: *The rich rule over the poor, and the borrower is slave to the lender.*

When you sign on the dotted line and take possession of, say a brand new car, boy, does it ever feel great! But then, thirty days later, you have to start paying for it. The late Dr. Joyce Brothers put it more dramatically: "Credit buying is much like being drunk. The buzz happens immediately, and it gives you a lift ... the hangover comes the day after." The latest statistics I could find about the average length of new car loans[19] literally shocked me—guess how long? The hangover lasts about sixty-nine and a half months—over six and a half years.[20] Believe me, that new car smell and feel will be long gone before that. What about a mortgage on a house? Thirty years is the most common length. And during that time, yes, you are a slave to the lender—in a very real sense, the lender "owns" you. If you don't pay—or pay on time—they will call and/or write asking "hey, slave, where's my money?"

In fact, although it was mistakenly sent out, read what appeared on the monthly home-equity loan statements sent to seven thousand Wells Fargo customers a while back:

   > You owe your soul to the company store. Why not owe your home to Wells Fargo?[21]

No amount of backtracking by Wells Fargo officials could eliminate the veracity—the truth—of that statement. If you borrow to buy your house, if you borrow to buy your car, if you borrow to buy the big screen TV and you don't repay, the lender has every right to repossess the item. Moreover, in many states, if it is not worth what you owe on it, you are still responsible for the difference—what's called a "deficiency judgment." In other words, you are still slave to the lender.

This leads naturally to point #2 about borrowing, our *responsibility*. Look at the first part of Psalm 37:21:

> *The wicked borrow and do not repay ...*

This verse comes in the midst of five contrasts between the wicked and the righteous. So, if the wicked borrow and do not repay, guess what's implied about the righteous, you and me? That's right: The righteous, when they borrow, *do* repay.

So, if you borrow, it is expected that you will repay. No rocket science here, right? Some of you may not like me putting it this way but don't blame the lender when you become a slave—no one was holding a gun to your head when you signed on the dotted line to buy your house, your car, your big screen TV, or even your groceries. You are dealing with lenders who made a reasoned business decision to lend to you so ... you have to pay it back and on the agreed-upon terms. Suck it up and however long it takes, either make all the payments or sell the item and pay off the loan.

Point #3 is our *goal*: Enough of being in debt, let's talk about getting *out*. Here's God's guidance, Romans 13:7-8:

> *Give to everyone what you **owe** them: If you owe taxes, pay taxes; if revenue, then revenue; if respect, then*

> respect; if honor, then honor. ⁸*Let **no debt remain outstanding**, except the continuing debt to love one another, for whoever loves others has fulfilled the law.*

This passage comes in the midst of general submission to authorities and how if you do right, you have no fear of those in authority but if you do wrong, verse 4 says "be **afraid**, for rulers do not bear the sword for no reason." The word translated "owe" in verse 7 literally means "financial debts, or taxes or obligations," so the verse is simply but forcefully reaffirming my previous point that we have a responsibility to repay our debts, whomever they are owed to.

But our goal, as verse 8 encourages, is to become financially "debt free" in everything except for the continuing obligation to love one another. The NASB translates the first part of verse 8 as follows:

> *Owe **nothing** to anyone except to love one another ...*

So, we are to owe nothing to anyone—again, the Greek word implies financial debts—but, as the text note in the NIV indicates, "to love is the one debt that is never paid off." A beautiful thought, don't you think?

So ... while borrowing is not a sin, our goal should be to get financially debt-free. You may not be there now—I confess that for many years I was not—but what a day it was when I was finally released from bondage! Wouldn't it be great to be debt-free, even including your home mortgage? It is possible, as we'll see below. Here's a hint: You don't get out of debt by borrowing more, you get out of debt by borrowing *less* and paying *off* more. To see this principle clearly, let's go to main point #2—and remember, it forms the meat of the chapter.

Main point #2: Borrowing to buy is *ex-pen-sive*. Remember that there is not one but two costs to debt. We'll first talk about the potentially larger cost and then about interest. I asked this question in Chapter 2:

> On average, how much more, percentage-wise, will the average person spend when they use credit cards?

Do you remember the answer?

Here's the number I want you to memorize, internalize, ingrain or whatever, into your brain: fifty to seventy percent! Say that aloud: *fifty to seventy percent!* Although there is quite a wide range of results from various studies, here's what we know:

⇨ A study by Dun and Bradstreet suggests the average person will spend twelve to eighteen percent more using credit. However, when they looked at vending machines, the average transaction size nearly doubled—that's twenty-four to thirty-six percent.

⇨ Actual results from Arby's, the first fast-food chain to accept credit cards back in 1988, found that the average credit card sale was $5.50 compared to the average cash purchase of $3.20. Do the math: that's an increase of seventy-two percent. In a later article in 1990, that dropped to "only" forty to sixty percent.

⇨ When McDonald's started accepting credit cards in 2004, the average sale increased from $4.50 to $7, an increase of fifty-six percent. In an article prior to McDonalds going "live," the credit card processing company spokesperson matter-of-factly said this: "We anticipate a 40% increase in the average ticket size for those franchises implementing credit card processing for the first time."

⇨ Here's the one I really like. In an article about McDonald's starting a new type of restaurant in Orlando, FL, there is this startling statement:

> According to American Express, customers who use credit cards spend up to 100% more than customers who pay cash.

Can you imagine that—one hundred percent! I could go on and on but the truth is simple: when you can buy on credit—and especially when using a credit card—the average person will spend more: Even a rough average of all these studies produces at least a fifty percent increase in spending.

Why is this? As mentioned in Chapter 2, there is little or no emotional connection between you and your money when you don't have to pull out the green stuff. That's why casinos use chips, cruise lines use ID cards, and why retailers want you to use a credit—or even a debit—card (as discussed below). In fact, I am amazed at myself, how often I don't even look at the credit card receipt—I just sign and put it in my wallet. Has that ever happened to you? But when you pay cash, you can "feel" and "see" the money leaving you. And, as the amount goes up, it hurts more and more to do so. Let me give you a personal example.

My Example

Back in the 1990s when my kids were young, we decided to buy a trailer and travel around the U.S. during the summers since, as an academic, I had the summers off. To provide a ready source of entertainment during some long drives, we decided to buy a "conversion van" to tow the trailer, one that had really nice seats and a TV. Knowing that I didn't have enough cash to buy a new van, I found a used one for about $15,000 on a dealer's lot. After settling on the final price, I told the salesperson that I would bring a check the next day. It was late afternoon that next day when my wife and I headed back to the dealership. About five minutes away, I pulled off the road and confessed to my wife, "I just don't know if I can go through with this." Although somewhat shocked, she understood. We both knew how long and hard it had been to save up that $15,000 and we were now faced with the dilemma of literally "sliding all that money across the table" to obtain this vehicle which would, the moment we drove it off the lot, continue depreciating rapidly. We sat there for about fifteen minutes just thinking and praying and wondering *was it worth it?* This was the only way to really evaluate the decision, as we were now comparing apples to apples: keep our hard-saved money or give it up to obtain this particular thing. Yes, we ended up buying the van, but we also learned how important it was to "consider the cost." Although I didn't literally "peel off the bills," just the process of going to the bank, filling out the withdrawal form, getting the cashier's check, and ultimately releasing it into the salesperson's hand was nearly as painful.

Because it is so important for *you* to experience the impact of this concept, let me repeat the "living on cash" challenge in Chapter 2: For just one month, pay cash—real cash, not a check, credit or debit card—for all of your daily expenses, including your grocery shopping, coffee purchases, gas purchases, eating out, etc. Yes, it might be a hassle turning your paycheck into cash and carrying it around but remember why it's worth it:

⇨ First, you will be flabbergasted at how much things cost—even groceries—because pulling out the hard-earned greenbacks really makes you focus on how much you are spending.

⇨ Second, for optional-type things—like coffee or even a nice dinner out—you will likely find yourself "economizing" because … things are so expensive! And buying food or drinks at the movie theatre? Forget about it! Those things can easily cost twice as much as the movie! How much is a small soda? Five dollars?

Magnifying the impact of the living-on-cash test is utilizing the little spiral notebook also discussed in Chapter 2 and jotting down your cash expenditures. You become so conscious of the cost of things, something magical happens: you start spending less. There will be so many things where you say to yourself, "I sure don't need that!" And the bigger the potential expenditure, the bigger the potential savings.

What about debit cards?

Given that debit cards are so prevalent these days, a common question arises: Instead of using cash, can't I simply use my debit card since the money comes right out of my bank account, I'll have a written receipt, and it's safer than carrying around cash?

There are both "pros" and "cons" answers to this question. First, the "pros:" The benefits of a debit card are mainly two-fold. Yes, you avoid having to carry around cash. And, ostensibly, you can't spend more than the amount you have in your checking account at that moment.

The "cons" however, are extensive: First, you actually can spend more than is in your checking account at that moment because, if you have overdraft protection, your bank can approve a transaction even if there are insufficient funds in your checking account. Why do the banks do this? So they can charge you an overdraft fee of up to thirty-five dollars! So, that three-dollar cup of coffee could end up costing you thirty-eight dollars or that one dollar candy bar could cost thirty-six dollars. You don't believe it? Banks make more than ten billion dollars each year on these fees!

Second, with some purchases—like gasoline, rental cars and hotels—your debit card information is taken prior to completion of the transaction. The problem is that the merchant doesn't know how much you are going to end up spending so, by design, the system looks to see if you have enough in your account to cover the *maximum* amount of the transaction—say fifty or a hundred dollars for a gas purchase, and more for a car rental or hotel stay—and if you have enough, it essentially *pre-authorizes* a purchase for that amount. So far, so good. However, the system also "blocks off" that amount so you can't spend it elsewhere and it can take several business days after completion of the transaction for the block to be removed. So, if you have bills automatically paid out of your account and you don't have enough funds over and above the blocked amount, guess what? You'll either be charged fees for overdraft protection if you have sufficient funds in another account or insufficient funds fees if you don't.

Third—and more importantly—you are still not pulling those hard-earned greenbacks out of your wallet or purse. As proof of why doing this is so important, in Orlando, FL, Prime Time Amusements set up hundreds of state-of-the-art video arcade games in three McDonald's restaurants where users purchased a debit card to play the games. Here are the unbelievable results [editorial comments and emphasis added]:

> With a cashless system, suddenly a customer can play games all day [imagine that!] without feeling as if they are constantly spending money. No worries about lost tokens or that feeling of *reaching into your wallet yet again*. By loading up a PlayCard with money, it is easier for the customer to concentrate

on playing and *much more profitable for the arcades.* The McDonald's Orlando arcades have more than *doubled their profits* in just a few short months, and the sales show no signs of slowing down. By eliminating cash and tokens … arcade owners will continue to feel as though they have [guess what?] … hit the jackpot.

Fourth, debit cards are turning into easy targets for thieves. While it would seem that they would be safer than carrying cash, thieves can actually clean out your entire bank account, not just the cash in your wallet! It can take weeks or months to track down the source of the missing cash and get the funds back into your account—assuming you report the loss or misuse of your card soon enough.[22] And, if you are part of that seventy-eight percent living paycheck to paycheck or you haven't funded your "oh thank God" emergency fund, what do you do in the meantime?

Finally, even though it's your money, the practice of bank's charging you to use your debit card may become more widespread. It's already common for banks to charge a fee when you enter your PIN as part of the approval process.

So … while it may seem archaic to carry and pay with cash, *there is no close substitute* to peeling the bills out of your wallet to get a sense of what you are really paying. That's why I can't over-emphasize why you should experience the thirty-day "living on cash" challenge for yourself.

Pay Cash to Buy a Car?

Let me go back to the car purchase situation to further illustrate how expensive buying on credit can be. When you buy—or even lease—a car using a payment plan, you are not comparing apples to apples.

In fact, most car salespeople are trained to ask you "how much can you afford *each month*." Not only is there no real discussion about the total cost of the car but there is little if any mention of the term of the loan, at least in the beginning. All the focus in on the monthly payment—and making that as reasonable as possible, so that you can drive that brand-spanking-new car home. That's again why the risk of spending more when using credit is so deceiving. As proof, look at the results of a survey by J.D. Power and Associates, a California-based auto market research firm:

> ... more than half of those buying a car on credit—like many home buyers—are more concerned with the size of the payment than the overall cost of the vehicle.[23]

Let's take this one step further—and this may be stepping on toes again. Why do you suppose so many new cars have high-end sound systems ... or fancy wheels ... or GPS navigation systems ... or TVs in the headrests and so on? Because the increase in the monthly payment is so small. Or even more enticing, instead of increasing the monthly payment, the salesperson simply blows some fairy dust over the vehicle and voila, you can have all that extra stuff for no change in the monthly payment! All the salesperson does is stealthily stretch the loan out over a longer time period. Let me give you two brief examples. Just to make it clear, my purpose is not to keep you from buying a new car, but to (again) show you how expensive credit can be.

Example #1: Is there a difference between paying $25 and $1,000? Duh, of course, but here's how the auto dealership can make you think you *are* getting a $1,000 item for only $25. An extra $1,000 item for the car—say, an upgraded sound system or a nice DVD player for the kids—may only add an extra $25 to the monthly payment; and without skipping a beat, the salesperson chides, "surely you can afford that, can't you?" Unmentioned is the fact that with the added interest, that $1,000 sound system ends up costing $1,200 or $1,300 bucks. A cash buyer would likely evaluate more carefully having to peel off ten more $100 bills than would the credit buyer who only has to justify an extra $25 per month.

Example #2: I'll warn you in advance, this example is going to be more dramatic and more troubling for some readers. As I mentioned earlier, to be able to "afford" the car you really want, the monthly payment is stretched out from forty-eight months (or four years) to sixty months (or five years—now the most common loan period). The example uses an average new car cost of $35,000:

Average new-car cost:	$35,000
Out-the-door cost with taxes and fees of $3,000:	$38,000
Down payment of 20%:	$ 7,600
Amount borrowed:	$30,400
Monthly payment, 48-month loan, 5% interest:	$ 700

That same payment, however, on a sixty-month loan will magically finance about $37,000 or $6,600 more car, easily covering all those fancy options I mentioned previously. And, in the pressure of the moment—or the delight of the eyes ... or added roominess of a bigger car ... or whatever—it can be easy to justify the higher cost for the vehicle since all those fabulous goodies "only" cost an extra year of those same payments. But, *do they really*? Here's what the numbers show:

AMOUNT BORROWED		TOTAL INTEREST PAID
$37,000 (60 months)		$4,880
30,400 (48 months)		$3,200
$ 6,600	⟵——— Increase ———⟶	$1,680
=21.7% more loan, but	———————⟶	52.5% more interest

Fifty-two and a half percent more interest—52.5%—that is a huge amount for that extra year of payments and a stark illustration of both costs of credit: how easy it is for us to be fooled into spending way more, and how expensive the interest can be in the process

So ... do you want to know how to save ten, fifteen, even twenty-five percent on your next car purchase? Some of you are going to grind your teeth on this one but here it is: as discussed in detail below in Recommendations, cut the use of credit and start paying cash ... for *everything*—and that includes cars. Instead of signing on the dotted line and paying seven hundred dollars every month, *save* that seven hundred dollars for forty-eight or sixty months, then use that money to buy your next car for cash. Instead of paying interest, you'll be earning interest. And you'll be able to pay cash for every car thereafter.

Now, I know some of you, after reading the above, are shaking your head back and forth, thinking, "Pay cash for a car? Yeah, right!" In this "I want it now!" society we live in, waiting for four or five long years to acquire a vehicle seems impossible—but that's only because we are so used to getting things *now*. To turn this issue around, think about this: Let's say you did scrimp and save for four long years to set aside $35,000—how many readers would even be willing to spend it all on a single purchase like a new car, which would likely lose half its value in two or three years? Yet, we do it all the time, spending even more by borrowing, because all we see is the monthly payment.

So ... here's what I must tell you as your financial trainer: If you wouldn't be willing to slide the $35,000 across the table but are willing to buy the car on credit because it seems so much easier, then credit has *seduced* you into buying more and paying more—it's as simple as that. That may sound harsh—and it is—but a car-purchase situation is the best example I have found to clearly illustrate how buying on credit can be so *ex-pen-sive*.

Let me put a capstone on this—admittedly controversial—issue by sharing with you two memorable quotes from the same author:

> It is marvelous, when we are eager to possess something, how we can argue ourselves into feeling that extravagances are economies; that expense is income; and that a liability is an asset. This is called rationalizing our desires. Watch it.[24]

Does that bring any of your buying experiences to mind? Here's what this author suggests:

> I say they postpone buying only once, save instead, and forever after get more for their money ... Your impatience makes you buy on the installment plan. It chains payments and charges around your salary because you will not wait one short year to start clean and continue clean forever after ... It seems easier for the average American to live today and die tomorrow than to enrich tomorrow's living by sacrificing today.[25]

Right on, wouldn't you agree? But there's something startling you should know about these two quotes. They are from a delightful little book written by Roger W. Babson, titled, "The Folly of Instalment Buying"[26] written in ... 19**38**. So, this issue of credit being *ex-pen-sive* and likely causing you to spend more is not a recent phenomena. That's why I said earlier:

If you buy something on credit that you wouldn't buy if you saved up for it beforehand, credit has *seduced* you.

The Second Cost of Debt

As you ponder and cogitate on that a bit, let's talk about the other cost of credit—interest. There's really not much I can say except to give you some snippets of information and recommendations. First, the more "secured" the loan, the lower the rate. That's why home equity loans are so low—if you don't pay, the bank simply takes your house! Unsecured debt, like credit cards, can have rates that can easily be 24-30% and more—I've actually seen rates up to 79.9% on really risky accounts.

Beyond the interest rate—and especially with credit cards—the minimum payment is set to keep you paying off for a long time. Because of this, recent legislation requires that credit card companies show you two things on your monthly statement: exactly *how* long it will take to pay off your balance paying only the minimum payment and how much you would have to pay every month to pay it off in only three years, both assuming you never charge another cent. Here's an example

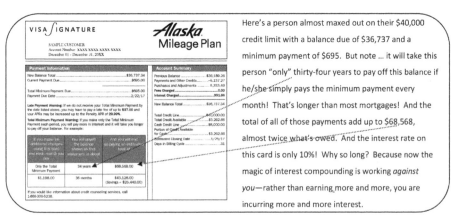

Here's a person almost maxed out on their $40,000 credit limit with a balance due of $36,737 and a minimum payment of $695. But note ... it will take this person "only" thirty-four years to pay off this balance if he/she simply pays the minimum payment every month! That's longer than most mortgages! And the total of all of those payments add up to $68,568, almost twice what's owed. And the interest rate on this card is only 10%! Why so long? Because now the magic of interest compounding is working *against* you—rather than earning more and more, you are incurring more and more interest.

Note that with any debt, the term can easily be shortened by making extra payments. There are several ways to do it—and you don't have to refinance anything. The easiest way is to simply prepay the next month's principal component of your payment. By doing so, you magically save that next month's interest charge and reduce the loan term by one month! To illustrate with a simple example, let's say you owe $1,200, borrowed at twelve percent per year (or one percent per month) with twelve monthly payments of $106.62. Below is a loan amortization table; even those with rudimentary Microsoft® Excel skills can create one. It simply shows how each payment is broken into principal and interest and the remaining balance to be paid:

Date	Payment	Interest Paid (12%)	Principal Paid	Balance
Jan 1, 20X1				$1,200.00
Feb 1, 20X1	$106.62	$12.00	$94.62	$1,105.38
Mar 1, 20X1	$106.62	$11.05	$95.57	$1,009.81
Apr 1, 20X1	$106.62	$10.10	$96.52	$913.29
May 1, 20X1	$106.62	$9.13	$97.49	$815.80
Jun 1, 20X1	$106.62	$8.16	$98.46	$717.34
Jul 1, 20X1	$106.62	$7.17	$99.45	$617.90
Aug 1, 20X1	$106.62	$6.18	$100.44	$517.46
Sep 1, 20X1	$106.62	$5.17	$101.45	$416.01
Oct 1, 20X1	$106.62	$4.16	$102.46	$313.55
Nov 1, 20X1	$106.62	$3.14	$103.48	$210.07
Dec 1, 20X1	$106.62	$2.10	$104.52	$105.55
Jan 1, 20X2	$106.60	$1.06	$105.54	$0.00
Total Interest Paid:		**$79.42**		

To shorten your loan by one month, find the principal to be paid the next month let's say March 20X1 ($95.57), so in February 20X1, include March's principal of $95.57 with your regular payment of $106.62, for a total of $202.19. When that payment amount is inserted into the table, replacing the $106.62 that had been there, note what happens:

Date	Payment	Interest Paid (12%)	Principal Paid	Balance
Jan 1, 20X1				$1,200.00
Feb 1, 20X1	**$202.19**	$12.00	**$190.19**	$1,009.81
Mar 1, 20X1	$106.62	$10.10	$96.52	$913.29
Apr 1, 20X1	$106.62	$9.13	$97.49	$815.80
May 1, 20X1	$106.62	$8.16	$98.46	$717.34
Jun 1, 20X1	$106.62	$7.17	$99.45	$617.89
Jul 1, 20X1	$106.62	$6.18	$100.44	$517.45
Aug 1, 20X1	$106.62	$5.17	$101.45	$416.01
Sep 1, 20X1	$106.62	$4.16	$102.46	$313.55
Oct 1, 20X1	$106.62	$3.14	$103.48	$210.06
Nov 1, 20X1	$106.62	$2.10	$104.52	$105.54
Dec 1, 20X1	$106.60	$1.06	$105.54	$0.00
Jan 1, 20X2				
Total Interest Paid:		**$68.37** (or $11.05 less)		

The balance owed is reduced by $190.19 ($94.62 original amount + the extra $95.57) and now the loan is paid off one month sooner, and March's interest cost of $11.05 has been saved.

If you do it for another month, you shorten the loan by one more month and save that month's interest charge of $9.13: Add April's principal amount of $97.49 to March's payment of $106.62, making it $204.11:

Date	Payment	Interest Paid (12%)	Principal Paid	Balance
Jan 1, 20X1				$1,200.00
Feb 1, 20X1	$202.19	$12.00	$190.19	$1,009.81
Mar 1, 20X1	**$204.11**	$10.10	**$194.01**	$815.80
Apr 1, 20X1	$106.62	$8.16	$98.46	$717.34
May 1, 20X1	$106.62	$7.17	$99.45	$617.89
Jun 1, 20X1	$106.62	$6.18	$100.44	$517.45
Jul 1, 20X1	$106.62	$5.17	$101.45	$416.00
Aug 1, 20X1	$106.62	$4.16	$102.46	$313.54
Sep 1, 20X1	$106.62	$3.14	$103.48	$210.06
Oct 1, 20X1	$106.62	$2.10	$104.52	$105.54
Nov 1, 20X1	$106.59	$1.06	$105.53	$0.00
Dec 1, 20X1				
Jan 1, 20X2				
Total Interest Paid:		**$59.24** (or $9.13 less)		

The only negative to this approach is that, since the amount applied to principal each month is increasing, as you can see, the longer you wait, the larger the extra amount you have to pay. But, if this were a fifteen- or thirty-year mortgage loan and you start early, your income might go up sufficiently or you could tweak your expenditures enough to cover the increase in principal each month. And since you are doing this voluntarily, if a special emergency comes up one month, you can suspend your extra payments. To generate these types of tables, just Google "loan amortization schedule" and input your loan information.

Instead of an increasing amount each month, some borrowers prefer a constant payment. No problem! Using a loan amortization program, simply put in your current loan balance, interest rate and *desired* term into the program. For example, let's say you have twenty-six years left on your mortgage and want to pay it off in fifteen. Put in the balance currently owed, the interest rate, and desired term of fifteen years and you have, cost-free, created your own fifteen-year mortgage—the increase in your payment is the amount going to directly reduce the principal each month. And most programs will let you print out your amortization schedule if desired.

To do this with credit cards, since the bank recalculates your minimum payment each month, the easiest way is to simply pay a flat extra amount or pay some multiple of the minimum payment.

There are other methods, but they are all variations on a single theme: any extra money you pay goes directly to reduce the principal; so the best advice is, in the words of the Nike shoe commercials, *just do it*! To provide some powerful motivation, let me briefly show you the magnitude of potential savings by comparing a thirty-year and fifteen-year mortgage loan of $250,000 at five percent:

	$250,000 loan @ 5%		
	30-year	**15-year**	**Difference**
Monthly payment:	$1,342	$1,977	**$635** higher/month for 15 year loan
Sum of interest paid:	$233,139	$105,857	***$127,282* 2 ¼ times more** for 30 year loan
Loan reduction after:			
5 years	$20,424	$63,608	**$43,184 more** loan reduction for 15-year loan
10 years	$46,636	$145,241	**$98,604 more** loan reduction for 15-year loan
Loan balance after:			
5 years	$229,576	$186,392	**$43,184 higher** loan balance for 30-year loan
10 years	$203,364	$104,759	**$98,604 higher** loan balance for 30-year loan

What stands out? *Over $127,000*—or two and a quarter times—more interest paid with a thirty-year loan! The difference is actually greater than this because with a fifteen-year loan, the interest rate would be about a quarter percent less, reducing the monthly payment by $32 per month and increasing the difference in interest paid to $133,149. Note also how much faster the loan balance goes down—and your equity goes up—with a fifteen-year loan, because every extra dollar you're paying goes directly to reduce the loan. To really drive this point home, here are graphs of the total interest paid and equity buildup:

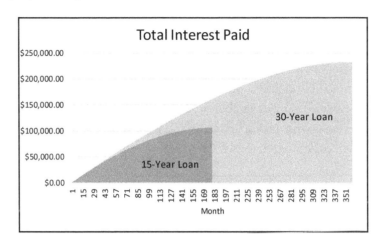

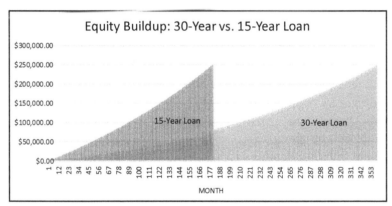

Of course, to achieve these savings, you have to pay more each month: In this example, $635 more per month. "Impossible!" you might say given your current financial position. My response? "Maybe, maybe not." Remember that tool we introduced in Chapter 2, the personal financial roadmap? Combined with living on cash and writing down your expenditures, can you re-jigger your expenditures ... or become more efficient ... or even cut out some expenditures in order to save $127,000? What could you do with an extra $127,000? Might that pay for a child's college education? Or help fund your retirement dreams? But, this takes implementation (again) of the "d" word, discipline.

To provide even more incentive, we are now living in an interest rate-increasing environment. Back in 1981, mortgage rates topped out at an incredible eighteen percent—I was "privileged" to have one of those. Maybe that was an aberration so let's look at the difference in interest costs with a comparison of a $250,000 loan at ten percent—and notice the humongous difference in interest paid:

	$250,000 loan @ 10%		
	30-year	15-year	Difference
Monthly payment:	$2,194	$2,687	$493 higher for 15 year loan
Sum of interest paid:	$539,679	$233,458	*$306,221* 2 ¼ times more for 30 year loan or more than the loan itself!
Loan reduction after:			
5 years	$8,570	$46,746	$38,176 more loan reduction for 15-year loan
10 years	$22,670	$123,658	$100,989 more loan reduction for 15-year loan
Loan balance after:			
5 years	$241,430	$203,254	$38,176 higher loan balance for 30-year loan
10 years	$227,330	$126,342	$100,989 higher loan balance for 30-year loan

Have I made my point? Just as interest compounding works magnificently *for* you when you are saving, it sucks money out of your wallet big time when you are borrowing. Restated simply:

> Save and your money **grows**; borrow and your money speedily **disappears.**

And that naturally but forcefully leads into **Main Point #3, Recommendations**.

Recommendation #1: First and foremost, buck the tide and start eradicating debt in your life. Or, in the words of Dave Ramsey, dump debt. *Anytime* you make extra payments, by avoiding that interest charge, your money is *earning* the interest rate on the loan. So, do you want a risk-free twelve to eighteen percent return on your money? If you don't know it already, look at your most recent credit card statement to see what your rate is and then start paying down your credit card balances early to earn that rate. Remember that the only way to get out of debt is by spending less and paying off more … and in the process, you earn a huge return on your money.

I wish I could stop there but we live in society where the nicer things in life are all around us. A former pastor used a memorable illustration of wearing a broad-brimmed hat with all kinds of fanciful toy items dangling from it: an ATV, a fancy car, a big house, a cruise ship, a power boat, skis, you name it. All of this "stuff" was hanging right in front of his eyes no matter which way he looked. And the mix keeps changing, with new and better items all the time! It may be hard to remember, but for those over the age of twenty or twenty-five, we lived without cell phones … and overnight package delivery services … and cable/satellite TV with hundreds of channels to choose from and on and on. No matter how much stuff we have, it seems that we want more and more of it … definitely not needs but wants and desires. Let me ask you this: when was the last time you banked your raise for any extended period of time? Or the last time you went through all your stuff and said, "nope, I don't need this anymore" or "we don't need to spend our money on this anymore" and sold off a bunch of stuff? For most of us, at the end of every year, we have *more* stuff than when the year began. Rarely if ever do we stop to consider our answer to the telling question, "how much is enough?" possibly because our lifestyle embarrassingly provides the answer: "just a little bit more."

Likely stepping on toes again, this is a disease called "possession itis" and it is quite virulent because it is so contagious—nearly everyone has some degree of it. But spend a couple of days in Haiti … or Nepal … or Ethiopia … or Somalia and you will quickly see how ridiculous this disease is. Most of us could easily—yes, easily—live on less. And yet, we want more ... that is possession-itis.

Recently, I came across a statement made by the apostle Paul that somehow, in all my readings of the book of Philippians, I had totally missed. Now, I frequently ponder if I will ever be able to echo his words. Coming in the midst of his thankfulness for their aid and gifts, he says this in Philippians 4:17-18:

> *Not that I desire your gifts; what I desire is that more be credited to your account.* [18] *I have received full payment and* ***have more than enough****.* ***I am amply supplied****, now that I have received from Epaphroditus the gifts you sent.*

When was the last time you said to yourself, "I have more than enough ... I am amply supplied?" Did Paul live the high life? Hardly! Born into a wealthy family, highly educated and in his own words, "a Hebrew of Hebrews," on a dusty Damascus road he met Jesus and gave up everything to follow Him. From that day forward, he lived the life of an itinerant preacher, suffering ridicule and torture and deprivation unlike any of us who have followed after him. Yet even though much of his Christian life was lived in dependence on the gifts of others, with few possessions of his own, he was able to say *I have more than enough ... I am amply supplied.*

Living in the world we do, with all the accoutrements of modern society swarming around us, it is so easy to forget that we don't really "need" all the stuff we have. Earlier in Philippians 4, Paul talks about how he learned to be content in any and every situation, whether well-fed or hungry, whether living in plenty or in want. Absent is any sense of craving ... or ... idolizing ... or chasing after ... or even lamenting not having a lot of stuff. Instead, he says in verse 13: *I can do all this through* ***him*** *who gives me strength.*

Let me make one last comment before providing some general guidelines on moving towards a contented life. This ties in nicely with Chapter 3 and the importance of understanding the necessity of giving before delving into the everyday issues of earning and spending. Paul makes a statement in verse 19 of Philippians 4 that you have likely heard or read many times. Yet, when you understand the context of Paul's statement, it should change how you should read the verse ... what words you emphasize. Without regard to context, we often just read the verse by itself, and we read it this way:

> *And my God will meet **all your needs** according to the riches of his glory in Christ Jesus.*

There is nothing wrong with reading it that way, for it is true. But, that's not really Paul's point. Verses 10-20 of Philippians 4 are titled "Thanking Them for Their Gifts," and Paul takes great effort to do exactly that. He says:

> (verse 10): *I rejoiced greatly in the Lord that at last you renewed your concern for me.*

> (verse 14): *... it was good of you to share in my troubles.*

> (verses 14-15): *... in the early days ... not one church shared with me in the matter of giving and receiving, except you only.*

> (verse 16): *... you sent me aid more than once when I was in need.*

> (verse 18): *... I have received from Epaphroditus the gifts you sent. They are a fragrant offering, an acceptable sacrifice, pleasing to God.*

The Philippians had apparently given to Paul often, sacrificially, and in generous measure. So, Paul tells the Philippians that, just as the Lord has provided *his* every need, as a result of all of *their* sacrificial giving to him (and I am going to insert one word to get the point across):

> ... my God **will** also *meet all* **your** *needs according to the riches of his glory in Christ Jesus.*

Can you see the difference? It's not just that God will meet all their needs but that as a *result* or consequence of following His leading and giving up some of their precious resources to provide some of Paul's needs, God is also going to take care of *them* ... He is still going to meet all of *their* needs.

So ... how are we to live our lives in the credit-saturated and temptation-filled society we live in? Two things should be abundantly clear at this point. First, we have far more than we "need"—much of our spending is directed towards the nicer things of life. Second, recall one of the key points from Chapter 2: as a steward/manager of all that you possess, you are going to be evaluated on that stewardship. Life here on earth is not about "he who has the most toys wins" but rather "he who utilizes God's resources to the most benefit"—that person is the one who hears those magical words "well done good and faith servant ... I will put you in charge of many things."

Recommendation #2: Know when to borrow ... and the consequences. Just as God's Word treats lending/borrowing as a commonplace "business decision" during Biblical times, there are going to be situations where the need to borrow is virtually unavoidable so recommendation #2 is composed of three guidelines.

Guideline #1: Understand the general economic maxim on borrowing:

> Borrowing only makes financial sense if the expected rate of return on what you acquire is greater than the after-tax cost of interest on that borrowing.

For a businessperson, this means that an investment can be made with borrowed funds if the item is expected to generate income greater than the cost of borrowing. For individuals such as you and me, our assets don't normally generate an income, so the rule means that the value of the asset should increase faster than the cost of borrowing. For example:

> If it costs ten percent to borrow, and therefore eight percent after tax (assume a twenty percent tax bracket), the asset had better be going up *more* than eight percent per year, or else you're losing money.[27]

That's why borrowing to buy just about any kind of depreciating asset—such as a car—is such a poor use of financial resources. In fact, a former editor of *Money* magazine bluntly called it "d-u-m-b!" Even with appreciating assets, you have to be careful. Using the same facts, if your house is not increasing in value at least eight percent per year—and these days are they?—you are losing money. Factor in maintenance, repairs, new furniture, etc., and renting starts looking a lot better. Plus, as we talked about, it might be easier to move if you don't have to sell. So, don't mindlessly sign on the dotted line just because the bank will loan you the money.

Guideline #2: Debt presumes upon the future. When you borrow, you promise to repay in the future and so, are relying on the adequacy of your future income to be able to make the payments. Most debt is entered into assuming that the financial resources to repay will remain the same or increase over time, and, as long as that occurs, repayment can be accomplished. Going into debt is similar to making an investment: No one invests believing that the investment will go down in value. But just as investments do, at times, go haywire, so do the economic conditions that a family finds itself in—and history is replete with examples of that outcome. We are, in a sense, gazing into a crystal ball and trying to see the future. Borrowing is not wrong but the future may not turn out as we thought. After the Great Recession of 2008, recall how many families owed more on their homes than those homes were worth—maybe you were one of them. If you absolutely must borrow—for example, to buy a home—then pay it off as quickly as possible as demonstrated with the thirty- vs. fifteen-year mortgage example earlier. There is no better Scriptural warning against presuming on the future than James 4:13-15:

> *Now listen, you who say, "Today or tomorrow we will go to this or that city, spend a year there, carry on business and make money." [14] Why, you do not even know what will happen tomorrow. What is your life? You are a mist that appears for a little while and then vanishes. [15] Instead, you ought to say, "If it is the Lord's will, we will live and do this or that."*

Finally, guideline #3: A debt-free lifestyle should be your ultimate goal. As a wise *oikonómos*, minimizing or living free from the two exorbitant costs of debt simply makes good financial sense. Our friend Roger Babson says it better than I can:

> The entire installment business is unnecessary. People could be taught to save and buy later as easily as to go into debt to buy in advance.[28]

Summary

Let me wrap up this thought-provoking chapter with a few overall comments. First and foremost, nowhere does God's Word say that borrowing is a sin. Moreover, there is no Biblical commandment that says we are to live life here as ascetics and abstaining from all the pleasures of life—in fact, His Word indicates that He may bless us in tremendous ways. But, the availability of credit makes it so easy to "bypass" the time-honored practice of saving up for something and then determining if it is still worth getting, as you are now comparing apples with apples. While buying on credit and borrowing are not sins, borrowing *is* presuming on the future, always a risky venture. Moreover, credit and borrowing can easily and woefully be overused or abused to get stuff we don't really need—stuff that ends up costing an arm and a leg when interest is included. So, before you make any major borrowing decision, first check with your Father, because good economic sense does not automatically equate to good spiritual sense—i.e., that it is His will for you. He may say, "Fine, go ahead." But He may also say, "no, you don't really need that item," or "I'm going to provide it another way," or "why don't you save up for it and once you have the funds, see if you still desire it."

Second, if you decide to borrow, count the cost. Never forget that credit is *ex-pen-sive*, both in terms of the interest cost as well as the likelihood of spending far more than you otherwise would without it. Whether using that innocuous little two inch by three inch piece of plastic or signing on the dotted line of a loan agreement, what was that range of percentages for how much more the average person will spend? Fifty to seventy percent. I want you to see that statistic in your mind every time you use your credit or debit card—50-70%. Maybe you think that you are more careful than the average person ... fine. All I ask if for you to take the thirty-day "living on cash" test and pay cash for everything. Maybe it will be less than 50-70% but I know it will be significantly greater than zero and more than the cost of this book. Living within our means—really within God's means—and even below our means, should be our goal. Instead of living to acquire more and more—and most of us already have too much—we should learn to be content and desire to give more and more.

Finally, most all of us have financial debts of some kind, whether for a mortgage, a car, school, whatever. Many no doubt sought the Lord's direction before taking on the debt and are dutifully making the payments. So, the last thing to remember is: Don't delay—start vaporizing your debt *now*! Using the debt snowball process discussed in Chapter 2, diligently work to get out of debt, out of servanthood to the lender. It may take a while, but it's a freeing feeling to make that last payment. And unless there is an awfully good reason to take on more debt, vow to trust the Lord to provide the funds in advance and not in arrears. I can't think of a better way to demonstrate wise stewardship.

To provide a capstone to this chapter, here are parts of two scriptures, one Old Testament and one New Testament, which capture the essence of the Bible's view of debt:

> Proverbs 22:7: *...the borrower is slave to the lender.*

and

> Romans 13:8: *Let no debt remain outstanding, except the continuing debt to love one another...*

APPENDIX 4: Common Questions regarding Debt and Borrowing

Q   What if you need a certain item now and don't have the cash to pay for it?

For example, maybe you're in sales and need a nice car as part of the job. Or maybe your current car is about to die. Let me suggest the following four general steps that apply to any major purchase:

1. Examine the marketplace and determine which item or items would best fit your *needs*, given what you will be using it for.

2. As a test of the reasonableness of the item or items selected in step #1, seriously evaluate whether you *would* spend that much if you had worked and slaved and sacrificed to save up the cash. Forget monthly payment amounts, forget interest rates, forget down payments and all that. Compare apples with apples:

    > Would you write a check for that amount, kiss the money good bye, and buy the item?

    This is, admittedly, a tough decision, but it's the only fair way to make the judgment that you're being a good steward and not spending more than you should. Continue in this process until you have matched the amount you're willing to spend with what item or items that that amount will buy.

3. Count the cost. As you've learned, the price for immediate acquisition via borrowing is high. If the item is something you always have to buy by borrowing, it can easily end up costing you ten, fifteen, twenty percent or more, especially

if you use a credit card each time. Knowing that cost going in can help you decide if completing the transaction is what the Lord wants you to do.

You've now done your homework, using the good brain He's given you. But, because His wisdom is far greater than ours, there's one last and most important step:

4. Seek His guidance. He promises to make our paths straight, if we'll let Him. New things, such as cars, are nice and there is nothing inherently wrong with desiring one, but His will may be for you to repair or maintain the one you have until you have saved up the cash. Don't let the ease of getting a "yes" to your credit application lull you into thinking that that automatically implies approval from your Father on high.

Q   What about credit card use in general?

Much has been written about the exorbitant interest rates charged on credit card purchases (as mentioned, up to 79.9%, with an average of about 18%). Most anything these days can be purchased with a credit card. But most of those things have two characteristics in common:

- They don't produce any income, and
- They don't increase in value.

So, buying them using a credit card, especially at the high rates charged, is bad financial management, because doing so does not meet the general economic guideline of borrowing. Recall that comment made by the former editor at *Money* magazine:

Unless absolutely essential, borrowing to buy a depreciating asset is D-U-M-B.[29]

What about convenience use of credit cards? Some people use credit cards and pay off the balance, in full, by the due date, and so do not incur any interest charges. This admittedly eliminates the need to carry a lot of cash, provides a good record of purchases, and for some, earns them rewards like airline miles. I would say that, if you have a good handle on your finances, in that you have and are living in accordance with your personal financial roadmap, using a credit card for convenience is okay. There is nothing inherently sinful about a two- by three-inch piece of plastic. But recall that troubling statistic mentioned previously: study after study has shown that the average person will spend fifty to seventy percent more when they use credit, *regardless* of when the balance is paid—this easily negates any usage awards that come with the card.

One way to rein in potential over-spending is to ask yourself every time you use the card, "would I make this purchase if I had to pay cash?" Another way is to use a debit card—which can also come with rewards—as the purchase price is deducted from your bank account almost immediately, usually within one or two days. For those who don't want to carry around a lot of cash but don't trust themselves with a normal credit card, this may be a better alternative. You don't get free use of the bank's money, but then you are less likely—note that I intentionally didn't say "unlikely"—to overspend. As we talked about, it just seems so easy to spend more if you don't have to physically peel off the bills.

In summary, when credit cards are used properly, they can be practical tools, minimizing the need to carry around a lot of cash. Use of them involves risks, but so does driving a car. If one can't control themselves in driving a car, that privilege should be revoked. So should it be with credit cards.

Q   What about using credit to buy a house? Let me offer four thoughts on this question.

First, although it seems we Americans believe it's a God-given right to own the roof over our heads, I can find no Scripture to support such a notion.

Second, however, for many people, buying a home has been the best investment they've ever made. During the last forty to fifty years, there have been several periods where homes have appreciated much faster than the inflation rate, creating true equity buildup. And because that equity buildup occurred with very little down (five to twenty percent), the leveraged rate-of-return has been very high. But let me caution you: many homeowners in Houston in the 1970s walked away from their homes because the market value had dropped below even the mortgage balance, not just the original purchase price. This same thing happened in California in the early 1990s and most recently, nationwide in 2008-2011. No one puts this risk in better words than King Solomon in Ecclesiastes 7:14:

> *When times are good, be happy; but when times are bad, consider this: God has made the one as well as the other. Therefore, no one can discover anything about their future.*

Third, on the positive side, because houses, in general, tend to meet the general economic guideline on borrowing, and because it is almost impossible to save up the entire purchase price ahead of time, borrowing to buy a house—again, after prayerful seeking of His will for you—is probably the safest type of borrowing one can undertake.

Fourth, recall the example on how much interest you can save using a fifteen-year mortgage—similar savings can be achieved with a "bi-weekly" mortgage. For the same house, yes, your monthly payment is higher so you may have to carefully restructure your other expenditures. Alternatively, if the payment amount on a thirty-year loan is truly all that you can afford, use Google or have your lender assist you in determining how much that same payment will let you borrow on a fifteen-year loan. Yes, it will be less. In our $250,000, five percent loan example, the thirty-year $1,342 monthly payment would finance only a $172,500 loan, about thirty percent less. But, instead of paying $233,139 in interest, you would pay only $69,000, a savings of an astonishing $164,000, almost as much as the house itself. And if interest rates keep increasing, that differential will also keep growing. So, the real issue may be this: can you buck the tide of the worldly maxim of "bigger is better" and be content with less house to achieve these amazing savings? A mortgage is the biggest and longest commitment you will likely ever incur—therefore, do so wisely and carefully.

Q   What about home equity and home equity line-of-credit loans?

These, as you likely know, are loans against the equity in your home, and if certain rules are met[30], the interest paid is fully deductible on your tax return. For this reason, and because many people have large, untapped amounts of equity in their homes, the banks are pushing these loans hard. Should you get one? Only after you have fully convinced yourself of one thing: the money you get is not yours, it's theirs. Approximately 30 days after receiving the money, you must start paying it back, with interest. And if you don't, they have the right to force you out and sell your house.

The marketing for these types of loans is very enticing. If you have a good reason to borrow—say for remodeling/expansion of your home or debt consolidation where the goal is to significantly reduce your interest rate along with foregoing any new borrowing—and you understand the costs and significant risks, these are a good vehicle. That's because there are very few fees and the interest rates are about as low as you can find (although many are adjustable rates with either very high or no caps). However, only the interest on the portion to remodel/expand your home is tax deductible. As with other types of borrowing, use extreme care so as to avoid the quite graphic consequence of Proverbs 22:27b, "if you lack the means to pay, your very bed will be snatched from under you."

Q   What about co-signing on a loan?

This is one area where God's Word is very, *very* clear. Co-signing is where you agree to, along with the primary borrower, sign the loan documents. The lender is requiring this because the primary borrower doesn't have sufficient credit-worthiness to satisfy them. The Biblical guidance can be put in three crystal-clear words: DON'T DO IT! The Biblical word is often translated "security" or "surety," the legal term still in use today, and literally means "to stand good for another." How good? Well, if they don't pay, guess who the lender comes after? *Y-o-u.* In fact, if there is any problem with the lender collecting on the loan, they'll likely come after you first because they know you *have the money.*

The applicable verses are as follows—and they don't really need any explanation:

    a. Strong command against it:

        Proverbs 22:26: *Do not be one who shakes hands in pledge or puts up security for debts.*

    b. Type of person who does it:

        Proverbs 17:18: *One who has no sense* [KJV—void of understanding] *shakes hands in pledge and puts up security for a neighbor.*

c. Results of being surety, or standing good for another:

> Proverbs 11:15a: *Whoever puts up security for a stranger will surely suffer* [KJV—shall smart for it] ...

> Proverbs 22:27: *if you lack the means to pay, your very bed will be snatched from under you.*

d. Strong command to get out (didn't know not to do it or forgot to follow #1-3)—note many allusions to snare or trap, which we will talk more about in Chapter 5:

> Proverbs 6:1-5: *My son, if you have put up security [surety] for your neighbor, if you have struck hands in pledge a stranger, you have been trapped by what you said, ensnared by the words of your mouth. So do this, my son, to free yourself, since you have fallen into your neighbor's hands: Go—to the point of exhaustion—and give your neighbor no rest! Allow no sleep to your eyes, no slumber to your eyelids. Free yourself, like a gazelle from the hand of the hunter, like a bird from the snare of the fowler.*

Q What about cosigning among *family* members?

a. The context of passages above, either directly or indirectly, is in reference to neighbors, friends or strangers—in other words, with nonrelatives. There seems to be no Biblical prohibition to co-signing for family members. However, the warning of Proverbs 22:27 still holds true when you co-sign for little Jimmy or Suzy for their first car:

... if you lack the means to pay, your very bed will be snatched from under you.

    b. As a cosigner, you are *as* liable as the signer, and the lender has legal right to collect from *either* of you, regardless of how the money was spent. So, if you cosign and the primary borrower doesn't pay, family member or not, you can expect a call and better be ready to pay.

Q What if you have the cash to buy—is there any wisdom in keeping the cash and borrowing? Let me offer four thoughts on this issue:

First, regarding the cost of borrowing, interest: From a strictly quantitative point of view, if one truly can afford to pay cash, but instead chooses to borrow, the differences may not be all that great: the difference in interest rate to be earned on money left in the bank (or return on the investment if invested), the interest rate to be paid on the loan, possible tax deductibility of interest paid, and income tax brackets all determine how close the two methods are. But, in general, it is cheaper to pay cash because the interest rate on borrowing is always higher than the interest rate on saving. And to remain consistent, you should have sufficient cash for *every* major credit purchase, not just one.

Second, two motivations are often put forward for this approach, of which the first is disingenuous and the second potentially quite risky:

- To be able to have a cash reserve in case of emergencies: This basically assumes there is insufficient or no other savings. In one sense, then, you really can't afford to pay cash, because if you did and you had an emergency, you'd be in trouble. It

is much wiser to set up a true emergency—oh thank God—fund, then another fund to pay cash for the item.
- The potential of earning more with the borrowed funds than the interest is costing you: This is risky, as you may actually earn less or lose part or all of the money—reread the words of King Solomon in Ecclesiastes 7:14 and the apostle James in James 4:13-15.

Let me share a personal life-lesson experience with you to make this risk realistic. Back when I was in graduate school in the early 1980s, interest rates were skyrocketing. I had easy access to student loan money which not only carried very low interest rates, the interest charges didn't start accruing until after graduation and I didn't have to start paying the money back until I graduated. At this same time, the price for silver bullion was skyrocketing. So ... in my unbridled and seemingly sophisticated earthly wisdom, I used some of the money—$5,000—to buy $20,000 of silver futures on margin, figuring of course, that I couldn't lose. For a time, I was up more than $5,000—doubling my money! But, as some readers may know, futures markets can move swiftly and if the market declines rapidly, it can be difficult to get out before you are wiped out, even owing money if your investment declines more than you have invested. I was lucky—I only lost my $5,000. But every monthly payment on that loan was a persistent reminder of my recklessness.

Third, if inflation occurs during the loan payback period, you must increase your savings/cash balance (in addition to making payments on the loan), otherwise, you will not have enough to truly "pay cash" the next time.

Finally, you still have the risk of that second and potentially far larger cost of borrowing: spending (acquiring) more than if you peeled the bills out of your wallet. That is because in this approach, you really are buying the item on credit.

In sum, the absolute best test of whether you really want or need an item is to save up in advance and then decide if you're willing to put it all on the table to buy the item. Then you can truly determine that 1) yes, this is what you "need" or are willing to pay for your "wants" and "desires," or 2) you may find you don't really "need" as much. Overcome the temptation to rationalize buying something on credit when you really don't have the cash to pay for it.

Q   What if the merchant offers 0% interest on the purchase?

This is most common with car loans but I have started seeing it with every-day type purchases like mattresses. In most instances, the merchant must pay for the merchandise long before the loan period being offered the consumer ends. Money is not free and the merchant is either paying for that merchandise out of their own funds and losing the interest earnings on it while you pay off the loan or they are obtaining some type of financing to pay for the goods and incurring interest. As a result, in nearly every situation where zero percent interest is offered, you can get a better price by offering to pay cash. The difference is the implied interest cost to the merchant. So, evaluate that cost, as well as the probability of spending more simply because you can buy the item on credit.

Q   What if you are in severe financial debt, i.e., barely able to make only the minimum payment on one or more credit cards?

This will admittedly be the harshest advice in this book. You must do three things, and you may need a Christian financial counselor to help you with steps 2 and 3:

1. However you got into this situation, you must humble yourself, seek the Lord's guidance and ask for His help. Just as no sin is too great for Him to forgive, no financial situation, no matter how bad, is too hard for Him to help

you through. He may not provide mammon from heaven, but the Psalmist writes an encouragement for Israel that is just as appropriate for us today, whatever our need:

> Psalm 50:15: ... *call upon me in the day of trouble; I will deliver you, and you will honor me.*

It may require significant sacrificing to get out of debt. It may mean some things have to be sold. It may mean you have to change your lifestyle. But the longer you wait, the harder it will become.

2. You must not take on more debt. You may need to undergo "plastic surgery," where you cut up your credit cards, or put them in water and store them in your freezer. Recall what I said earlier: You don't get out of debt by borrowing more, you get out of debt by borrowing *less* and paying *off* more.

3. You need to formalize the "paying off more" by putting together a workable plan for repayment, starting with the smallest one first. If you are delinquent on any of your accounts, you will need to write to the creditor, explain your situation, and show them your plan of payments. Then, *you must stick to the plan.*

Just as you likely did not get into this situation overnight, it is going to take time to work your way out. You might even stumble along the way but don't give up. It is a freeing feeling to see debts get paid off. Untold others before you have done it and you can also. As the Psalmist wrote: "Call upon me in the day of trouble; I **will** deliver you, and you **will** honor me."

Q What if things are so bad that you are considering bankruptcy?

Before answering the question, let me provide some statistics and information about bankruptcy law. Over the twelve-year period 2006 – 2017, there were almost thirteen million consumer bankruptcies, or about one million per year, although in recent years, that number has declined to about 800,000 per year. Declaring bankruptcy can provide a fresh financial start for those who cannot pay their debts, either because of insolvency or insufficient income to meet creditor demands. Bankruptcy generally works in one of two ways: your assets are sold to pay your debts under Chapter 7 of the U.S. Bankruptcy Code, or the court establishes a repayment plan under Chapter 13 of the code.

Under a Chapter 7 liquidation, you can achieve a fresh financial start more quickly than under a Chapter 13 repayment plan, which can last up to five years. However, under Chapter 13, you may be able to save a home from foreclosure, reschedule secured debts and extend them over the life of a Chapter 13 plan (possibly lowering the payments), or consolidate debt payments to a trustee who then handles distribution to creditors.

Is this a viable option for a believer? Recall our discussion about non-need borrowing and the implied message in Exodus 22:25:

> *If you lend money to one of my people among you who is needy,* ***do not treat it like a business deal****; charge no interest.*

With ordinary, non-need lending, the transaction is going to be the result of a structured, agreed-upon transaction between a willing lender and a willing borrower, with an interest rate appropriate for the amount of risk that the lender is taking. The lender knows—without a doubt—that some borrowers are going to default. They may try to harass you with phone calls and letters, they may even try to sue you. But ultimately, if you don't or can't pay, it is a risk and loss that they took on willingly.

The bankruptcy laws allow you to speed up the process a bit by putting it in the court's hands. Because we talked about how the righteous, when they borrow, do repay, if you decide—or are encouraged—to file for bankruptcy, I would strongly recommend the Chapter 13 repayment process for three reasons. First, as you read above, it may allow you to keep your home. Second, as we talked about in the chapter, no one was holding a gun to your head when you signed on the dotted line—you voluntarily took on the debt and promised to repay. The Chapter 13 process provides a way for you to keep that promise. And third, as mentioned in Chapter 2, getting out from a heavy debt load is not going to be easy or quick. But, experience can be a great teacher and honoring your debts is part of honoring your God. Remember that great verse in 1 Samuel 2:30: "Those who honor me I will honor." When you honor Him, I guarantee that you will be amazed at how He honors you in return.

But there are situations where the borrower gets into dire straits through the act of another: a business partner loots the business or causes losses for which you are responsible; a divorced spouse doesn't honor their financial commitments; uninsured medical costs spiral out of control. These are not situations where the debtor simply wants to use the bankruptcy laws to avoid paying an acknowledged debt. In all of these types of situations, the debt burden may be so large as to be ultimately unpayable, no matter how much the debtor may desire to try to pay them off. Again, because the lender took on the debt as a knowledgeable businessperson—knowing the risks—suffering a loss at times is part of ordinary lending. So, a fresh financial start can be the best solution. Moreover, I have known individuals who went this route and because of their desire to "honor their debts" still made an attempt to repay part or all of it as the Lord blessed even though there was no legal requirement to do so.

If you decide to go one of these two routes be aware that your credit score will get hammered: a Chapter 13 bankruptcy stays on your credit report for seven years while a Chapter 7 bankruptcy stays on for ten years. So, in either situation, the repercussions last for a long time because most lenders will not be fooled again and lend to someone with a bankruptcy on their record.

5

MANAGING MAMMON FOR THE LONG-TERM

> Risk comes from not knowing what you are doing – Warren Buffett

> An investor without investment objectives is like a traveler without a destination – Ralph Seger

> If your investments are limited to this earth, you are the world's worst investor - John Hagee

For some readers, this may be the chapter you have been looking forward to—maybe you have already peeked at it a bit! So, let me start with some overall comments. First, there is only one correct way to start on this journey: Your giving and your spending must be less than your income. While the Lord may lead a few to spend and give away all their income, that is not the norm. In other words, you need to have put in practice all that we talked about in chapters 2-4, which deal primarily with the short term, before even considering the long term. So, as prerequisites, you should be:

- Giving regularly as your Lord has guided and blessed you. Recall that the purposes of giving are not only to glorify and honor Him but to acknowledge that He is your God and that He does, in fact, own it all.
- Monitoring your spending using your personal financial roadmap.
- Controlling and reducing your use of credit. In addition, you should not be in arrears on any debt since we've seen that as a good *oikonómos*, you have an obligation to repay. You cannot expect God to bless your investing if you are using funds that legally belong to another.

Second, to prepare your heart and mind for all that God has to share in this area, I need to remind you of that quote by Billy Graham—do you remember it?

> If a person gets their attitude toward *money* straight, it will help straighten out almost *every other area in their life.*

Investing is an area where, unless you do have your attitude toward money straight, it is so easy to go from using money to loving money, from investing to provide for needs to investing to provide for "greeds," from managing God's resources to hoarding God's resources—all with potentially deadly consequences as you'll see. As just a brief introduction, both King Solomon and the apostle Paul provide us with stern warnings about these risks:

> Ecclesiastes 5:10: *Whoever loves money* **never** *has enough; whoever loves wealth is* **never** *satisfied with their income. This too is meaningless.*

> 1 Timothy 6:10: *For the* **love of money** *is a root of all kinds of evil. Some people, eager for money, have*

wandered from the faith and pierced themselves with many griefs.

One bright-line indicator of loving money and it becoming your god is having investible funds but doing little or no giving. Said another way, if you can't trust the Lord enough to give out of your short-term income, you'll likely not give out of your long-term earnings either. As proof, read what Jesus says in the parable of the shrewd or wise manager in Luke 16:10 and I'll use the Phillips translation here because it is so telling:

> *The man who is faithful in the little things will be faithful in the big things, and the man who cheats in the little things will cheat in the big things too. So that if you are not fit to be trusted to deal with the wicked wealth of this world, who will trust you with the true riches?*

So … as we go through this material, remember that your goal must never be to simply make money—or make more money—because that is a never-ending quest. Instead, your primary focus should always be on generating additional resources to provide for the needs of your household—as we'll talk about—and being able to give more to Him.

Along those lines, there are some whom God gives a special ability to make money—maybe to make a *lot* of money—so that it can be used to have a huge impact in spreading His message and building His Kingdom. If that is you and you are choosing not to honor Him with your giving, I need to remind you of the dire consequences spoken by Jesus Himself in Matthew 16:26 27:

> *What good will it be for someone to gain the whole world, yet forfeit their soul? Or what can anyone give*

> *in exchange for their soul?* ²⁷ *For the Son of Man is going to come in his Father's glory with his angels, and then he will reward each person according to what they have done.*

You may still invest and be successful in worldly terms but ultimately it will all be meaningless when you meet Him face-to-face. As an antidote, recall what I said in Chapter 3: You can't have your head straight on the reasons for making money until you have your heart straight on the reasons for giving it away. So, give—and give generously—before you try to make.

A Caution

Finally, back in Chapter 1, I told you that God's Word deals more with financial issues than any other topic. One consequence of that, however, is that it can be easy to misinterpret what it says. We saw that potential in Chapter 3 when we looked at the topic of giving and we are going to see it again with investing. To be honest, for many years of my Christian life, I fell into that trap because I neglected that all-important concept of context. In terms of a pithy phrase, "if you miss the context, you mess up the message." Let me give you a simple example.

> In the parable of the Workers in the Vineyard in Matthew 20:1-16, the landowner pays the workers that are hired in the eleventh hour the same as those who started early in the morning—much to their consternation after a long, hard day's work. Now, is that suggesting that the employers reading this book do the same? Hardly! The whole point of the parable was that Jesus has the right to accept into His kingdom those who have served Him for

years as well as those who accept Him in the last moments of their lives on their deathbeds.

There are two well-known parables of Jesus that are often used to conclude that God's Word—and Jesus Himself—endorse or encourage investing. But when I stepped back and examined the context of those parables, it became clear that, to the contrary, Jesus was simply using a common investing situation that the listeners could understand to illustrate His point. So that you can see it for yourself, let's look a bit at these two parables. These are generally titled the Parable of the Bags of Gold (*Talents* in many translations; we looked at this briefly in Chapter 2) in Matthew 25 and the Parable of the Ten Minas in Luke 19.

In both parables, Jesus uses the example of entrusting money to servants while the master goes away. Some of the servants invest the money, making more, and then when the master returns and settles accounts with them, they give it all back. In both parables, the master replies with those magical words mentioned in earlier chapters that we'd all like to hear: "Well done, good and faithful servant! You have been faithful with a few things; I will put you in charge of many things. Come and share your master's happiness!" And in both parables, one servant does not invest but instead either buries the money in the ground or hides it away. The angry master takes that servant's money away, gives it to one of the successful servants, and in one of the parables, even casts the derelict servant into the darkness where there is "weeping and gnashing of teeth."

So, can you see that it is very easy to conclude that the parables are indeed promoting or endorsing investing by us, His servants? But let's examine the context. For the Parable of the Talents in Matthew 25, here are the headings going back to the beginning of Matthew 24:

- 24:1-35: The Destruction of the Temple and Signs of the End Times
- 24:36-end: The Day and Hour Unknown

and

- 25:1-13: The Parable of the Ten Virgins

All these deal with Jesus' return and being ready for that return. The heading after the Parable of the Talents is The Sheep and the Goats (25:31-46), which deals with separating the true believers from the pretenders at the final judgment. Chapter 26 discusses how, after Jesus had said all these things, the Jews plotted to arrest Him.

So ... is the Parable of the Talents really about investing? Or, like the Parable of the Ten Virgins that precedes it, is it simply using a situation to which the listener could relate to hammer home the concept of being ready for the return of the Master? Think about that for a moment.

What about the other parable, the Parable of the Ten Minas? It is preceded by the story of Zacchaeus, the tax collector who actually gave away all of his wealth as a result of meeting Jesus, followed by Jesus' triumphal entry into Jerusalem. Again, the parable seems simply to be using an illustration the listeners could relate to in order to convey the concept of being ready for the Master's return and doing everything possible to be ready for that return.

So ... can you see what I mean? Over and over, context is critical to drawing correct conclusions. Now, you might be thinking, "well, can't we draw some good advice from these parables about investing?" The more I thought about that very question, the more I dug into all the verses in His Word that seemed to have something to do with investing. And here's what I found. Overall, God's Word neither promotes nor prohibits investing. Instead, it simply presents the concept as a "matter of fact" or "this is what we observe." Pictorially, it can be viewed like this tightrope illustration:

On the left side, there are verses that view investing, saving, and providing very positively:[31]

> Proverbs 10:4b: ... **diligent** *hands bring wealth.*

> Proverbs 13:11b: ... *whoever gathers money little by little makes it* **grow***.*

> Proverbs 21:5a: *The plans of the diligent lead to* **profit** ...

> Ecclesiastes 11:1-2 (this verse even uses the word "invest"): *Ship your grain across the sea; after many days* **you may receive a return***. Invest in seven ventures, yes, in eight; you do not know what disaster may come upon the land.*

And probably the most important verse:

> 1 Timothy 5:8: *Anyone who does not **provide for their relatives**, and **especially** for their own household, has denied the faith and is worse than an unbeliever.*

But the right side has verses that communicate something very different; be aware that not only am I listing more verses here, there are many more in His Word that view saving and investing negatively:[32]

> Job 31, 24-25, 28: *"If I have put my **trust** in gold or said to pure gold, 'You are my security,'* [25] *if I have **rejoiced over my great wealth**, the fortune my hands had gained ...* [28] *then these also would be **sins** to be judged, for I would have been **unfaithful to God** on high."*

> Psalm 37:16: *Better the **little** that the righteous have **than the wealth of many wicked***

> Psalm 62:10b: *... though your **riches increase, do not set your heart on them**.*

> Proverbs 16:16: *How much **better** to get **wisdom** than gold, to get **insight** rather than silver!*

> Proverbs 22:1: *A **good name** is more **desirable** than **great riches**; to be **esteemed** is better than silver or gold.*

> Proverbs 23:4-5: ***Do not wear yourself out to get rich**; do not trust your own cleverness.* [5]*Cast but a*

glance at riches, and they are ***gone***, *for they will surely* ***sprout wings*** *and fly off to the sky like an eagle.*

Proverbs 28:22: ***The stingy are eager to get rich*** *and are unaware that poverty awaits them.*

Ecclesiastes 4:8b: *There was no **end to his toil**, yet his **eyes were not content** with his wealth.*

Ecclesiastes 5:10: *Whoever loves money **never** has enough; whoever loves wealth is **never** satisfied with their income. This too is meaningless.*

Luke 12:15: *Then he [Jesus] said to them, "**Watch out!** Be on your guard against all kinds of **greed**; life does **not** consist in an abundance of possessions."*

And a passage that we will spend more time on in a bit:

1 Timothy 6:9-10: *Those who **want to get rich** fall into **temptation** and a **trap** and into many **foolish and harmful desires** that **plunge** people into **ruin and destruction**. ¹⁰ For the **love of money** is a root of **all kinds of evil**. Some people, **eager** for money, have **wandered from the faith** and **pierced** themselves with many griefs.*

Pretty heavy verses on the right side of the picture, don't you think? To simplify the illustration just a bit, let me crystalize the key thought for each side:

> Proverbs 10:4b: ... *diligent hands bring wealth.*
>
> 1 Timothy 5:8: ... *provide for their own household.*
>
>
>
> Ecclesiastes 4:8b: *There was no end to his toil, yet his eyes were not content with his wealth.*
>
> Luke 12:15: *Watch out! Be on your guard against all kinds of greed; life does not consist in an abundance of possessions.*

So, the real question is this: The rope between the two sides, what does that represent? What did Billy Graham say? Get your *attitude* straight towards money. The only difference between "need" and "greed" or "using" money and "loving" money is our attitude. As we have discussed previously, there is nothing inherently sinful about the multi-colored piece of paper we call money. Moreover, we actually need it as an easy "medium of exchange" in the marketplace. But there is something about *us* that causes us to want more and more of it, to trust in it, and even to love it, creating that "tug of war" tension between using money and loving money. Look at the word picture contrast that King Solomon draws for us in Proverbs 18:10-11:

The name of the LORD is a fortified tower; the righteous run to it and are safe. **The wealth of the rich is their fortified city; they imagine it a wall too high to scale.**

But how wrong they are. Instead, God's Word makes it abundantly clear that the more stuff you have—whether money or things—creates a barrier that actually makes it *harder* to trust in Him. Why? Because when you have everything you need, it will be that much harder to see your need for God. That very wealth which He gave you—or the abilities to earn wealth—can be the very thing that causes you to … turn away from Him. Remember the rich young ruler and how he was unable to give up his wealth to obtain the true and lasting riches Jesus was offering him. And likely you know the famous and oft-cited verse in Revelation 3:20? Jesus says: "Here I am! I stand at the door and knock …" What you might not remember is the context for that verse. Just three verses earlier, the people in the church of Laodicea say, "I am rich; I have acquired wealth and do not … **need … a … thing**." Jesus replies to them—and to us today—in verses 17-18 that they do not realize that they are "wretched, pitiful, poor, blind and naked," needing white clothes to cover their shameful nakedness and salve on their eyes so they can truly see. *That's* why He says, "Here I am! I stand at the door …" Such is the deception of wealth—please, please, please, don't ever forget it.

To put a capstone on these introductory yet crucial concepts, I encourage you to read parts of four verses out loud and really concentrate as you read them:

> Psalm 62:10b: *Though your **riches increase**, **do not set your heart on them**.*

> Ecclesiastes 5:10a: *Whoever loves money **never** has enough.*

> Proverbs 23:5: *Cast but a **glance** at riches, and they are **gone**, for they will surely sprout **wings** and fly off to the sky like an eagle.*

Ecclesiastes 7:14a: *When times are good, be happy; but when times are bad, consider this:* **God had made the one as well as the other.**

Investing is not wrong, and believers have been doing it for millennia. Sometimes they make money and sometimes they lose it—there are no sure bets. Moreover, other than giving money to further the gospel, there is no such thing as a "Christian" investment. Yes, there are Christian financial advisors who can guide you, but you can still lose it all. Even lending money to build churches is risky; as evidence, the magnificent Crystal Cathedral in Southern California filed for bankruptcy back in 2013.

One more thing about those two so-called "investing" parables we looked at. If you want to draw some guidance about investing from these parables, remember this: In both parables, the investing was always done for the Master, not for the servant—the servant gave it all back and kept nothing for himself. None of funds were used to finance the servant's lifestyle. No doubt he was paid a wage for his services, but the reward for successful efforts was not being able to keep the money; instead, it was being put in charge of even more important things—things we talked about in Chapter 3. Again, that is why it is so important that we be very careful about the conclusions we draw from His Word.

The Goal: How to Fish

So, with that as background, let's look at what guidance God's Word does provide about investing. As the range and complexity of investment possibilities is ever-increasing, an analogy is appropriate. Just as there are many kinds of fish in the ocean, the overriding goal will be to teach you *how* to fish—or make wise decisions on investing—and not simply tell you what to invest in. With this in mind, the Bible provides both general and specific guidance.

Here's a warning in advance, however: the general guidance not only sets the tone but includes two of the most life-threatening graphic illustrations in all of God's Word.

THE MESSAGE OF 1 TIMOTHY 6

The general guidance deals with the alarming risks of loving money and is expounded upon in 1 Timothy 6. This passage goes much deeper than two passages we read in Chapter 2—one regarding the parable of the shrewd manager in Luke 16 and the other describing the interaction between the rich young ruler and Jesus regarding how to inherit eternal life in Mark 10. Moreover, the warnings in 1 Timothy 6 are even given in duplicate to make sure we understand the risks.

In verses 6-8 of 1 Timothy 6, Paul has just finished talking about the concept of contentment and how it is the greatest gain possible in the Christian life. In the remainder of the chapter, he addresses two types of individuals and their identifying characteristic. In verses 9 and 10, Paul focuses on the first type, and in verses 17-19, the second type. Paul compresses a lot of information into verses 9 and 10 so we need to unpack them very carefully. Look at verse 9 first:

> *Those who want to get rich fall into temptation and a trap and into many foolish and harmful desires that plunge people into ruin and destruction.*

Paul doesn't name the identifying characteristic yet—that comes in verse 10. Instead, he uses verse 9 to "set the stage." First, he identifies the symptom of that characteristic: *the wanting to get rich*. This is one of the few places where the NIV really misses the intensity of the Greek word used here. The "wanting" is actually a "craving" or "obsession" to get rich. Read how other translations put it:

> Amplified: ... *those who* **crave** *to get rich*

Complete Jewish Bible: ... *those whose **goal** is to be rich*

Phillips: *For men who **set their hearts** on being wealthy*

Living Bible: ... *people who **long** to be rich*

The Passion Translation: ... *those who **crave** the wealth of this world*

Rarely is this craving or longing simply to have more money—it's really about all the nice things, and comforts, and security that money can provide.

That leads to Paul's second point and the introduction of the first of several dangers he wants to warn us about in verses 9 and 10: falling into *temptation*. Open a magazine and there is a picture, in living beautiful color, of a gorgeous something:[33]

This one just makes me drool to look at it because I have desired owning a plane ever since I learned how to fly at age thirteen. For you, it might be a certain car or a nicer home or even some expensive jewelry. Whatever it is for you, it is an example of temptation and what you and I face every day. Remember, though, that even Jesus was tempted, so that temptation itself is not wrong. But it can create in us a hunger for something.

THE FIRST TYPE OF TRAP

It can be difficult to determine which comes first, the craving to be rich or the temptation, but verse 9 clearly says that if you have this desire, the "wanting to be rich," you *will* fall into temptation. And when you combine desire with temptation, do you know what they form? In his third "stage-setting" comment, Paul presents the first of his two extremely graphic illustrations alluded to earlier: those who want to get rich fall into ... *a trap*. According to *Unger's Bible Dictionary*, there were two types, and we'll see both in verses 9 and 10: Traps were either set in the path or hidden underground. The image conveyed in verse 9 is that of the first type, the above-ground trap, that looked like this:

These kind of traps had two sharp-toothed opposing sides that were forced apart, laid on the ground, and lightly fastened with a trap-stick; some food was also included for attraction. As soon as a bird or animal touched the stick, the opposing sides sprang together and either enclosed the bird in a net or caught the foot of the animal.

So … the point of this very graphic illustration? To give you and me a mental picture of how serious are the risks of "wanting to be rich." Traps spring quickly, and it's difficult, if not impossible, to extricate one's self. This "wanting to be rich," when combined with temptation, forms a potentially deadly snare that can trap us while we're unawares:

How deadly can this trap be? The latter part of verse 9 contains Paul's fourth "stage-setting" comment—and another danger: people who want to be rich fall into "… many foolish and harmful desires that *plunge men into ruin and destruction*." The KJV uses an even more graphic word for "plunge": drowns. So, Paul is saying that this "wanting to be rich" can cause desires that literally "drown" us in ruin and destruction.

While temptation is not wrong, as most are willing to admit, it can be a danger that is very hard to resist. Think about one drink for an alcoholic, one bet for an addicted gambler, one peek at a pornographic image, one flirtation with someone who is married. Acted upon, we can step into a trap that can be nearly impossible to escape. And that single temptation can lead to "many other foolish and harmful desires," with potentially disastrous outcomes.

Note one last thing about verse 9. That falling into "many foolish and harmful desires" is characteristic of those who are not content, who seemingly want more and more—the exact opposite of the type of individual Paul describes in verses 6-8 who exhibit the greatest gain possible in the Christian life, "godliness with contentment."

THE DISEASE

Even after all of that, Paul's not done. In verse 10, he's going to identify the characteristic alluded to earlier—which is actually a disease—and expand the discussion by 1) rewording the symptom of "wanting to get rich," 2) presenting another danger, and 3) providing his second graphic illustration of the other kind of trap with its dreadful consequences. Here's what verse 10 says:

> *For the love of money is a root of all kinds of evil. Some people, eager for money, have wandered from the faith and pierced themselves with many griefs.*

The disease? The *love of money.* Money itself is not evil but the *love* of money is a root of all kinds of evil. It causes desires that provoke people to lie, cheat, connive and steal just to get money. No doubt you are aware of how people fight with family members over inheritances just to get money. Paul calls this desire "eager for money," which is the restated symptom of wanting to get rich in verse 9. Then he describes another danger: this love of money—and its symptom of an eagerness to get rich—causes some to "*wander from the faith.*" What does this mean? Jesus says it best in Luke 9:25, where He says:

> *What good is it for someone to gain the whole world, and yet lose or forfeit their very self?*

For some, the pursuit of riches here on earth becomes so all-consuming that they can't see "the forest from the trees." They desire—or already have so much here—that they begin to think that that is all there is to life, and spiritual things are but a passing thought. Recall the ominous words uttered by those in the Laodicean church in Revelation 3:17:

> *I am rich; I have acquired wealth and* ***do not need a thing.***

Possibly just as ominous is the thinking of the rich in Proverbs 18:11:

> *The wealth of the rich is their fortified city; they imagine it a wall* ***too high to scale.***

And remember that after Jesus told the parable of the shrewd manager in Luke 16—with its lesson that we can't serve two masters—it says this in verse 14:

> *The Pharisees, who loved money, heard all this and were* ***sneering at Jesus.***

Maybe you have heard the story of a frog sitting in a pan of water that is slowly heated up. The increase in temperature is so gradual, so unnoticeable, that the frog is eventually boiled to death. "Wandering from the faith" can be just as gradual, and potentially just as lethal, because in the end, you are separated forever not only from your wealth but from the very One who gave it to you in the first place. The apostle Paul even illustrates this separation, this ultimate danger, in the latter part of verse 10 in 1 Timothy 6:

> *Some people, eager for money, have wandered from the faith and* ***pierced themselves with many griefs.***

The "piercing" here is Paul's second graphic illustration, as he is describing the other kind of trap, the "underground" one, that looked like this:

A pit was dug in the ground, filled with sharp stakes, and covered over so that a person or animal who stumbled onto it would likely become impaled and suffer greatly before dying.

Are you grasping the seriousness of the warnings here? In back-to-back verses, God (through Paul) is illustrating to us as graphically as possible that this "wanting to get rich" is like a steel-jawed trap that, with the slightest bit of pressure—desire or temptation—can snap shut and trap us in many foolish and harmful desires leading to ruin and destruction. Alternatively, God uses the gruesome image of a pit placed strategically in our path of travel, invisible until one fateful step is taken onto its flimsy covering, collapsing onto hidden and life-threatening stakes. The cover over the pit represents the insidious love of money, so deceptive in its ability to lead us away from dependence on God. The sharply-pointed stakes symbolize anything that possess the destructive potential to superficially substitute for a life-generating relationship with Him. They could be such common-place but idolatrous desires as the next promotion, the bigger/nicer house, the fancier car, the second home, the boat or RV, etc., or more obvious evils of greed, trusting in wealth, stealing, lying and so on. Either way, God says this misplaced love is a root of all kinds of bad things in our lives, ultimately drawing us away from Him, and leading to a piercing of our physical life with spiritual death.

Admittedly, these are heavy words. But the words, and the graphic illustrations they portray, are from our loving Father, and given in duplicate to ensure that we understand how deadly the disease of loving money can be.

The Way Out

Thankfully, Paul also tells us how to avoid this disease, or if contracted, the guaranteed "antidote" or "cure." Look at verses 17-19 of this same chapter of 1 Timothy where he deals with the second type of individual, whom he identifies as "those who are rich in this present world:"

> *Command those who are rich in this present world* [that's you and I] *not to be arrogant nor to put their hope in wealth, which is so uncertain, but to put their hope in God, who richly provides us with everything for our enjoyment.* [18] *Command them to do good, to be rich in good deeds, and to be generous and willing to share.* [19] *In this way they will lay up treasure for themselves as a firm foundation for the coming age, so that they may take hold of the life that is truly life.*

This is an amazing passage with a lot packed into it. Note that Paul simply acknowledges that there are going to be rich Christians. However, he has some pretty strong words for them. Likely speaking to the disease of loving money and how to avoid it, he doesn't "request" or "advise" but, using a Greek military term, he literally *commands* or *orders* them not to do two things. First, do not be arrogant. Other translations use *high minded, proud, conceited, egotistical, contemptuous* or *haughty* implying that the rich can be tempted to think they are better than others. Second, taking it a step further, Paul warns them to not put their hope in their wealth. With all of the current emphasis on 401Ks and retirement planning, this is perhaps the greatest temptation for wealthy twenty-first century believers. Yet, no matter how large the amount of earthly treasure, Paul reminds us in this passage that it is *so uncertain*. During the 2008 great recession, many retirees lost fifty, sixty, even seventy percent of their retirement funds and were forced to go back into the job market, with little expectation of finding any meaningful work.

To overcome the disease of loving and trusting in money—and the temptations and dangers that accompany it—Paul commands four "to dos"—and these are an inoculation against the disease as well as an antidote for those who have contracted it.

- First, while material possessions are among those many things that God has given for our enjoyment, our hope must always be only in Him. Similar to the many rich people talked about in Hebrews 11—which we read about in Chapter 1—*our* faith, *our* longing or craving in a good sense, should be for that heavenly city to come.
- Second, we are to "do good," or live righteously, not lying, cheating, stealing, etc., but living honest, God-honoring lives.
- Third, we are not to do a good deed only now and then but we are to be *rich* in good deeds, making them a way of life.
- Finally, regarding all of those material blessings He bestows on us for our enjoyment, we are, in turn, to be generous and willing to share with others. Bringing in what we learned

in Chapter 3, we are not to be tight-fisted, chintzy or give out of obligation. Read how other translations put this last "to do" in verse 18:

> Phillips: ... *be ready to give to others and to sympathize with those in distress*

> Living Bible: ... *give happily to those in need*

> The Message: ... *be rich in helping others, to be extravagantly generous*

And the glorious result for doing all of this? Reread 1 Timothy 6:19 carefully. I have taken the liberty to substitute the word "you" and "yourself" for "they" and "themselves" to hammer home the message:

> *In this way **you** will lay up treasure for **yourself** as a firm foundation for the coming age, so that **you** may take hold of the life that is truly life.*

Why Command?

Why do you suppose Paul *commands* the rich—remember that includes you and me—to do these things? Don't miss this—Paul's whole point centers around this word *command*. This thing called money can do such weird things to us and have such a hold on us—especially as we get more and more of it—we have to literally be *ordered* not be arrogant, *ordered* not to put our hope and trust in wealth, and yes, *ordered* to be generous in giving it away. Otherwise, what will likely happen? We may be successful in accumulating wealth, but that very success—like the rich young ruler in Mark 10 or the Laodiceans in Revelation 3—can blind our eyes to our ultimate need for Him in our lives. And without a relationship with

Him, we have no heavenly foundation. Without that foundation, we will not share in the eternal life that He intended for us … the life that God says—through Paul—is *truly* life. Admittedly blunt and heavy words but remember, they are *His* words and *His* warnings, not mine.

Let me put it this way. Money—especially a lot of it—is like a hot potato: you have to be careful how you handle it. But, you still are responsible for *how* you handle it. Remember that convicting verse in Luke 12:48:

> *From everyone who has been given much, much will be demanded; and from the one who has been entrusted with much, much more will be asked.*

With that as sobering background, we're now ready to examine the specific guidance in God's Word regarding investing. If you are a little hesitant at this point because of all that we just covered, that is a good thing. But as you'll see, His Word does provide guidance to help allay those fears. As mentioned, the overriding goal is to teach you *how* to invest—or not invest—and not attempt to analyze the ever-changing mix of specific investments, although the guidance here will use some as examples.

A Definition

To set the stage, let me define the term "investment." That's because the word is thrown around pretty loosely these days. Some people even try to "justify" a purchase by calling it an "investment." The proof of the pudding, however, is that an "investment" satisfies one or two of the following three tests:

1. It will generate regular income, OR
2. It is expected to increase in value, AND

3. It will eventually be sold to yield the profit.

So, how about artwork, Persian rugs, jewelry, coins, antiques, etc.? These likely do not generate any income so they had better go up in value, and you have a plan for them to be sold at some point. Even if they are passed on to your heirs, unless somebody finally sells the items, they are nothing more than pieces of art ... or rugs ... or antiques. The same thing goes for your house unless you rent out part or all of it. Until someone sells the house, it is nothing more than a place to live. Borrowing against an item is not yielding the profit because the money must be repaid—with interest! So, refer to this test whenever you are trying to evaluate your motives for buying something you are trying to justify by calling it an "investment."

The guidance in God's Word can be broken into three major topics: *Motives for Investing*, the *Risks of Investing* and finally, *Guidelines for Investing*. These topics include both "dos" and "don'ts" or "avoids."

MOTIVES FOR INVESTING

God's Word is very clear that there are both right and wrong motives for investing.

Two right motives: First, the more excess resources we have, the more we can glorify Him and make Him known to the world. Said another way, the more we can "invest to impact," becoming a bigger conduit to fund God's projects. Instead of a little "garden hose," you become a four-inch ... or sixteen-inch ... or forty-eight-inch pipe delivering massive amounts of assistance where the Lord has led you to give. Think of those who have or are giving away large amounts of their income—some up to ninety percent (R.G. LeTourneau, Pastor Rick Warren, Pastor Francis Chan, Warren Buffet, Bill Gates). And for the believer who has the gift of making loads of money investing and puts this kind of giving into practice, note what the apostle Paul says God will do in 2 Corinthians 9:10-11, a passage we touched upon in Chapter 3:

> *Now he who supplies seed to the sower and bread for food will also supply and* **increase** *[NASB, ESV: multiply!] your store of seed and will* **enlarge** *the harvest of your righteousness. ¹¹You will be made rich in* **every** *way so that you can be generous on* **every** *occasion, and through us your generosity will result in* [listen to this!] *thanksgiving to God.*

There is much more I could say about this type of giving but I think you get the idea.

Second, we can invest to provide for our families, both now and in the future. In 1 Timothy 5:7-8, Paul provides guidance that can easily be overused, but properly understood can guide our investing:

> *Give the people these instructions, so that no one may be open to blame. ⁸Anyone who does not provide for their relatives, and especially for their own household, has denied the faith and is worse than an unbeliever.*

Although the context of this passage deals specifically with widows and when they should or should not be supported by the church, there are two reasons why this passage can be appropriately applied to other types of familial provision:

1. The wording of verse 8, specifically *"relatives"* and *"household"* implies *more* than just *widowed* relatives.
2. The Greek word for *"provide"* in verse 8 is *pronoeo* (*pro-no-eh'-o*), and literally means:

> "To foresee or think ahead, to provide by seeing needs in advance, or to make provision for."

There are many such kinds of needs—education, housing, clothing, etc.—so that providing for a widow is only one example. Including caring for widows in verse 4, verse 8 could be paraphrased to read as follows:

> If anyone does *not* think ahead to provide for their family by seeing things in advance, of which providing for widows is one example, they are not putting their faith into practice, and are worse than an unbeliever, who does provide, despite their lack of belief.

Although the comparison to unbelievers is startling, it does convey the importance of providing for the family. But there is a "tension" here. Can you guess what it is? What is a *reasonable* amount of providing? As we have talked about, should the reference point be the environment around us, the environment we grew up in, or what? I can't answer that question for you because it is different for each of us. But I'll tell you the easy route to take and that is to say to yourself "I don't want to have to think about it" and simply model your lifestyle after what you see around you. As your financial trainer, I would suggest to you that if you do take that approach, you should think about the contrast between what we have here and what over two-thirds of the world's population has, living on ten dollars per day or less. And I would remind you again of what Romans 12:2 says—I label this as one of those pesky "guilt-inducing" verses:

> *Do not conform to the pattern of this world, but be transformed by the renewing of your mind. Then you will be able to test and approve what God's will is— his good, pleasing and perfect will.*

This verse—if you really ponder it—makes you question just about every motive for everything you do. For our purposes here, yes, we are to provide for our families but we should carefully and continually seek His will on what level of provision is sufficient. Moreover, we must not let the culture around us dictate, influence, or pressure us in how we acquire ... and spend ... and invest our resources.

Five wrong motives: The late Larry Burkett provided a commonsense list of wrong motives in *Your Finances in Changing Times*:[34]

1. Because *others* advise them to (investment decisions made solely on advice of others, with no consultation with the Lord—often get-rich-quick schemes).
2. *Envy* of others.
3. The *game* of making money.
4. Accumulation for *self-esteem*—the "bigger pile" syndrome.
5. Accumulation for "*protection*"—having enough to cover all calamities.

All these motives can be summarized in just three words and you should be able to guess them yourself: that destructive *love of money*. And the supporting verses are ones we have already read. But now, look at them from a bit different perspective:

> Job 31:24, 25, 28: *If I have put my trust in gold or said to pure gold,* **'You are my security,'** **25** *if I* **have rejoiced over my great wealth***, the fortune my hands had gained ... 28 then these also would be sins to be judged, for I would have been unfaithful to God on high.*

> Proverbs 18:11: *The wealth of the rich is their fortified city; they imagine it a wall* **too high to scale.**

> Revelation: 3:17: *You say, 'I am rich; I have acquired wealth **and do not need a thing**.' But you do not realize that you are wretched, pitiful, poor, blind and naked.*

And maybe the one that captures the wrong motives as clearly as possible:

> Ecclesiastes 5:10: *Whoever loves money **never has enough**; whoever loves wealth is **never satisfied with their income**. This too is meaningless.*

The best advice on how to avoid these wrong motives can also be put in three words: never forget that it's ... *not ... your ... money*! You are simply an *oikonómos*—manager—of all that you have, and your Master *will* want an accounting in the end. Recall that the more you have, the greater the expectations. So, don't start worshipping your wealth and your ability to make it—that is a sure recipe for disaster in the Christian life.

Risks of Investing

Even if you have the right motives for investing well-ingrained into your heart and mind, you still need to be continually aware of the significant risks involved. Although these are presented from a Biblical perspective, they really are pretty much common sense. But without a Christian world view, they may not be so obvious. Although there may be more, I have identified six of them. The first one is absolutely huge—so huge that there is no way for me to overstate it—so I put it as bluntly as possible.

1. Never ever forget that you **can** *lose ... it ... all*. In fact, I have an ever-enlarging file of articles about investors, both rich and poor, Christian and non-Christian, who did lose it all. Put another

forthright way, investing for Jesus is no guarantee of profit. We live in an imperfect world run by imperfect people. You may investigate it, you may pray about it, you may talk with others about it, you may even implement recommendations from a Christian financial planner, but you may still lose part or all of your investment. Remember how housing is often presented as an "investment?" During the 2008 housing crisis, it was not uncommon for homes to lose fifty percent or more of their value, especially in California. Let me share a personal—and still painful—example: I purchased a rental condo in Waikiki, Hawaii, in 2007 for $250,000, just about the top of the market. Near the lowest point of the crisis, equivalent units in the building sold for less than $90,000. In 2019—twelve years after the crisis—I got tired of waiting for it to recover in value and sold it for $170,000.

How about so-called "super-safe" tax-free investments like the bonds of states and municipalities? Well, Orange County in Southern California declared bankruptcy back in 1994. And in 2013, the city of Detroit, Michigan filed the largest municipal bankruptcy in history, owing more than $18 billion.

Sure, I hear about how much some have made—what I almost never hear is how much they lost along the way. Just as in baseball, no one bats 1,000. So, no matter how pure your motives—funds for little Suzie's education, funds for retirement, funds to buy a house, or whatever—never forget that you *can* lose it all. I don't understand why God allows some things to happen, but He does. Realize—and internalize—that as the Lord did with Job, He may take it away from you. None of us knows the future, nor what it holds. King Solomon— the wisest and richest man who ever lived—puts it bluntly as possible in Ecclesiastes 7:14:

*When times are good, be happy; but when times are bad, consider this: God has made the one as well as the other. Therefore, no one can discover **anything** about their future.*

So, in crystal-clear terms, although no one makes an investment expecting to lose money, always remember that there are no ... sure ... bets. Never risk money—like funds for your mortgage/rent or next week's groceries—that you truly cannot afford to lose.

2. If you are successful with your investing, you may *put your trust in wealth and your ability to earn it.* This is kind of the opposite of #1—and we have talked a bit about this before. There are lots of verses on this, but the best one is one we have read previously, Job 31: 24-25, 28:

> *"If I have put my trust in gold or said to pure gold, 'You are my security,'* [25] *if I have **rejoiced over my great wealth**, the fortune my hands had gained ...* [28] *then these also would be sins to be judged, for I would have been unfaithful to God on high."*

And I would suggest that the more successful you are, the bigger this risk will be. In a section titled "Do Not Forget the Lord," read the harsh warning God gives through Moses in Deuteronomy 8:17-18:

> *You may say to yourself, "My power and the strength of my hands have produced this wealth for me."* [18] *But remember the Lord your God, for it is he who gives you the ability to produce wealth, and so confirms his covenant, which he swore to your ancestors, as it is today.* [19] *If you ever forget the Lord your God*

and follow other gods and worship and bow down to them, I testify against you today that you will surely be destroyed.

Did you follow that? God is the One who gives you the ability *to* produce wealth. And the warning for forgetting this? *You will surely be destroyed.* As we discussed back in chapters 1 and 2, not only is everything ultimately His, as His *oikonómos*, He has entrusted some of His precious resources to us. Never should we start thinking that we are investing *our* money. He may have endowed you with a gift for recognizing and investing in successful ventures but remember that in the Parable of the Talents and the Parable of the Ten Minas, those profits were ultimately laid back at the Master's feet.

Risks #3 and #4 are somewhat related:

3. You may work *too hard* to get wealth;

4. You may become *entangled* with your investments.

Making money does not come easy—it takes time to investigate and understand investing alternatives, especially if it's an area you are not very familiar with. You might get lucky once with a "tip" from a friend … or a barber … or whomever, but in the long run, you must have a good understanding of what you are doing. As unbelievable as this may sound, about seventy percent of all mutual fund managers—two out of three paid professionals—do not outperform the overall market—and they are supposed to know what they are doing.

So, with the stock market, you must be willing to spend time learning about stocks. In the residential real estate market, you must be willing to be a landlord—just ask me, I know. Whether it is coins … or Persian rugs … or fine art … or a business, it all takes time to master. So risk #3 is that it is easy to work too hard to get wealth.

Moreover, because almost nothing in life ever seems to go the way we think it will, risk #4 is that you could become "entangled" with your investments. For several years now, I have wanted to sell my real estate investments but there just haven't been any buyers. And, as we have learned, stewardship involves management—investments do not tend themselves. Like unpulled weeds that can overtake the nicest lawn or garden, mismanaged investments can destroy the best-intentioned financial roadmap. And invisible but ever-looming catastrophes can cause you to worry. I can't tell you the number of times I have awakened in the middle of the night because of worry about my rental real estate, whether due to difficult tenants, keeping the property rented, or whatever. Listen to how the wise one, King Solomon, lays it out in Ecclesiastes 5:12:

> *The sleep of a laborer is sweet, whether they eat little or much, but as for the rich, their abundance permits them no sleep.*

So, like it or not, the more you have, whether in things or investments, the more you are going to become entangled and worry about them.

5. You may become *overly emotionally involved* with your investments. Know for a fact that your investments *are* going to go up and down in value. Those fluctuations can have an unsettling impact on your emotional state unless you have a mature confidence and conviction that God's sovereignty extends even to your investments. Absent that maturity, your investments can start controlling you, becoming an idol, shifting

your involvement from wise stewardship to outright love of money.

6. You may not know when to *stop* accumulating. I don't need to say much more about this final risk. As we read before, Solomon says just two verses earlier in Ecclesiastes 5:10:

> *Whoever loves money **never** has enough; whoever loves wealth is **never** satisfied with their income. This too is meaningless.*

Those are the risks to be aware of. And the main one is what? Never forget that you *can* lose it all.

Guidelines for Investing

Assuming you have the proper motives and are well aware of the risks, let's now turn to the Biblical guidelines on *how* we should invest. Let's look at the "dos" of wise investing first. Discussion of some points is brief since they are self-explanatory. And the order is in terms of priority, since again, we need to have our head and heart properly aligned with His desires and avoid that nasty trap of loving money.

1. Do seek *God's* counsel: Because much of investing deals with everyday issues of buying and selling, it can be easy to leave Him out of this process, thinking that we have to rely primarily on worldly wisdom in our endeavors. And yet, He desires to be part of and guide us in every aspect of our lives. Moreover, we must never forget that we are investing *His* funds! Although these verses have much general application, note how they can also guide us in the investing arena:

Psalm 37:23-24: *The Lord makes firm the steps of the one who delights in him; though he may stumble* [and yes, you will stumble when you invest], *he will not fall, for the Lord upholds him with his hand.*

Proverbs 3:5-6: *Trust in the Lord with all your heart and lean not on your own understanding; in all your ways acknowledge him, and he will make your paths straight.*

Proverbs 16:2-3: *All a person's ways seem pure to them, but motives are weighed by the Lord. Commit to the Lord* [listen here!] *whatever you do, and he will establish your plans.*

Proverbs 16:9: *In their hearts humans plan their course, but the Lord establishes their steps.*

Here's the best one, I think, because it so clearly conveys how He wants to be personally involved in every part of our lives—read the last part ever so carefully:

Psalm 32:8: *I will instruct you and teach you in the way you should go; I will counsel you with my loving eye on you.*

2. Do seek *Godly counsel*: There are many wise Christian men and women out there who know much more than I do about specific investments. A vital part of making sound judgments is obtaining as much counsel as possible. Put another way, if you aren't a carpenter, would it be wise to build a house on your own? In addition, what better way is there for the body to function together than for those that are more knowledgeable in one area

to advise and counsel those with less knowledge in that area. There are two great verses here:

> Proverbs 15:22: *Plans fail for lack of counsel, but with many advisors they succeed.*

> Proverbs 18:15: *The heart of the discerning* [literally, a wise planner] *acquires knowledge, for the ears of the wise seek it out.*

3. Do seek your *spouse's* counsel: (If you are married, I cannot stress this one enough.) Many seek counsel from the Lord and earthly advisors but not from their spouses, usually justifying it by saying their spouses wouldn't understand the investment. This may be true with some very complex investments but even those can be broken down into their basic elements.

To make sure *you* understand what you are getting into, you need to be able to break the proposed investment into those basic elements for yourself, because you cannot exercise sound judgment without knowledge. Put bluntly, it you can't put it into your own words, *you* don't understand it!

Once you are sure you understand it yourself, explain the investment to your spouse. He or she may not understand it as well as you do but they need to at least give their blessing or put their trust in your decision—remember that you are dealing with their financial future also. More simply, it's also their money, so what gives you the right to invest it without their blessing? This is critical because some investments do turn sour and much marital disharmony can result if one spouse is kept in the dark about the potential for loss or the riskiness of a certain type of investment. Although some spouses may be less sophisticated in business matters, give God a chance to work through them.

They can at least act as a sounding board and may, in fact, raise questions that you, in all your excitement about the investment, may not have seriously thought about. Although in 1 Peter 3:7 Paul is dealing specifically with wives, it should be obvious that it goes both ways: "treat them ... as heirs with you of the gracious gift of life." Why does Paul say this? Listen carefully! "So that **nothing** will hinder your prayers." So, don't assume that your spouse doesn't care to participate; encourage them to be involved in the investment decision process as much as they would like.

4. Do develop an *investment strategy*: Incorporating all the counsel from steps #1-3, and *prior to* any investing, you need to map out the kinds of investments you will be willing to consider. For example, do you want to focus solely on the stock market? Are there certain industries that you'd like to avoid like tobacco or gambling? How about real estate—commercial or residential? Renting out or flipping? Or how about coins—maybe Bitcoin? What about stamps or antiques? The list goes on and on. And, how much risk do you want to undertake?

Lost investment dollars cost you in two ways. First, the capital, and second, the potential earnings on that capital, are gone forever. Investing with a well-defined strategy can help limit potential losses caused by ignorance or by taking chances that are much riskier than you desire ... or can afford. As one of my long-time friends—an investment professional—has said many times, don't listen to "tips and rumors," especially from friends and relatives! Look at the wisdom that Solomon offers:

> Proverbs 13:16: *All who are prudent act with knowledge, but fools expose their folly* [literally, foolish acts].

Proverbs 14:8: *The wisdom of the prudent is to give thought to their ways, but the folly of fools is deception.*

Proverbs 14:15: *The simple believe anything, but the prudent give thought to their steps.*

5. Do stay with *what you know*—or can learn fairly easily. This "do" is related to #4 and is a crucial one: You can lose big money quickly if you are in an area where you have no frame of reference to determine good deals from bad deals:

    - Different industries have different risk characteristics and economic outlooks, making stock market investing very tricky.
    - Different residential or commercial districts in the same city can dramatically impact the potential for investment growth ... and this can change over time.

Instead of simply being responders, acting on investment possibilities as they randomly come before us, we need to be researchers, identifying those areas where we may have some expertise, can gain it, or feel comfortable trusting someone else with it. This is critical for success because you can't know a good deal until you have a frame of reference to measure it against—and that takes knowledge and experience, either yours or someone you trust. Furthermore, expertise in a particular investment category takes time to acquire yet can reap huge dividends if used shrewdly.

Fortunes have been made in all types of investments but usually by those who know what they are doing. Luck plays a part in being in the right place at the right time but you have to be able to recognize that you are there. The best verse to consider is one we read above, Proverbs 13:16:

All who are prudent act with knowledge, but fools expose their folly.

6. Do evaluate the *risk*. Only with knowledge are you able to evaluate the riskiness of a particular investment. Risk is not wrong, but it can give your investment a wild ride—recall the story in Chapter 4 about my ill-fated foray into the silver futures markets. Be aware of the one unchangeable, non-negotiable, unavoidable, and universal rule regarding risk:

> The ***greater*** the potential for ***gain***, the ***greater*** the ***riskiness*** and potential for ***loss***.

As a wise *oikonómos*, you must measure and contemplate the risk involved in a particular investment. Although the context of Luke 14:28-29 is awareness of the cost of being a disciple, it also has good, general application. Jesus asks a probing question that, answered wrongly, leads to embarrassing results:

> *"Suppose one of you wants to build a tower. Won't you first sit down and estimate the cost to see if you have enough money to complete it?"* [29] *For if you lay the foundation and are not able to finish it, everyone who sees it will ridicule you ...*

Always remember that the opposite side of the potential-for-great-gain coin is labeled "potential for great loss." Investing literature rarely emphasizes this risk enough because, again, who makes an investment expecting to lose money?

To give you sense of the **riskiness** of various types of investments, here's a useful diagram. On the left side are the safest types of investments and on the right, the riskiest. I suggest you come back to it when evaluating the risk of a particular investment.

7. Do *diversify*. This is a well-known but rarely acknowledged *Biblical* maxim to minimize risk. It means to "spread out your investments" over several different types, as nobody can pick all winners. It is not unusual for a stockbroker to advise "don't put all your eggs in one basket," so investors invest in more than one stock, industry, or country, reducing the likelihood that bad news or performance in one will be reflected as greatly in another. With stocks, the easiest way to accomplish this is with a professionally-managed mutual fund. With real estate, it could be different locales and so on. And yes, God's Word speaks to this issue although the term "investment" is not used. In the book of Ecclesiastes, there are two excellent illustrations of the practice:

> 11:1-2: *Ship your grain across the sea; after many days you may receive a return.* ² *Invest in seven ventures, yes, in eight; you do not know what disaster may come upon the land.*

> 11:6: *Sow your seed in the morning, and at evening let your hands not be idle, for you do not know which will succeed, whether this or that, or whether both will do equally well.*

Amazing, isn't? That is the concept of diversification—way back in Old Testament times! And modern-day portfolio managers thought that they were so inventive! In fact, there's a classic example of diversification in the very first book of the Old

Testament, one that gets down to a very personal and practical level. Genesis 32:7-8 reports Jacob's preparation in meeting his brother Esau for first time since Jacob stole patriarchal blessing. This blessing was rightfully Esau's as the firstborn—you can almost sense his foreboding. Not knowing how Esau would react, it says:

> *In great fear and distress Jacob divided the people who were with him into two groups, and the flocks and herds and camels as well. [8] He thought, "If Esau comes and attacks one group, the group that is left may escape."*

So, heed the ancient Biblical advice and diversify your investments.

8. Do *monitor performance*. No investment tends itself, as was mentioned earlier. Wise stewardship requires supervision and that involves both monitoring and steering to make sure investments are meeting expectations. Moreover, investing, managing, and monitoring takes time. The challenge is to not have it take too much time ... or cause too much worry ... or create too much entanglement. Two extremes cause tension: On one side, since we really own nothing here, it is possible to have a rather cavalier "easy come, easy go" attitude about things. This view is a result of misinterpreting parts of Matthew 6:25-27 where Jesus says:

> *"Therefore I tell you, do not worry about your life, what you will eat or drink; or about your body, what you will wear ... [26] Look at the birds of the air; they do not sow or reap or store away in barns, and yet your heavenly Father feeds them ... [27] Can any one of you by worrying add a single hour to your life?"*

The other side is worrying too much, being consumed with your wealth and how your investments are doing:

> Ecclesiastes 5:12b: ... *as for the rich, their abundance permits them no sleep.*

> Proverbs 23:4-5: *Do not wear yourself out to get rich; do not trust your own cleverness. [5]Cast but a glance at riches, and they are gone, for they will surely sprout wings and fly off to the sky like an eagle.*

Tension actually can be a good thing, as it can keep you on your toes ... and on your knees. You are well aware of the upcoming evaluation of your stewardship but thankfully it will be coming from a loving Father, not a tyrannical taskmaster. Two passages provide guidance here. The first one is a reminder to do your monitoring to keep on top of things while the second one provides some perspective in this uncertain process:

> Proverbs 27:23-24: *Be sure you know the condition of your flocks, give careful attention to your herds, [24] for riches do not endure forever, and a crown is not secure for all generations.*

> Ecclesiastes 7:14: *When times are good, be happy; but when times are bad, consider this: God has made the one as well as the other. Therefore, no one can discover anything about their future.*

There is no easy road to acquiring or maintaining wealth. Just as we must monitor our kids, our performance at work, the quality of our marriage relationships, even the oil level in our cars, so must we monitor our investments, lest they be lost through some misfortune.

9. Do earn money *honestly*—this should be obvious. There are a huge number of verses on this one, likely because the eagerness to get rich and the love of money make it so tempting to use any means to get wealth. We are never to forget that our lives—all parts of our lives—are to be as lights shining on the mountaintop for all to see. Here are some sample verses, but pay especially close attention to the passage from Jeremiah:

> Proverbs 10:9: *Whoever walks in integrity walks securely, but whoever takes crooked paths will be found out.*
>
> Proverbs 13:11: *Dishonest money dwindles away, but whoever gathers money little by little makes it grow.*
>
> Jerimiah 17:10-11: *"I the Lord search the heart and examine the mind, to reward each person according to their conduct, according to what their deeds deserve." [11] Like a partridge that hatches eggs it did not lay are those who gain riches by unjust means. When their lives are half gone, their riches will desert them, and in the end they will prove to be fools."*

Now, with all that in place, what do you do if your investments actually start going up? The last three guidelines deal with this gratifying outcome.

10. Do establish, in advance, a *purpose* for successful increase in the value of the investment. Investing without purpose is not Biblical and to do so increases the likelihood that the accumulation is being done for one or more of the wrong motives discussed previously. Having a purpose also helps you avoid the "love of money" risk we talked about before and keeps you focused on why you made the investment in the first place. It needs to be more of a justification than simply "well, it looks like a good deal:"

- Pay off specific debts
- Go towards family provision
- Additional giving
- Retirement planning
- Some agreed-upon special purpose

11. Do set a *maximum gain/loss/holding period*. Although this generally applies to investments that do not generate a periodic income, in this rapidly changing world, no investment is impervious to disaster. You likely recall that once-mighty companies Kodak and Sears recently filed for bankruptcy because they didn't adapt to the changing marketplace. Moreover, an investment's potential for gain is not constant:

- Individual stocks are subject to a myriad of factors, as are gold and silver.
- Real estate can become a bad investment if the value decreases due to tax law changes, deterioration of the neighborhood or an excess of supply.
- Particular coins, baseball cards, or other trading cards go in and out of favor, etc.

When investments increase in value, setting a maximum gain helps you do two things. First, it helps you refocus on the original purpose for making the investment (see #10 above). Without that definite purpose, as King Solomon warns, there is a potentially grievous evil—hoarding. Recall that in Old Testament times, wealth was measured primarily with how much "stuff" you had:

Ecclesiastes 5:11: *As goods increase … what benefit are they to the owners except to **feast their eyes on them**?*

Ecclesiastes 5:13: I have seen a grievous evil under the sun: **wealth hoarded to the harm of its owners** ...

And in the book of Job, while the accumulation of wealth without purpose is implied, note the ultimate harm to come in 31: 25 and 28:

> ...*if I have rejoiced over my great wealth, the fortune my hands had gained* ... [28] *then these also would be **sins** to be judged, for I would have been unfaithful to God on high.*

Second, setting a maximum gain *locks it in* so that it becomes realized and doesn't disappear due to declines in value. It is a well-documented fact that most stock market investors are reluctant to sell their "winners" and end up giving back much of their gains due to market reversals—recall risk #5 warning against excessive emotional involvement. The wise one, King Solomon, shares another "grievous evil under the sun," likely one he experienced himself:

> Ecclesiastes 5:14: ... *wealth lost through some misfortune, so that when they have children there is nothing left for them to inherit.*

The Easy-to-Read translation puts it this way:

> *Then something bad happens and they lose everything. So they have nothing to give to their children.*

This advice also applies when setting a maximum loss for an investment. As we said when talking about the need to diversify, no one can pick all winners, not even Warren Buffett. Setting a maximum loss to trigger a sale, say ten, twenty, or thirty percent, helps to prevent a catastrophic loss. Yes, you might miss out on some gains, if the investment recovers. However, much money has been lost by investors waiting in vain for an investment to recover as it goes down and down. Cutting losses and redeploying the funds is most often wiser than hoping and praying for recovery. About the only exception to this recommendation is if what's termed "intrinsic value analysis" remains positive—a determination that the fundamentals of the investment are intact and the market is overreacting. In this case, a knowledgeable investor or their advisor may actually recommend buying *more* of the investment to lower average cost. However, especially with the stock market, studies have shown that most retail investors won't do this due to fear of even larger losses.

Finally, setting a maximum holding period for an investment accomplishes two things. First, if an investment is not performing up to expectations, the funds can be shifted to an investment with more potential. Second—relating primarily to investments that don't generate a periodic income—unless it *is* ultimately sold, it becomes nothing more than a "thing." As mentioned earlier, it is just something to be owned. For example, a valuable coin collection is just a bunch of coins if no one ever sells them—they have no benefit other than something to look at. Persian rugs and artwork are the same. Yes, they might be able to be used as security for a loan but remember, that money has to be paid back with interest.

Here is one last comment that will lead into the final "do." The setting of maximum gain/loss/holding period recommendations discussed above apply primarily to ownership of individual items like a single stock, a piece of artwork, a particular coin, etc. If you have a portfolio of items—especially one that is well diversified and professionally managed—then a careful periodic review should normally be occurring. Not only will that review determine appropriate holding periods for all investments in the portfolio, it will also include selling "winners" that have reached their reasonable potential gain, selling "losers" that have little likelihood of recovery, and reinvesting the funds from both types of sales. Because of the ongoing nature of the buy, hold, and sell activity with a portfolio of investments, it can be gratifying to watch that portfolio increase in value over time, which leads naturally into the last "do."

12. Do *give a portion of the increase to the Lord*. If the investment generates an income, give as He leads. When the investment is sold at a gain, give as He leads. And, if an investment increases in value, consider giving a portion to the Lord. I would even suggest that you determine the amount or percentage *before* you make the investment. Why? So you can use this giving as both a reminder that He is the one who gives you the ability to make money in the first place and to honor Him as owner of all. It can be very tempting to say, "well, I'll reinvest the whole amount; that way I'll have more working for the Lord." This can sound so reasonable, yet it can be a weak rationalization to avoid giving and be evidence of loving money. So, don't do it.

As further justification for giving, especially for investments that are still held and the ultimate total gain unknown, recall a type of Old Testament giving called "firstfruits," where the Israelites gave at the beginning of the harvest, before they even knew how large the harvest would be. Look at the amazing blessing:

> Proverbs 3:9-10: *Honor the LORD with your wealth, with the **firstfruits** of all your crops;* [10] ***then*** *your barns will be filled to* [not just filled but what?]

***overflowing**, and your vats will* [what?] **brim over with new wine.**

And that is the perfect example of the Biblical promise: "give in faith and watch Him bless." If you want the Lord to bless your investing, give back a generous portion to Him periodically.

THE "DON'TS" OF INVESTING

Finally, let's look at the major "don'ts" of investing, of which I identified four, with the first one being absolutely essential:

1. *If you don't have peace, don't invest.* In addition to evaluating the risk and staying with what you know, the long list of "dos" includes three types of counsel: God, wise believers and your spouse. If after all that listening and evaluating you don't really understand it, you feel uncomfortable about it, or you just don't have peace about it, then, using the good brain God gave you, exercise your sound judgment and don't invest. Just because something looks like it will make money cannot be the sole criterion for a believer—of greater importance is the potential impact the source of that money may have on your testimony. For example, do you want to be known as someone who made their money investing in casinos or tobacco companies or even the emerging cannabis industry? There are so many places to invest these days—why not pick investments with a positive influence on society? For example, in the stock market, there is a whole segment of "socially responsible investing," also known as sustainable, socially conscious, "green" or ethical investing. These types of firms seek to consider both financial return and social/environmental good to bring about a positive change. Here are two passages to guide your thinking, one dealing with our testimony and one dealing with motives:

Proverbs 22:1: **A good name** is more desirable than great riches; to be esteemed is better than silver or gold.

Proverbs 16:2: All a person's ways seem pure to them, **but motives are weighed by the Lord.**

Yes, you may miss some good investments but they won't be the last ones. And, along the way, you may avoid some big losses. As one financial writer put it,

 I'd rather *miss* a boat than be on a *sinking* one!

2. Avoid *hasty* investment decisions—this is a biggie. There are a few rare instances where speed in investing is crucial:

- Being first in line to buy a successful business can be an example.
- Buying commodities like gold, silver or bitcoin is another.
- In some hot real estate markets, being the first to see and make an offer on a house is a necessary prerequisite to being able to buy one.

However, speedy decision making requires one key element to be successful over the long term. When that key element is present, you have informed investing, which is very different from hasty investing. In terms of a pithy phrase:

Informed investing acts on *knowledge*, whereas hasty investing acts on impulse.

Knowledge enables you to act quickly if the situation warrants, whereas impulse forces you to act without knowledge. So, unless you *really* know what you are doing—and even then, it's risky—do not rush into an investment. Probably the best example is a time-share presentation—have you ever been involved in one of these? I will just mention two things here. First, the *only* way you can get even somewhat of a good deal is to a) have a lot of knowledge about the presentation process going in and b) already have a lot of information about the property. In most situations, you will be lacking in one or both. Second, in 99.9% of all cases, you can get a much, *much* better deal in the resale market. Heed this advice from Solomon:

> Proverbs 13:16: *All who are prudent act with knowledge, but **fools expose their folly**.*
>
> Proverbs 21:5: *The plans of the diligent lead to profit as surely as **haste leads to poverty**.*
>
> Proverbs 19:2: ***Desire without knowledge is not good**—how much more will hasty feet miss the way!*

The New English Translation puts Proverbs 19:2 even more succinctly:

> *It is dangerous to have **zeal without knowledge**, and **the one who acts hastily makes poor choices**.*

And believe me, impulse investing has produced far more losses than knowledgeable investing.

3. Avoid *highly leveraged* investments. This is where you put down a small amount and finance/borrow the rest. The futures

markets—like gold and silver—operate this way. This is also how the housing market operates:

> Say you buy a $100,000 house, making only a ten percent (or $10,000) down payment and borrow the other $90,000. You are making a leveraged investment because if the value of the house increases only ten percent or $10,000 to $110,000, you will have doubled your investment—as your equity is now $20,000 and you have a return of one hundred percent. Ahh, but what happens if the house decreases in value only ten percent, down to $90,000? Your ten percent equity has been wiped out and you have suffered a one hundred percent loss. Such is the nature of leverage and there is an old adage that goes with it:
>
> > What gets levered on the way up gets hammered on the way down.

Leveraged borrowing is not wrong but it can give your investment a wild ride—and many sleepless nights. The general rule is that if the expected gain, say fifteen percent, is greater than your after-tax cost of borrowing, say ten percent, then the investment makes sound financial sense. But remember, you are dealing with *expected* gains: the less you have invested, the smaller the decline to wipe you out.

Some people make a living out of investing in highly leveraged investments (commodities, futures, options, etc.), but are experts who are able to literally track their investments minute-by-minute, because it can only take minutes to wipe you out. Yes, big profits can result from small investments but the risk level (look back at the diagram on page 229) strongly suggests that these should not be anyone's primary type of investment. Only those who have other significant, less-risky investments should consider committing a small portion of their portfolio to these riskier types of investments. The big gains may materialize but if not, the big losses won't wipe you out. So, overall, unless you have the knowledge, time, and leading of the Lord to invest this way, I would recommend you avoid highly-leveraged investments. And, yes, this even applies to your personal home—and why I strongly recommended a fifteen-year mortgage to get it paid off as quickly as possible.

For Scriptural guidance, recall the discussion about 1 Timothy 6:9-10 and those wanting/eager to get rich. Also remember the latter part of Proverbs 13:11: "… whoever gathers money **little by little** makes it grow."

4. Avoid highly *speculative* investments. These are generally high risk and often highly leveraged investments at the far right end of that investment scale on page 229 like oil wells … or commodities markets … or movie production … or the latest fad investment like Bitcoin. Similar to leveraged investments, highly speculative investments can achieve huge gains, but they also have the potential for huge losses—in some cases, even more than your original investment amount. So, these should never be a very large part in any portfolio but can add diversification that we talked about earlier. Recall Ecclesiastes 11:2:

> *Invest in seven ventures, yes, in eight; you do not know what disaster may come upon the land.*

The New Living Translation puts it this way:

> *But divide your investments among many places, for you do not know what risks might lie ahead.*

Final Comments:

This has been a fairly detailed—and likely for some, a fairly complicated—chapter. What do I really, *really* want you to remember? Just two points:

- No matter how much research you do, how much advice seeking, how much praying, never forget—you *can* lose it all. Not that this will happen every time—it may not even ever happen to you. But, when you start experiencing success with investing, it can be really easy to start thinking, "hey, I'm pretty good at this!" and think you can do no wrong. Never forget that disaster can be just around the corner and that money lost is lost *forever*. My investment professional friend, who has advised investors for nearly forty years, sums up this point as follows: "Do you understand risk? The answer is almost always 'no.'"
- Because you can lose it all, never forget that *it's not your money*. You are a steward, a manager investing your Master's funds. After providing for your needs—however you want to define those—you should be very careful and seek His guidance on what you do with the rest.

To help you in this process, here's some encouragement:

- Be a learner. Read financial magazines, a newsletter, take a class and use the internet. There are so many different investments out there, you cannot expect to become an expert in very many of them. When you find something interesting, watch it for a while. Do some "pretend" investments with it to see how they work out and test your understanding.
- Once decided, act. Procrastination and hesitation are twin handcuffs that prevent believers from doing what the Lord encourages them to do and this is no less true in the

investing arena. We should never be like the servant who was afraid of his master and went and hid his talent in the ground, yielding nothing. At first, start small. You can buy a single share of stock—or a thousand shares – for about five dollars these days. Buy one or two coins … or one small rental property … or whatever—you get the idea. If you lose, you haven't lost a lot but hopefully you have learned a lot. If the investment goes up, you gain confidence to keep going—just keep a check on your attitude.

- Realize that *all* investing presumes on the future and even the best advised investment can falter or fail. Another way to say this is: Don't expect all winners. Even the best traders lost big in the 2008-09 stock market crash. Hard economic times hurt even the best of companies and best of locales. We need to continually remind ourselves that our true treasure is the one kept safely in heaven. And, as we read in Ecclesiastes 7:14:

    When times are good, be happy; but when times are bad, consider this: God has made the one as well as the other.

- Finally, continually remind yourself to keep the correct perspective. As it says in Psalms 62:10b:

    ...though your riches increase, do not set your [what?] *heart on them.*

Remember that this *will be* a lifelong struggle because of the temptation for us to start loving money and for it to become our god.

Is there a verse that can summarize this chapter? Yes, and it's a good one, as we introduced it in Chapter 2 and re-read it earlier in this chapter. Read Proverbs 13:11 aloud, emphasizing the bolded part:

Dishonest money dwindles away,

but whoever gathers money **little by little**

*makes it gr****ow!***

So, don't invest dishonestly, don't get hasty, and take your time to make the best-informed investments possible. If the Lord blesses, turn around and honor Him in return.

RETIREMENT: IS IT EVEN BIBLICAL?

A man is not old until regrets take the
place of dreams - John Barrymore

Often when you think you're at the end of something,
you're at the beginning of something else - Fred Rogers

God's retirement plan is out of this world - Author Unknown

Ah, retirement! What does that magical word conjure up in your mind, especially if you have not yet reached that milestone? For some, it would be a time of freedom from the daily drudgery of work, of being able to do whatever they want, whether it is traveling, golfing, visiting the grandkids, or just sitting outside and finally being able to really enjoy the sunset. For others, given their present financial situation and obligations, it is little more than a hazy dream. And for many who are in that stage of life, unfortunately, it hasn't turned out like they had hoped.

Due to the amount and type of Biblical commentary on this topic, this chapter is going to be different from what you have read thus far. As a head's up, God's Word does not deal much with the "how" of retirement—the nuts and bolts of planning and saving for that time—at least not directly. However, since the nuts and bolts are an important part of the process of eventually being able to retire, the chapter will spend some time on those practicalities.

More important to understand are the "why" and "what" of retirement. By this I mean "why," as a believer, should retirement even be a goal to strive for, and "what" are you going to do in retirement? While His Word speaks to both issues, the "what" is actually the more important one to understand.

A Brief History of Retirement

To set the stage for understanding and applying the Biblical input on retirement, it is helpful—and maybe even a bit enlightening—to review the history of the concept. It is, in fact, a relatively recent phenomenon. Here's how retirement worked for most of human history:

> Work until you die—or until you can't work anymore.[35]

That was the old-age plan for the bulk of the world's workers for much of human history. Starting in the late 1800s, there were a few companies that began offering some benefits but it was not until the 1920s—about a hundred years ago—that a variety of American industries, from railroads to oil to banking, started promising their workers minimal support for their later years. In the 1930s, when the federal government began work on what would become social security, some of the potential programs suggested would have had workers off the clock at age sixty, or even earlier. The economics of that didn't quite work, though, and so when the Social Security Act (SSA) was passed in 1935, the official retirement age was arbitrarily pegged at sixty-five. The hidden secret of that golden promise was that the life expectancy for American men at that time was only ... fifty-eight, so few could ever have expected to get any benefit.[36] It wasn't until the late 1940s that life expectancy finally hit sixty-five. Even so, Social Security was never planned to provide everyone with a worry-free, comfortable retirement. Instead, it was designed to be a "safety net," providing something for those who didn't—or couldn't—set aside money on their own. And now that life expectancy rates keep going up, the government has found it necessary to occasionally bump up what's termed the FRA—or full retirement age eligible to receive full benefits—to keep the system solvent. The FRA is now sixty-seven, if you were born in 1960 or later.

About the same time that the SSA came into being, company-sponsored pension plans started becoming more available, peaking at about forty-five percent coverage of private-firm employees around 1970. And what about the ubiquitous 401k—or 403b for those in education? Those got their start in the early 1980s, about forty years ago.

So ... realize that only in the last fifty or sixty years—and only in the really rich countries like the U.S.—has there been the *potential* for large segments of the population to have the chance to leave their income-generating jobs and live off their retirement funds. Appreciate the fact that, as a result, even being able to think about and plan for this possibility is a real privilege. It is not a birthright, nor is it something that will automatically happen in your life. Put bluntly, you don't *pray* for retirement, you *work* for it.

Has it been a "success," i.e., are those in retirement "living the dream?" Let me give you some startling statistics and you decide.

According to the latest data from the Social Security Administration, in 2019, about forty-five million people were retired, or about fourteen percent of the U.S. population. Seems like a lot, yes? How are they doing? To set the stage for what I am about to tell you, let me provide one number for you—the average monthly payment paid by Social Security in 2019: $1,461 per month or $17,532 per year. That's $337 per week, or about $8.40 per hour. If you're currently working, you know that you can't really live on that amount.

So, here's **startling statistic #1**: About fifty percent of married elderly Social Security beneficiaries and seventy-one percent of unmarried ones get *fifty percent or more* of their income from Social Security.

Startling statistic #2: Twenty-one percent of married elderly Social Security beneficiaries and forty-four percent of unmarried ones get fully *ninety percent or more* of their income from the program.

So … not much of a retirement, is it? How about private pensions? About one in three workers today has a "defined benefit" pension plan, where the payout is generally based on years worked and final salary. The average payout is about $9,500 per year, or a whopping $850 per month. And what about 401(k)s, which are the predominant type now? Although data is hard to come by, a 2015 Government Accountability Office study found that those aged sixty-five to seventy-four have $148,000 in savings. If that money were turned into a lifetime annuity, it would only amount to a payment of $649 per month. Overall, the average median retirement income for all retirees from all sources is an under-whelming $1,500 per month, or $18,000 per year. Not much to fulfill the "American Dream," is it?

Startling statistic #3: That same 2015 government study found that twenty-nine percent of Americans aged fifty-five and older don't have ***any*** retirement nest egg or even a traditional pension plan.

Startling statistic #4: Of the seventy-one percent that do have retirement funds set aside, the average balance is about $100,000, which will provide a whopping $3,000-$4,000 *per year*—that's about $250–$340 *per month*, barely enough to cover groceries.

So, while there's a lot of *talk* about retirement, it should be pretty obvious that few reach that stage in life with much to live on and so their options are pretty limited. What did I say before? You don't *pray* for retirement, you *work* for it.

Now, as mentioned earlier, this chapter is not primarily about *how* to plan and save for retirement, but obviously, if you really do want to be able to retire at some point, you're sure going to have to do better than the statistics above. To motivate you in that process, let's deal with the "why" and "what" of retirement.

The "Why"

Likely most of you are still in the working mode. Being realistic, that involves striving and slaving away to struggle to have enough to rent or buy a house, buy a car, and—if you are married with kids or the desire to have kids—to somehow squirrel enough away to help pay for their college educations. On top of that, there is the pressure to also have amounts deducted from your paycheck in order to receive the matching funds from the company 401K plan. And as we have already talked about, of course before all of that, you surely want to try to give generously to your church and/or other Christian ministries. No wonder, as was mentioned in Chapter 2, over three fourths of us are living paycheck to paycheck. Maybe more amazing, that survey from CareerBuilder.com also reported that ten percent—one out of every ten—of those making over $100,000 per year were also living paycheck to paycheck.

So, given the financial realities facing the majority, a fair question would be "why even think about retirement at all?" The popular press is not at a loss for answers. Whole issues of "Money" and "Kiplinger's Personal Finance" magazines are annually devoted to the topic. Most often, a lifestyle of leisure and pleasure—golfing, travel, taking it easy—is presented as the goal. And ... the earlier, the better. But God's Word has something very different to say. If you are able to leave your income-producing job, that post-employment life can be an amazing time and opportunity of real *purpose*, a time of finally being able to truly have an impact here on God's good earth and literally "make your mark" for all eternity. A couple of quotes from some well-known individuals in Christiandom frame this thinking:

> Runners in a distance race ... always try to keep something in reserve for a final sprint. And my contention is that, so far as our bodily health allows, we should aim to be found running the last lap of the race of our Christian life, as we would say, flat out. The final sprint, so I urge, should be a sprint indeed. (J.I. Packer)

> There are no *sunset* years for the Christian. Until the day you die, you have a race to run and a ministry to finish. (John Piper)

MY STORY

For years and years, I have supported many Christian organizations like Samaritan's Purse and the Institute for Creation Research. I have also supported individuals in the Navigators, Cru, and others. But I have long desired to be on the ground floor, ministering "face-to-face" in some capacity. While it would seem that as an academic with the summers off, becoming involved—especially with short-term missions—would have been easy. Yet, so often it seemed that *life* intervened, whether it was family vacations ... or research agendas ... or just pure procrastination. On a positive note, during those years as an academic, I desired to somehow combine my secular training in accounting and finance with service to the Christian community. Starting back in 1976, I began developing a seminar on personal finances from a Biblical perspective—which ultimately resulted in this book. While the seminar enjoyed some success, my academic schedule often got in the way—the seminar was designed to be a Friday night and all-day Saturday offering, and travel times made that difficult. When I took my last academic position in Alaska, it became virtually impossible during the academic year because of even longer travel times. Complicating the picture, in 2007 my oldest son and I started a summer tourism business in Alaska so ... there went my summers. Yet, the seminar was never far from my thoughts.

Now, I'm not one to say that God speaks audibly to me all the time but there have been several times when I absolutely *know* He spoke to me. One of those times was in 2013 when I was once again mulling over my unmet expectations–including the seminar. This may sound a little gross but I audibly heard God say to me, "OK Mike, if you want the seminar to go, it is time to poop or get off the pot." I knew exactly what that meant: in order to pursue the seminar, I would have to leave my teaching position. I was not interested in pursuing another academic position in the lower forty eight states—I had been through the tenure process three times already—so it would mean quitting. Feeling strongly that this was His will, I made an appointment with the Dean the next week to formally indicate that the coming Spring term would be my last ... and why. In so many words, he told me that because of a shortage of qualified accounting professors, I was basically irreplaceable so ... how can we work this out? The end result was that he worked out a special deal with me to teach my Spring term classes online—which I could do from anywhere. That allowed me to establish a second home base in Arizona, begin updating the seminar and start making connections. It also provided time for some "hands-on" short-term missions work, as I started getting involved with Youth with a Mission (YWAM) building homes for the poor in Baja California, Mexico, which I loved. But since I also had to spend time teaching my classes and be back in Alaska in mid-April for the summer tourism business, the three and a half months went by pretty quickly.

So, in the Fall of 2016, after a lot of thought and prayer, I came to a fairly radical conclusion—and one that I hope a lot of readers will also come to at some point: *I have enough money* ... I don't need to keep working just to make more money. Could I use more money? Sure, who can't. But I came to the realization that there were more *important* things—things of a higher priority with eternal significance—that I could, and should—be doing. So, Spring 2017 was my last at the University.

I now have mid-October through mid-April as my huge block of time to *really* make an impact (summers are still in Alaska—but they help fund my missionary endeavors). Besides continuing involvement with YWAM, I have aligned with another organization where one of my long-time mentors (and someone I have supported for over 20 years) works; I have become involved in teaching third-world pastors and church leaders how to disciple believers and multiply the church. So far, I have been to Brazil and Nepal. And I don't need to raise support as I can self-fund my involvements because ... I didn't pray for retirement, I worked for it! So, my life is split between glorious summers in Alaska and wonderful warm winters in Arizona as my base. More importantly, I feel like I am now really, *truly* involved at ground zero on the missions field. And like my previously-mentioned mentor once said, 'I'm all in until the end." By the way, that mentor is in his late seventies and still going strong.

OTHER EXAMPLES

Let me share a few more examples of people "making their mark." Do you recall the name Norman Vincent Peale? He was best known for his book, "The Power of Positive Thinking." He answered the "why retire" question as follows:

> "I tell everybody to do what I did: Find *another* career when you're 65. If you retire and go to Florida and play golf all morning and all afternoon, you're going to deteriorate."[37]

By the way, Reverend Peale died at age ninety-three, so that second career spanned *twenty-eight years!* If the Lord allows you to live that long, what could you accomplish in twenty-eight years, especially if you could focus full-time on that endeavor?

Or how about David Hartman? He was host of the ABC TV show Good Morning America, and on his last day, Rev. Peale appeared on the show and told him—and listen carefully to this:

> Now's your chance. You can go out and *really* do something in the world.

Here's a fairly recent illustration of Rev. Peale's advice. Although a bit extreme, a recent article in Business Week[38] contains a story about two guys, Dustin Moskovitz and Justin Rosenstein. As some of you may know, Moskovitz was a roommate of Mark Zuckerberg and co-founder of Facebook. Now thirty-five [in 2019], he was at one point the world's youngest billionaire (he's eight days younger than Zuckerberg). In 2008, he and Rosenstein left Facebook to start a workplace productivity software company, and in the article, Moskovitz is quoted saying:

"Some people would say, 'you have hundreds of millions of dollars, obviously what you do now is go live a hedonistic lifestyle or retire. What we want to do is contribute to the world and make everyone more effective.'"

Pretty heady words but from a Biblical perspective, they are right on. Instead of frittering the time away, they have chosen to use their financial freedom to, in Rev. Peale's words, really do something in the world. Providing great confirmation to this thinking, look at what God tells us can happen in Psalms 92:12-15:

> *The righteous will flourish like a palm tree, they will grow like a cedar of Lebanon;* [13] *planted in the house of the LORD, they will flourish in the courts of our God.* [14] ***They will still bear fruit in old age, they will stay fresh and green**,* [15] *proclaiming, "The LORD is upright; he is my Rock, and there is no wickedness in him."*

There are many examples of this very thing: Moses didn't even begin his work for the cause of God until age eighty—and kept at it until one hundred twenty! Billy Graham, unable to walk due to Parkinson's and a fall, still conducted a crusade in NYC at age eighty-six! Mother Teresa kept at it until her death at age eighty-seven. Bill Bright, founder of Campus Crusade for Christ—now Cru—kept at it until his death at eighty-one. And what did the Apostle Paul say near the end of his days?

> *I desire to depart and be with Christ, which is better by far; but it is more necessary for **you** that **I remain in the body**.* (Philippians 1:23-24)

Although Paul's exact age at the time of his upside-down crucifixion is unknown, he is thought to have been about sixty-eight, when the average life expectancy was only thirty to thirty-five, so he was also quite an old man.

And the common denominator in all of these lives? They kept working at something important ... *until they died.*

The "What"

Moving on to the answer to the "what" question—the all-important "what are you going to do in retirement"—leads us to examine the Biblical input on retirement. Any idea how much there is—a little or a lot? For starters, from beginning to end, there are *no* examples of any able-bodied person working to a certain age and then leaving his or her position or occupation and "taking it easy" for the rest of their days. Not a single one. What we do find, however, are people serving the Lord—like Paul—basically until the day of their deaths. For example:

- Abraham continued directing the affairs of his vast family until his death at one hundred seventy-five, as did Jacob and Joseph.
- As mentioned, Moses died when he was one hundred twenty, after leading the Israelites out of Egypt and guiding the people during their forty-year sojourn in the wilderness. He died soon thereafter, yet Deuteronomy 34:7 says:

  "... *his eyes were not weak nor his strength gone."*

- After leading the Israelites into the Promised land and "clearing all of it of foreign peoples, save one [who made a treaty of peace]," Joshua reconvened the people at Shechem and led them in a sacred ritual of covenant renewal in which

they pledged to fear and follow the Lord God. Dying soon thereafter at the age of one hundred ten, no greater tribute could be paid to him than as it says in Joshua 24:29, he was "the servant of the Lord."
- King David ruled until his death at seventy, although he was not in the greatest of health (2 Kings 1:1). Solomon also ruled until his death.
- In the New Testament, the apostles served in their capacity until their death, whether timely or not.

As far as Biblical commentary on retirement, there is one—only one—direct reference in the entire Bible. Yet, what it says *is* extremely relevant and timely for us today. That single reference is in Numbers 8:23-26, so pay close attention to it. The Lord is giving instructions to Moses about setting apart the Levites for service in the Tabernacle and it says:

> *The Lord said to Moses, "This applies to the Levites: Men twenty-five years old or more shall come to take part in the work at the tent of meeting, but at the age of* [here it comes] *fifty, they must retire from their regular service* [KJV—shall cease waiting upon] *and work no longer. They may* [KJV—shall] *assist their brothers in performing their duties at the tent of meeting, but they themselves must not do the work. This, then, is how you are to assign the responsibilities of the Levites."*

So ... what do *you* note from this single Biblical passage on retirement?

This passage contains three trains of thought: First, similar to requirements in other passages,[39] the Levites were to work. Working to provide the necessities of life is quite Biblical. Second, at age fifty, they were to retire (wouldn't that be a nice age!) and cease from their normal, God-appointed duties. I'm not sure why God picked the age of fifty, but recall that the Levites had to deal with all of the sacrifices—literally wrestling with animals and killing them—and that must have been rough, even dangerous, work, so maybe by age fifty, they were pretty well worn out. But third—and here's the Bible's answer to the "what" question and the critical point for us today—they were not to spend the rest of their years twiddling their thumbs. Instead, they were to stay involved and *assist* their younger brethren, no doubt providing advice and help when needed. The old folks, rather than being held in low esteem, were to be held in high esteem. And do you know what? One of the biggest complaints of modern-day retirees is that they feel worthless, because they are no longer an important cog in the machinery. Said another way, many find that:

> The end of a fulfilling job means the end of a fulfilling life.

God did not want that to happen to the Levitical priests, so they were encouraged to stay involved by helping in their area of expertise, but not leading, as they once did.

What Retirement Shouldn't Be

So, all of this is pretty simple yet profound advice. But here's what the world and the advertising media say: Go to Florida, go to Arizona, get an RV, golf, travel, take it easy—you've earned it. In fact, here are some definitions of the word "retire:"

- To withdraw
- To stop working
- To take out of circulation
- To withdraw from use or active service or active participation

- To recede or disappear
- To cease
- To dispose of, discard, cast aside, toss out, throw away

I don't know about you, but none of those definitions sound appealing to me. More importantly, here's what study after study has shown happens to men who retire from a dynamic and high-paced job if they don't get actively involved with something that will utilize their skills and talents: Their brain and body atrophy and within three to four years, they die.[40] They work and work and work, saving up for that golden time and don't even live long enough to enjoy it. Even worse, the more dynamic their pre-retirement life and less dynamic their post-employment life, the faster they go.

WHAT RETIREMENT SHOULD BE

The solution, stated in a pithy and more positive fashion, is *stay challenged ... and stay alive!* Combining this with the last part of the Numbers 8 passage, if we are privileged to be able to retire, the Biblical guidance in a nutshell is:

> We don't just retire, or as the KJV puts it, cease; but,
> we should retire to something *else*.

In other words, retirement should not be the goal or the endpoint; rather it should be the start ... of something new, of something truly rewarding and *impactful*. What I mean is this: For many years, I have searched for a more empowering word to replace the lifeless-sounding "retire" and "retirement." The best one I have come across is a military term suggested recently by my long-time investment-professional friend: *Redeploy*. It means to be assigned to a new place or task—and that's exactly what retirement for a Christian should be all about—going places and doing things that have an eternal impact for His Kingdom. Recalling the words of Rev. Peale, this is your chance to really "make your mark" for Him on the world. Alternatively, this is your chance to "leave your legacy."

Moreover, especially for those who are in a job situation that they really view as just a paycheck, of putting their time in, retirement can be when you can finally "redeploy" all your time and energy towards something that really counts. Instead of it being a time focused solely around you—"I want to do this, this and this"—it can be a time where you make yourself more available to do things that further the Kingdom and provide pleasure in the process. For example:

- Love to golf? Get involved with the Christian Golfers' Association
- Love to travel in an RV? Get involved with a ministry like Roving Volunteers in Christ's Service
- Or just love to travel? Join one of the hundreds of Christian-based tours around the world or serve in a short-term missions capacity in several different locations.

And on and on. Let me put it this way: Don't you think it would be more fulfilling to be part of bringing fresh, clean drinking water to villages in third-world countries than simply devoting yourself to having the greenest lawn, the cleanest car and the lowest golf handicap in the neighborhood?

So ... as you think about that time in life, really think about how you'd like to use it. We all have unique gifts and talents—pray about how He would like you to utilize yours during that special time. This is yet another area where, if you really believe that God does have the best life planned for you, His desires on how you use that time have to be the most fulfilling that you can ever imagine. And for those who are currently retired, let me encourage you to take some time—and prayer—to "re-confirm" with your Master that you are utilizing this time as He would desire, time that will give you fulfillment beyond your wildest hopes and dreams. Don't come to the end of your life and look back saying "if only" I had done this or this or that. As the actor John Barrymore once said, "a man is not old until regrets take the place of dreams." So, start making your mark *now*!

More Statistics to Motivate You

To be able to do that, let's talk about the financial realities of retirement—or redeployment, the term I will use frequently—planning. As I said previously, retirement does not happen automatically—it has to be earned. To prove that to you, let me share a few more alarming statistics:

- Northwestern Mutual's 2018 *Planning & Progress Study*, which surveyed 2,003 adults, found that twenty-one percent of Americans have *nothing* saved at all for their golden years, and a third of Americans have less than $5,000. To put that into perspective, it means that a third of U.S. adults could last only a few months on their savings if they had to retire tomorrow. The study also found that the average amount Americans have socked away for the future is just $84,821—far less than the $1 million typically recommended by experts to supplement Social Security, pensions, and any other sources of funding you may have. Young people who haven't had as much time to save aren't skewing the statistics in either direction as the report found that thirty-three percent of boomers have $25,000 or less in retirement savings. In picture form it looks like this:[41]

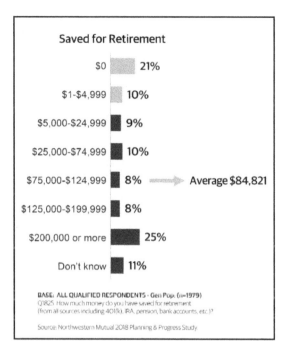

- The statistics in a recent 2018 story on cnbc.com paint an even more dismal picture:[42] Nearly *half* of Americans are at risk of retiring broke according to a survey by GOBankingRates, which found that forty-two percent of Americans have less than $10,000 tucked away for their golden years.
- Another report from the Economic Policy Institute (EPI),[43] using 2013 data, also found that many Americans are highly unprepared for retirement. The EPI looked at the mean and median retirement savings of working-age families, which it defines as those with wage-earners between thirty-two and sixty-one years old. The mean retirement savings for these families is $95,776 in 2013 dollars. That sounds considerable but that number doesn't tell the whole story because an average can be easily skewed upward by several large amounts. Since so many families have zero savings,

super-savers can pull up the average. The better measure is the median savings, or those at the 50th percentile, where half the sample is below and half above. That median for all working-age families in the U.S. is *just $5,000*.

I could go on, but what clearly stands out from these statistics? Most people are far from having enough to really "retire." For many, instead of planning and saving for tomorrow, they are living as if there is no tomorrow, spending all they have—and even more using credit.

Another Compound Interest Example

To reinforce the calamitous consequences of that kind of lifestyle, let me show you another illuminating interest compounding example of how costly it is to wait until your later years to *really* begin saving for your redeployment time period. Most investment advisors have some variation of this example, as it was made popular by a *Money* magazine article back in the 1980s.

Case #1: Sandi, twenty-one years old, invests/saves $2,750 per year for only ten years [ages twenty-one to thirty] at an average annual return of nine percent. She makes no further contributions.

Case #2: Jim, thirty-one years old, invests/saves the same $2,750 per year, investing every year for thirty-six years [ages thirty-one to sixty-six] at an average annual return of nine percent.

So, at age sixty-seven, the normal retirement age for those born in 1960 or later:

➢ Which one will have more money?

➢ By a little or a lot?

> How much different do you think?

Sandi, the twenty-one-year old, who saves for retirement for only ten years, setting aside only $27,500, will be a *millionaire*, as she has $1,013,339 sitting in her account at age sixty-seven (plus social security and/or a company pension).

Jim, the thirty-one-year old who saves for thirty-six long years and sets aside $99,000—almost four times as much—will have only $707,784 at age sixty-seven (plus social security and/or a company pension).

So, even though Sandi only saves for ten years, she winds up with over $300,000 more ($305,555) or forty-three percent more than Jim. In picture form, it looks like this:

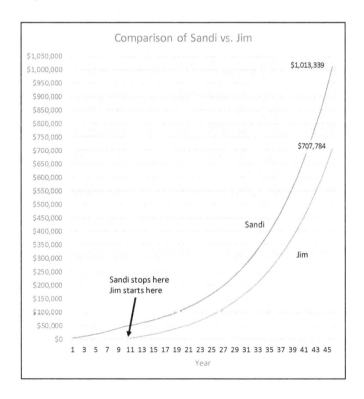

What if you wait until age fifty to start saving for retirement? To yield the same $1,013,339 as Sandi, you will have to save $28,517 per year—or *ten times* as much per year—every year for the next sixteen years.

What about waiting until age fifty-five to start saving? Now you will have to save $55,244 per year—*twenty times* more per year—every year for the next eleven years.

Or, how about this: What if Sandi just keeps on saving $2,750 per year until she is sixty-seven? And why not since, as her salary grows, this will become easier and easier. How much will she have? $1,721,123, almost one and three-quarters of a million dollars. What did it cost her? Forty-six years x $2,750 per year, or only $126,500, possibly about one year's salary for some of you.

Let me put it even more simply: If we take that $2,750 and divide it by 365 days in a year, we get about seven dollars and fifty cents per day. That's what, two small cups of fancy coffee at Starbucks? For those of you who like going to the movies, it's one ticket. For those of you who like Carl's Jr, it's a six-dollar burger and a drink. That much, spent every day on things that disappear, could end up costing you almost one and three-quarter million dollars if you are twenty-one today. I like the way Dave Ramsey puts this issue for the younger folks: "It is easy for everybody to become a millionaire!" If you start when you are older, yes, you'll have less—or you will have to save more—but I think you get the point ... such is the magic of interest compounding that we also saw in Chapter 2. And regardless of what interest rate you assume or the annual amount saved, the outcome is always the same (But remember, in Chapter 2, I informed you that the long-run average return from the stock market is actually ten percent.) Starting early not only yields huge amounts, but also much larger than those who delay.

So ... are you astonished by those numbers? Here's my point ... again: Retirement *must be earned*. The longer you wait to start setting aside for this season of life, the harder it is going to become. We still have some key issues to resolve but the main point will always be, it has to be earned. But as we also saw, it does not have to be all that hard! If you start early—in our example at age twenty-one—you simply need to save about seven dollars and fifty cents per day ... or about fifty three dollars per week or two hundred thirty dollars per month. You could even have it taken directly out of your paycheck! Need I remind you that this is also additional motivation to get your personal financial roadmap implemented?

SOME DETAILS ON THE "HOW"

Let's now spend some time on the nuts and bolts of redeployment—the "how" question I mentioned in the beginning. Here's a question that might be in your mind: Is Jim's $707,784 enough? How about Sandi's $1,013,339? Or even the $1,721,123?

In essence, in the "how" of redeployment planning, the key issue is: How much will you need? You're likely not going to like my answer. Stated bluntly, *I don't know* ... because the sufficient amount depends on answers to four primary questions or issues—and the most important one is unknowable! Moreover, the answers to the other three will be unique for each person or couple. Let's deal with the toughest one first.

The Unknowable Question: *How long will you live?* Unless you are like King Hezekiah in Isaiah 38:5 whom God told would live fifteen more years, all I can say is that you're not going to know. Yes, you can consult life expectancy tables but those are broad averages. What most retirement programs assume is that you will live until ninety. After that, you are on your own!

The Other Three Questions

Now as to the other three questions/issues, these *are* quantifiable:

1. *When* are you going to retire (i.e., at what age),
2. What are you going to *do* during the redeployment time of your life (this will address the "what" issue mentioned in the beginning of the chapter)

And finally,

3. How much will you *need* to finance the when and what.

Issue #1, *when* to leave your paying position, depends on several factors, including your health and current job satisfaction, but primarily on:

"What standard of living do you want to plan for?"

If you have planned well, many of your fixed expenses, such as your home mortgage and car payments, may have ended. In addition, many employment costs such as work clothing, business lunches, and transportation expenses, will disappear. Plus, there shouldn't be any more of those "I'm too tired to cook" eating out meals! So, for most folks, they can maintain their existing standard of living on about seventy to eighty percent of their pre-retirement income, and even less if everything is paid off.

However, you can't fully answer the first question, when to retire, until you narrow down the other two. Issue #2—*"what you're going to do"*—impacts greatly on the "when."

As we talked about previously, the redeployment stage of life provides a huge block of time—for Rev. Peale, it was twenty-eight years! And there are many more of us even living past the age of one hundred these days. In fact, Proverbs 9:10-12 tells us that:

> *The fear of the Lord is the beginning of wisdom, and knowledge of the Holy One is understanding. For through me your days will be many, and* [listen to this!] ***years will be added to your life****.*

So, as we talked about before, you may need to spend some serious time thinking and praying about exactly what it is you'd like to do during your redeployment to get the most benefit and impact out of it. Ideally, this time should either be used to start working on the legacy you'd like to leave or continue making significant progress towards that goal you have already established.

Finally, the "when" and "what" of redeployment must be tempered against the third issue, *how much will you need*? This is where the planning becomes tricky and unique to each person's plans. Because of this, I can't give you "the number" on how much is enough. However, in this amazing internet-based age we live in, there are numerous on-line retirement calculator sites that can help you determine your unique "number"—just Google "retirement calculator." A few observations are in order.

First, the amounts that the online retirement calculators produce can seem daunting and efforts needed to reach those amounts can be almost overwhelming. In addition, that insidious "love of money" can easily raise its nasty head because the amounts *are* so large. Jesus provides a warning for us in another of His many financially-oriented parables, that of the rich fool building bigger and bigger barns so that he could "take life easy; eat, drink and be merry" [Luke 12:19]. Do you recall God's harsh response to him?

> Luke 12:20-21: *"But God said to him, 'You fool! This very night your life will be demanded from you. Then who will get what you have prepared for yourself?'* ²¹*"This is how it will be with anyone who stores up things for himself but is not rich toward God."*

Again, this is why, if the Lord blesses you sufficiently, and you, in turn, plan appropriately so that you are able to store up enough to leave your paying job and do other things, you need to prayerfully seek His will so your time and resources are used to honor Him.

Second, as part of your redeployment plans, you may continue to generate some amounts of income—say a small business, rental properties, a portable business or whatever—and this can greatly reduce the amount of redeployment funds necessary. And yes, you can lose some social security benefits it you start receiving them early and you make too much, so there's some planning involved. But you know that planning is Biblical, don't you? Once you reach your normal retirement age, however, there is no limit on how much you can earn. However, regardless of when you start receiving social security, depending on your total income, up to eighty-five percent of your benefits will be taxable.

Third, in general, here's how social security works: Depending on your current age, retiring before the normal retirement age of sixty-six to sixty-seven means that monthly benefits from social security and/or your company-sponsored plans will be less than if you waited until sixty-seven, since you've paid in less and will be receiving longer. With social security, it's about twenty-five to thirty percent less if you elect to start receiving benefits at age sixty-two.

While this seems like a huge "hit," offsetting this is the fact that if you start receiving benefits at age sixty-seven, it takes nearly twelve years of unreduced benefits, and therefore age seventy-nine, simply to catch-up in total dollars received with a co-worker who started receiving benefits at sixty-two.[44] So, you literally have to look into the crystal ball and guesstimate how long you think you are going to live—always a dicey proposition. What also needs to be factored into this decision process is that if you have self-created retirement funds (IRAs, 401-Ks and 403b plans), you can start withdrawing from these without penalty at age fifty-nine and a half. So, if you don't really need the social security dollars in the early days of your redeployment, it can make good sense to delay starting the process, as the payout keeps growing by about eight percent per year the longer you wait. Not only is that a pretty nice return these days, if you can wait until age seventy when you have to start drawing, your monthly payment will be an astounding 75% larger than the amount starting at sixty-two. If your situation involves a lot of these considerations, I strongly recommend you get together with a reputable investment/retirement planner to determine the best option.

Fourth, whether or not you generate extra resources during redeployment, the nitty-gritty of redeployment financing involves choosing one of three alternatives. Regarding your actual redeployment resources, you either:

1. Live off the income they generate (Social security, pension, IRAs, business income, etc.) and leave the principal intact,
2. Live off the income and principal, with little or nothing left at your demise, or
3. Some combination of the two.

BENEFITS/DRAWBACKS OF EACH METHOD:

Alternative #1 is the most expensive, because it requires a fairly large pool of resources to provide sufficient income. Since the principal remains at death and becomes part of your estate, this is by far the safest approach.

Alternative #2 is the least expensive to fund, but it is also the riskiest because you might outlive the fund.

Alternative #3 is the mid-range option. Here, a portion of the principal is utilized to fund the redeployment years, along with the income that is generated, and the remainder either provides a cushion in case one outlives one's expected lifetime or provides for a more modest estate. One nice benefit to this alternative is that you, the wage earner, enjoy some of the fruits of your labor, as do your heirs. What I mean by this is that in alternative #1, you enjoy the income, but you never enjoy the principal, as it is passed on to someone or something else, so in a sense, you worked for it but someone else enjoys it. This isn't wrong, and many people do it, but it implies a triple burden:

a. You, of course, have to earn it and save it;
b. The person(s) or party(ies) you leave it to need to be instructed on its proper use, else your hard-earned dollars may be wasted;
c. And if, like many believers, you plan to make charitable contributions from your estate, there is an important "give now while you are living vs. give at death" choice that you need to be aware of. In simple terms, tax laws favor giving while you are living because you then get one and possibly two tax benefits—an income tax deduction on the gift now and, should your estate be taxable, lower estate tax due to a smaller estate. If you wait to give only through your estate, you lose the income tax deduction. We will discuss more about this in the next chapter.

So, while option #1 is fairly safe, it does involve some troublesome issues and trade-offs.

Don't Wait Too Long

Aside from the numbers, let me mention one other knotty issue to consider. Many are the woes of those who worked and slaved and strived to have a rewarding retirement only to arrive at that stage in life unable to enjoy it. This possibility is a powerful reason why you should try to experience some of your "retirement dreams" *prior to* retiring, because you never know when sickness, illness or death, either yours or your spouse's, may radically alter your plans and desires. One way to do this is, especially if your plan involves sticking around your local area, is to consider literally "easing out" of your present job, reducing your involvement and hours, if possible, and increasing your involvement in your redeployment lifestyle. Moreover, this is also a great way to test out your plans, as I must tell you that many folks have found that when their pre-redeployment hobbies or interests become their post-employment fixation, they lose their appeal.[45]

Summary

Whether you are currently retired or still working towards that time, always remember two things: First, we live in a time where it is a privilege to be able to even think about leaving our income-producing job and doing something else ... to be redeployed by our Master. As a Christ-follower, that something else can literally be life-changing. Those homes I help build in Baja California, Mexico—cement floors, wood walls and ceilings, two or three bedrooms, a kitchen, and solar-powered roof panels—most often replace one-room, dirt-floor shacks made of cardboard and black plastic bags with no windows or electricity. The recipient's lives—many times a field-worker mother with small children—are literally transformed ... as is mine when I witness the unbelievable joy in their eyes when we give them the keys to their new home.

So … how about you? What would you like to do to help "change the world" and glorify God with the "freedom" years of your life, freedom that most of the world can't even imagine? Spend some serious time thinking and praying about it because, second, remember that retirement … redeployment … *doesn't just happen* … it has to be earned. It doesn't have to be hard, it just has to be consistent—the "d" word again. But it can be so worthwhile—so impactful—and such a glorious final chapter of your life here on God's earth. Why not finish your life here echoing the words of my missionary mentor: "I'm all in until the end!" I can think of no better passage to motivate you than what we read in Psalms 92:12-15:

> The righteous will flourish like a palm tree,
>   they will grow like a cedar of Lebanon;
> [13] planted in the house of the Lord,
>   they will flourish in the courts of our God.
> [14] They will still bear fruit in old age,
>   they will stay fresh and green,
> [15] proclaiming, "The Lord is upright;
>   he is my Rock, and there is no wickedness in him."

7

WHEN YOU GO TO BE WITH THE LORD

> The only thing we take with us when we're gone,
> is what we leave behind – John Allston

> What you leave behind is not what is engraved in stone
> monuments, but what is woven into the lives of others – Pericles

> A man's dying is more the survivor's affair
> than his own – Thomas Mann

We now come (finally!) to the last chapter. Someone has said that "last words are lasting words" and that is my goal here. We have covered a lot of critically important issues involved in being able to ultimately hear those magical words from our heavenly Father, "well done good and faithful servant." There is one final area, however, where approximately *seventy-five to ninety percent* of us—believers included—fail to implement even the most rudimentary steps: estate planning. That failure can have calamitous consequences:

- Spats and squabbles among family members that linger for years.
- Care or nurture of your children being delegated to individuals who not only may not be believers but have no idea of your desires and hopes for their future.
- Distribution of cherished and/or hard-earned assets to individuals to whom you never had any intent of giving anything.
- Waste of significant financial resources in the process.
- And maybe most importantly, tarnishing of your Christian testimony forever.

All of these outcomes can easily—and I mean easily—be avoided. Yet because most make the decision to do nothing, they happen over and over. After most bad decisions that we make—like poor investments, taking on too much debt, or mismanaging our lives in some way—with enough time and effort (the "d" word—discipline), we can work our way out and get on the path of recovery. But if you make the decision not to plan your estate—which is really simply an avoidance in making a decision—there is an irreversible consequence: Once the process of disbursing your assets begins, there is absolutely nothing you can do to intervene and modify it. This potentially horrendous family upheaval process will be out of your control because … you will have died without a will.

You might think I am being overly melodramatic—as you'll see, one of my goals in this last chapter will be to convincingly prove otherwise. We'll see how, with very simple techniques you can:

- Avoid the family squabbles.
- Have your kids provided for as you intended.

- Get your treasured items to those who will truly treasure them.
- Leave a lasting impression of the necessity of having a saving faith in the Lord Jesus.

Moreover, as the last act of a wise and trustworthy *oikonómos*, you will save thousands of dollars in the process.

You may not have given the topic of estate planning much thought but amazingly, it is an issue God's Word addresses in some depth. Probably no verse captures its message more succinctly than Proverbs 13:22:

> *A good person leaves an inheritance for their children's children.*

HEZEKIAH'S ASTOUNDING STORY

As the phrase indicates, estate planning involves *planning*. As an introduction, let me acquaint you with a extraordinary event from the Old Testament that you might hope will come true in your life. The story is about King Hezekiah who, by way of background, was one of the very few kings who "did right in the sight of the Lord." In many, many ways, as documented in 2 Chronicles, chapters 29-32, he encouraged and led his people to live by the Law and trust in Jehovah.

Isaiah, chapter 38, is the scene of the extraordinary event. Hezekiah is now on his deathbed, after having been king for fourteen years. Verse 1 provides some background:

> *In those days Hezekiah became ill and was at the point of death. The prophet Isaiah son of Amoz* [same Isaiah who wrote the book of Isaiah] *went to him and said,*

> *"This is what the Lord says: Put your house in order, because you are going to die; you will not recover."*

No sugar-coating, just the cold, hard facts—coming from God Himself through one of the most famous and reliable prophets in the entire Old Testament. By most accounts, Hezekiah is probably only about thirty-seven or thirty-eight years old at this time—verse 10 quotes Hezekiah saying "in the prime of my life"—so he has likely not been thinking much about death yet, possibly like many of you. And being a good King, he probably has a plateful of things he would still like to accomplish during his reign. But Isaiah bluntly tells him: Put your house in order because you *are* going to die ... soon!

BACK TO THE ROPE ILLUSTRATION

Rarely does anyone receive such direct knowledge concerning their future. For some, even the mere mention of death sends shivers down their spine. For others, death is an acknowledged reality, but is usually tucked away in a dark recess of the mind and not often dwelt upon. But if I can get you to think about it just a bit, let's go back to the rope illustration introduced in Chapter 1. The red tape—all of about an inch or so—represents the time spent here on God's earth; the rest of the rope, intended to be unending, is the time spent in eternity with God in Heaven. So, whether your unique red tape is an eighth of an inch, because you die young ... or a half an inch, where you die in your prime like King Hezekiah ... or maybe even an inch an a half—indicating living to a hundred years or more—the tape still ends.

But ... not really! As a Christian, death here is just another event in our eternal existence. Note how the apostle Paul frames the tension of being here verses being there in Philippians 1:21-24:

> *For to me, to live is Christ and to die is* [what?] *gain.*
> *²² If I am to go on living in the body, this will mean fruitful labor for me. Yet what shall I choose? I do not know! ²³ I am torn between the two: I desire to depart and be with Christ, which is better by far; ²⁴ but it is more necessary for you that I remain in the body.*

Can you sense Paul's tension? In essence, Paul is not afraid of death, as he would really like to be with Christ. But he realizes that the time is not yet right because there was still more ministry for him to accomplish here, essentially additional "molding" or "finishing" work to do with the Philippians so they could progress in their faith.

Hezekiah's response is in the same vein as Paul's but a bit less direct. Hezekiah prays the following in verses 2 and 3 of Isaiah 38:

> *Hezekiah turned his face to the wall and prayed to the LORD, ³ "Remember, LORD, how I have walked before you faithfully and with wholehearted devotion and have done what is good in your eyes." And Hezekiah wept bitterly.*

AND LOOK WHAT HAPPENED!

Although it seems a bit bold to me, note that Hezekiah "reminds" God of the life he has led and the good he has done (and he did do much good in leading the people back to the Lord). He weeps bitterly, literally a "great weeping" or "lamenting grievously." Why did he weep this way? Because under the Old Covenant there was not yet a clearly revealed assurance of glory in the life after death (see 2 Timothy 1:10). Instead, Hezekiah would have regarded an early death as evidence that God was very *displeased* with him. But instead of being displeased, look at what God does—the extraordinary event—in verses 4-5:

> *Then the word of the LORD came to Isaiah:* [5] *"Go and tell Hezekiah, 'This is what the LORD, the God of your father David, says: I have heard your prayer and seen your tears; I will add fifteen years to your life . . .*

Talk about effective prayer! In the parallel passage in 2 Kings 20, it says Isaiah had hardly left the middle court when God tells him to go back and tell Hezekiah that, no, he is not going to die. Instead, he will be healed and live *fifteen more years*!

Such an answer to prayer was also granted to Bob Pierce, founder of World Vision and later Samaritan's Purse. Struck with leukemia late in life, he prayed that the Lord might allow him to live several years longer—to continue the mission of meeting emergency needs throughout the world—and find a successor. Contrary to doctor's opinions, he did live several more years. Did he find a successor? Yes—none other than Franklin Graham, Billy Graham's son.

But ...

Pretty amazing stories ... but I left out one part: Both King Hezekiah and Bob Pierce still died. I hate to be the bringer of bad news but most likely, you will not know when your time is up. Some are taken early in life, some after seven, eight, maybe even nine decades. Possibly through prayer your life will be extended. However, a French essayist of the 1500s, Michel de Montaigne, offers some pretty practical advice:

> Beyond the age of 35, one should *always* have one's boots on and be ready to go!

Just to make sure that it is absolutely clear—even though this is a book on how God views money and how we can be a good *oikonómos* managing His resources—the most critical element in "having your boots on and being ready to go" is having saving faith in His Son, Jesus Christ (recall the appendix to Chapter 2). Without that ticket, the train is going to leave the station without you!

The Key Message For Us

But, there's also some stuff you need to do *before* you get on the train, especially if the Lord calls you home before your loved ones. Amazingly, all the way back in Isaiah 38, written about 700 B.C.—or 2,700 years ago—God tells us through the prophet Isaiah exactly what it is we need to do. Look again at verse 1, where it says:

> *Put your house in order, because you are going to die...*[46]

What does it mean to "*put your house in order*"? The phrase literally means to:

> Put or get your *affairs* in order.

Not to sound too morbid, but every day we live, we are one day closer to that time. And the essence of this command is to be as much help as possible to those we leave behind. Losing a loved one is difficult enough. Not having your affairs in order not only compounds the sorrow but makes the process of adjusting to life without you even more difficult. So, what very practical affairs need to be put in order?

- Wills, inheritances, caring for the kids, who gets what, etc.
- A power of attorney and an advanced medical directive—documents that empower one or more people to make decisions and take actions regarding your assets or medical care when you aren't able to.
- Both spouses should be aware of the location of wills and other important documents, as well as funeral and burial

plans of the other, financial decisions that need to be made soon after death, and so on.

How many of us do it? Care to harbor a guess? Here are two shocking truths to underline, highlight or whatever: More than two-thirds, or two out of every three adults, don't have a valid will. Even worse is that an estimated eighty to ninety percent of parents with young children have no formal instructions specifying who will care for the children in the event of both parents' death, and who will manage the children's finances.

A Wake-Up Call

To dramatize the perilousness of neglecting the writing of a will, let me share two potential consequences or outcomes of dying without a will and leaving behind young children. If you have young children, think about them as you read these:

- In a case in 1985, an orphaned brother and sister, ages nine and twelve, whose parents died without a will, were shuttled back and forth between a maternal aunt in Georgia and their paternal grandparents in Pennsylvania, says Lynne God-Bikin, a lawyer in Norristown, PA. For over a year, state courts argued over both the merits of the case and which state had jurisdiction. Finally, the grandparents reluctantly opted to give up their attempts rather than subject the children to further dislocation.[47]
- Even in cases in which the selection of a guardian is fairly routine, serious financial problems can arise. If the parents have made no arrangements for inheritance of their estate, a judge usually appoints both a guardian for the children and a separate trustee for their assets. This trustee may be unaware of—and even at odds with—the parents' and guardian's financial priorities. In many states, the guardian

must hire a lawyer and petition the court annually to be reimbursed for even the most routine child-rearing expenses, such as tax payments and Girl Scout uniforms.[48]

Maybe this is not a problem because you don't have kids or they're fully grown. But, did you know that not having a will can make Uncle Sam an unintended beneficiary? You read that correctly. Not having a will can make Uncle Sam one of your heirs, primarily due to estate taxes that can be easily avoided. Yet another consequence is potentially even more troublesome. When you die without a valid will (or "in-tes'-tate"), you're really dying without your own *customized* will, because the legislature in every state has drafted a "ready-made, one size fits all" will for those who don't take the time to do their own. Very likely, it won't "fit" your situation very well:

- Relatives you had no intention of giving assets to may, in fact, get a large portion of your estate.
- Cherished items may go to those who will cherish them, not for their remembrance value, but their resale value.
- Dear friends and charities aren't on the state's list.
- Finally, because it can take years to distribute the assets, many thousands of dollars can be wasted on needless attorney fees. And all the while, your loved ones have to somehow cope, wondering when the process will ever end.

Even if you have a will, unless it is drafted properly and in accordance with the state in which you currently reside, disgruntled family members, distant relatives or even friends can contest it. Let me cite one more outrageous example to set the stage for stating the two paramount purposes of this chapter:

- Historians are still not sure who were the real beneficiaries of the will of Daniel Clark, a wealthy merchant who owned a good deal of New Orleans when he died in 1813. Clark left most of his property, valued at $18 million [remember, this was 1813], to his business partners, ignoring the claim of his illegitimate daughter Myra, who, under Louisiana law, was entitled to half his estate. Myra contested the will, and the battle raged through the Civil War, Reconstruction and fifteen appeals to the U.S. Supreme Court. Finally, in 1891 [78 *years* later] the Supreme Court awarded $577,000 to Myra's estate, but by then she'd been dead for six years and had spent more than a million dollars pursuing her case.[49]

Pretty amazing, don't you think? Does it happen today? The singer Aretha Franklin died without a will, leaving an estate valued at $80 million. A valid will has not been found for the singer Prince and three years after his death, none of his estimated $200-$300 million estate has been distributed to his six siblings. Martin Luther King, Jr died without a will. In all these situations, there have been fights over the assets. In fact, I have a thick file of articles on fighting over inheritances—and they are simply more evidence of how nasty and vicious the love of money can become.

As part of the will-making process, you'll also need a power of attorney and an advanced medical directive. These are essential, so that if you become incapacitated due to an accident or simply due to the passing of years, your choices about who should manage your finances and who should make healthcare decisions will be made clear. Otherwise, without a power of attorney, the court will appoint someone to make financial decisions for you and your problems become part of public records! And without an advanced medical directive, chaos can rein in determining your care because not only may your relatives not know your desires—such as whether or not you want to be resuscitated or kept alive on machines—those relatives can squabble endlessly over the type of care, often arguing for opposing treatments.

The Two Paramount Purposes

So, to prevent all these potentially nasty and divisive outcomes, the overriding purpose of this final chapter is to motivate you to do two simple things that will make the lives of those who survive you and love you all that much more bearable. To be perfectly clear, these are not requests—they are commands:

- First, overcome whatever obstacles you have, whether mental, physical, or financial, and *get a valid will drafted*, along with a power of attorney and advanced medical directive.
- Second, if you have minor children, *name a guardian*—both financial and physical—in that will.
- → Become a member of that elite club made up of those who have their affairs in order.

Don't wait another week—it's not expensive, especially compared to the cost of dying without a will. As Sir Thomas Browne, a seventeenth century physician wrote:

> "What you leave at your death, let it be without controversy, else the lawyers will be your heirs."[50]

A fairly straightforward will costs from two hundred to five hundred dollars—about the cost of a nice suit—and, yes, it can be done online or via inexpensive software programs. While software programs are only recommended for *very* basic situations, they do fit a lot of people's situations. The point is to get it done.

Here's another way to look at this admittedly delicate issue: Do you have the oil changed in your car regularly? Do you religiously go to the dentist twice a year? Are you diligent in going to the gym consistently? Listen to this somber quote regarding money:

> People will spend forty years earning it, twenty years living off it, but they won't spend two hours planning how to pass it on. (Anonymous)

According to Paul Rosenblatt, now a retired professor of family social science from the University of Minnesota, no family situation brings more angry squabbling than divvying up Dad's estate. He cites a study that found:

> ... where there was no will, family arguments were four times as likely to occur. In one family, he says, "feelings were still strong over an inheritance dispute that had occurred 37 *years* ago."[51]

So, again, wise *oikonómos*, what are my two paramount purposes in this chapter? Get a valid will drafted and name a guardian for minor children. Don't procrastinate any longer. Do it because unfortunately, in this area, hindsight is impossible. And although you may be living in eternal glory, your loved ones can be left trying to pick up the pieces of the mess you left behind.

The rest of the chapter deals with avoiding that mess through a detailed discussion about general estate planning concepts including (a) how your property is distributed and taxed when you die, (b) the role of life insurance, and (c) basic estate and tax planning techniques. While I am not an attorney and can't legally advise you, the discussion below will inform you of the major issues and provide you with much of the information necessary to get your estate planning ball rolling. If you think your situation is even a tad complex, you'll need to see a qualified estate planning attorney. As you go through this material, keep in the back of your mind that not only is the process of getting your affairs in order Biblical—and therefore something that a wise and responsible *oikonómos* must do— this will be your last chance to communicate with and demonstrate your care and concern for those you love and the ministries you want to honor.

The Federal Estate Tax

First, the big picture. Due to the Trump estate tax reform bill passed in late 2017, the exemption for federal estate and gift taxes was doubled and indexed to inflation. While President Trump wanted to eliminate estate taxes completely, the bill essentially exempted most estates, as an individual can shelter $11.4 million in 2019 and a married couple doing effective planning would double that to $22.8 million. However—and this is a huge however—the changes are only effective until the end of 2025, so that if not extended, the exemption would revert to the $5 million base (indexed for inflation) that existed previously. "Whew," you might be saying but don't close the book yet! Currently, eighteen states have either estate or inheritance taxes and not all conform to the federal exemption amount.

Moreover, even if your estate has no estate tax to pay, unless you plan carefully, all your assets will go through the *probate* process—the legal process by which an estate is administered and distributed—and the costs (discussed below) can be significant. And yet, with proper planning, much or all of that can be avoided.

General Guidelines

In order to choose the strategy within the confines of your objectives and financial position, we'll cover four basic issues:

1. Distribution vs. taxation of your property when you die;
2. Care of your children, both financially and physically;
3. The role of insurance, primarily life insurance and
4. Basic estate planning and tax-saving techniques.

Regarding the first two issues, the discussion is primarily from a worldly perspective, since those issues deal with technicalities of what happens legally with your property and children here in the U.S. With issues 3 and 4, however, there is some Biblical input that we can draw on to guide our decision making. In any case, I've tried to make all of these issues as simple and understandable as possible.

Issue #1 - Distribution vs. Taxation of your property when you die: This is a potentially confusing area. That is because the property you own is subjected to one set of rules whereas the value of that property is subjected to a different set of rules. Let me clarify by looking at each set of rules separately.

Rules on Property Distribution: Depending on how title is held, the assets themselves may go:

1. Directly to the designated beneficiary(ies) and are unaffected by the existence or lack of a will. This is most easily done if the property is held in joint tenancy.

or

2. They become part of your estate and are distributed according to the instructions in your will (or the state's version if you die without one):

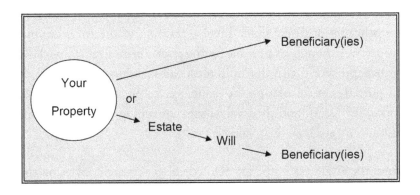

Which process looks simpler? Obviously, the one with fewer steps. Moreover, there is one big drawback to alternative #2: Estates, which are the legal owner of a deceased person's property and liabilities, must pass through the aforementioned probate process. That process involves the court, attorneys, significant delays in distributing the assets—six months to two years is not uncommon—and becomes a matter of public record. As an example, it is public knowledge that the actress Natalie Wood left a $6 million estate that included twenty-nine fur coats. Probate is an expensive procedure, averaging about four to eleven percent of the gross value of an estate. So, even a relatively small estate of $1,000,000 (yes, this *is* small when you see what's included), would be charged, on average, $40,000 to $110,000.

Yet, with relatively simple estate planning techniques, much of this can be avoided. But because most folks die without a will, more of their estate than necessary is subject to the probate process, its delays, and needless expense.

So ... my point yet again? Get that will made and make the process for your heirs simpler, faster, and much cheaper. That's why I indicated previously, the cost of dying without a will is far greater than the cost of getting one.

Rules on Taxation of the Value of Your Property: Now, let's look at the other set of rules, which involve taxation of the *value* of your property. Although it's possible for the assets themselves to avoid the probate process, their value is, in most cases, included in your estate for purposes of calculating the estate tax. So, try to keep these two issues, the assets, and their value, separate and at the back of your mind as we see how their value is taxed.

First, the estate tax is the tax the federal government levies on the transfer of property at death—I can deal here only with federal taxes as each state has its own rules and procedures. Second, it is paid by the estate of the deceased and not by the recipients. Third, the value of almost all assets, either owned or controlled by you, is included in your estate, even the value of those assets that avoid probate by passing directly to the joint tenant(s) or beneficiary(ies). In general, here's an example of what's included: The value of your share of joint property such as:[52]

Real estate (if you've held the property very long, you could have substantial equity),

+ **bank accounts, stocks and bonds** (value increased significantly due to gains in the stock market?),

+ **businesses, mutual funds**,

+ the **full** value of:

- life insurance (yes, this is included as long as you own it and have the right to change the beneficiary; also, don't forget your employer-provided group policy),
- retirement accounts, pensions and the like, are also included, and can easily amount to sizable sums;

+ finally, the value of **separately owned property** (a car in your name, investments, property owned prior to marriage, etc.)

- Subtracted from this would be **your share of any liabilities**, **debts** and **mortgages** or **loans** against your property.

= Your **net estate**. In 2019, estates larger than $11,400,000 pay federal estate taxes on the excess at rates that rapidly top out at forty percent.

Let's say that you're virtually positive that your estate will be less than $11,400,000. Let's even assume that most of your property is held in joint tenancy so that it passes automatically to your heirs (homes, vehicles, life insurance, etc.). Do you still need a will? YES! for two, and possibly three critical reasons:

First, whatever property does go through probate can be distributed however you choose. But, special bequests are impossible under intestacy rules. And while anybody can claim to be an heir even if you have a will, a properly drafted one will be much harder to contest. And, an uncontested will gets probated much faster.

Second, the longer it takes, and the more assets in the estate, the more it costs.

Third, and this will be the most important reason if you have minor-aged children: as noted earlier, the naming of a guardian, both financial and physical, can be done only in a will, which leads to the second basic issue.

Issue #2 - Management of Your Minor-Aged Children: Here's another iron-hot poker to get your will made. Although you might think it is very unlikely that you and your spouse will die together, it happens all the time. If you have not named a guardian for your kids, not only will they be left without their parents, but as one lawyer bluntly puts it:

> "How are they going to know who takes the children home from the funeral?"[53]

Do you remember the percentage I gave you on how many parents with young children don't do this? A whopping ninety percent. Don't follow the crowd here. Selection of these individuals, whether they are to be relatives or friends, should be a matter of prayerful concern, and the party(ies) selected should, and many would say, must, be consulted and agree to the arrangements.

If you don't name a guardian and you both die without a will, guess who does decide who will get the kids? The state. If one of you survives, but your deceased spouse dies intestate, the surviving spouse normally gets custody and life goes on.[54] If, however, you both die without a will, the court-appointed guardian(s) will also face strict court supervision. This is because a judge usually appoints both a (a) guardian of the person (physical custody) and a (b) separate trustee for their property (their share of the estate), who may be unaware of—and even at odds with—the deceased parents' and guardian's financial priorities.

Moreover, as stated before, in many states, the guardian must hire a lawyer and petition the court annually to be reimbursed for even the most routine child-rearing expenses, such as tax-payments and Girl Scout uniforms. Look at how ridiculous it can get:

> Trustees appointed by the court "are usually not as generous" with the children as family members would be, says George Stolberg, senior vice president of Fidelity Bank of Philadelphia. "They'll bend over backwards to make sure principal isn't lost."

> Guardians face a tough time accounting for "every glass of milk and one-quarter of the potatoes you serve at dinner," says William Norden, a New York lawyer.
>
> In a case in Illinois, guardians of a twelve-year-old disabled girl received only $5,200 per year for her care. Even though the assets totaled six figures, petitions by the guardians to increase the amount received were rejected in court."[55]

So, again, don't put it off another week. Get your will made. If you have minor-aged kids, you can avoid all of these hassles by naming a guardian. Surely you are more qualified to decide who should care for your kids, both physically and fiscally, than the courts? Let me put it this way:

* Want your kids to be cared for by good Christian relatives or friends? Put it in your will.

* Want your kids to be provided for uniquely as he or she needs, say to have the chance to be able to go to the best schools they can qualify for? Put it in your will.

The courts cannot read your mind once you're dead—they need to see it in black and white. So, *do it.* You'll feel better, your kids will be cared for if both you and your spouse go at the same time, and you'll be part of that exclusive club whose members have their affairs in order.

Those two points comprise the absolute basics of estate planning. Get a will made and you are in the top third of society. Name a guardian for your kids and you will be in the top ten percent of the class and truly have your affairs in order.

At this point, using a baseball analogy, we have accomplished the difficult process of getting a hit (even the best hitters only get on base a third of the time!) by getting our will made and making it to first base. Naming a guardian for our kids advances us to second base. We now want to get to third base and ultimately to home, scoring a run.

Issue #3 - The Role of Life Insurance (and insurance in general): There are really only three issues or questions involved, and we need to resolve the first one before dealing with the other two. First, is insurance Scriptural? Any passages come to mind?

Looking at all of the major translations, the word "insurance" does not appear.[56] However, its close cousin, "provide for," does occur in general usage unrelated to insurance in some translations. The only potentially relevant passage is one we have already looked at. Look again at 1 Timothy 5:8, where you'll recall that Paul is dealing specifically with care for widows but, as we learned in Chapter 5, really includes a much wider group:

> *Anyone who does not **provide for** their relatives, and especially for their own household, has denied the faith and is worse than an unbeliever.*

You might think that using this passage as justification for insurance is a bit of a stretch. But let me share again the literal meaning of the Greek word used for the phrase "provide for." The Greek word is "pro-no-e-o" and means the following:

> *"to perceive in advance," "to note beforehand," "to foresee;"* also *"to know in advance,"* then *"to care for," "to make provision for," "to take thought for."*[57]

What are you doing when you think about any insurance, especially life insurance? You're trying to "perceive in advance" or "make provision for" in case you go to be with the Lord earlier than you or they expected. I think the challenge here is walking the tight rope between "depending upon the Lord" at one end and "using the good brain God gave you" at the other:[58]

The Lord says He *will* provide. But does that mean we don't have a part in the process? How about when you are sick: Do you depend solely on the Lord to heal you or do you take advantage of all the advances man has made in the medical field using the good brain God gave you? Even more basic, do you walk everywhere you need to go or do you utilize that basic invention of man, the automobile? And in the realm of family, do you just sit around praying and hoping that God will provide food and the basics for living?

I think you get my point. Every day, we live our lives in a delicate balance between dependence upon the Lord and doing all we can to be part of that process. Author Patsy Clairmont puts the issue this way:

When you're in the middle of a lake and a big storm starts brewing, you pray towards heaven but row towards shore!

So, yes, I would suggest that insurance is Biblical and can be a wise use of the Lord's funds. Is it to replace Him? Of course not. Is it to be used to protect against every possible type of loss? If it was, what need would there be for God? But it can be used wisely to help protect us from the unexpected or the catastrophic. However, it should never be used to completely insulate us from ultimately depending on Him. In essence, we never get off the tightrope, but instead keep balancing between the two ends.

Let's now talk about the second major issue with life insurance: What is a reasonable amount? One cartoonist answers this question as follows:

The basic answer is to provide enough to maintain your dependents' current lifestyle for a few years and set aside enough to cover large future items, like paying off a mortgage or funding college expenses, etc. Believe me, if you provide them with a better lifestyle after you die, they might be glad you're gone (just kidding!).

How much life insurance is reasonable? Providing an exact number is impossible because everyone's situation is different. Life insurance is normally used to replace lost earning power. As you get older and more of the people you provided for begin providing for themselves, the peril lessens, as does the potential size of the loss, which implies a declining need for life insurance as time passes. Ultimately, if during your lifetime, no one is dependent on your earning power or should you outlive those who did depend on it, you would have no need for life insurance to offset this peril.

If you do need life insurance, here are some guidelines. In general, including the insurance provided by your employer, and depending on your stage in life, somewhere between three and ten times your annual salary should be sufficient. If there are special needs, such as paying estate taxes (large estates), providing funds to buy out a deceased owner's interest in a business, or providing special medical care to a dependent, more might be warranted. There are many resources online to help you—just Google "estimating life insurance needs."

Even when you have a reasonable number, you still face the third main issue: what type of insurance? This question seems to be getting harder and harder to answer because there are so many different products out there, and it is virtually impossible to compare, since no two policies have exactly the same features. But very simply, there are two types: those that are pure insurance and nothing else, and those that are insurance plus investment. Which is more expensive? You tell me: If you are trying to buy something, and one version has one feature and another has that same feature plus another one, which one is likely to be more expensive? The one with two features.

Pure insurance is called term insurance. You buy protection and nothing else. If you die, your beneficiaries collect. If you cancel the policy or let it lapse by not paying the premium, you get nothing.

- Its main benefit? It's cheap. You likely can afford most or all of what you need.
- Its main drawback? The premium payments may not be fixed. As you get older, the risk increases that you will die, so the cost of your coverage increases. While a company may publish future premium rates, these are not guaranteed. Depending on the mortality experienced by the company, actual rates can be higher or lower than initially estimated.
- Balancing this major drawback is that you can get a fixed premium for up to thirty years. However, this means that in the early years, the premium is higher than the actual coverage so that the excess can be applied to the later years when the premium is less than the cost of actual coverage. In simple terms, the longer the policy term, the higher the rate. So, you will need to balance how much insurance you need versus the monthly cost for longer and longer fixed terms.
- Also making the term length decision difficult is the trade-off between the declining need for insurance as you age, which argues for shorter terms, versus an increasing difficulty qualifying for a new policy if your health worsens. This is why dependence on the Lord's direction and seeking man's wisdom is so important.

All other types of policies, including the familiar "whole life," are insurance plus investment. Because they are more expensive than term insurance—anywhere from five to ten times more—obtaining a reasonable amount is out of reach for many people. But in simple summary terms, I will say this: If you do have the funds to buy whole life insurance, you can often come out ahead by buying term insurance and conservatively investing the difference on your own.

To summarize, the main points regarding insurance are:

1. A reasonable amount can be supported Biblically. Evaluate your insurance needs by deciding what kind and how much you need. Keep in mind that:

    God protects ... you are to provide.

2. Shop around—even term insurance rates vary wildly—try to find a Christian salesperson you trust or do your comparison shopping on the Web; simply Google "term life insurance rates."
3. Main point: *Do it!* Get adequate coverage to "provide for your own."

Issue #4 - Basic estate planning and tax saving techniques: Whole books are written on this topic so my goal here is to make you aware of the key issues. Because each state treats estates differently, I deal only with federal estate tax issues. You'll need the advice of a competent attorney to help minimize state estate taxes, or whatever they're called in your state. In addition, be aware that some states start taxing estates at much lower levels than the federal rules.

- *Portability:* As mentioned earlier, at least until 2025, everyone can shelter $11.4 million of net assets from federal estate and gift taxation and that amount is indexed to inflation so it will grow over time. If you are married, together you can shelter $22.8 million. If the law is not extended, however, the exclusion will drop back down to an inflation-adjusted $5 million per person. Are you pretty sure you won't have to worry about either amount? Just to be safe, there is one thing you need to do. Estate tax law contains something called "portability." What this means is that if you are married, when one spouse dies and has an estate of less than $11.4

million, the unused portion is transferred to the remaining spouse, increasing their exclusion by that amount. However, this is not automatic—it must be "elected." This means that on the deceased person's estate tax return, the box for this must be checked. Big deal, you might be thinking but here's why this is important. If the deceased's net assets are less than $11.4 million, a federal estate tax return does not have to be filed—and therefore, by default, no election is made. If the surviving spouse's estate turns out to be bigger than $11.4 million, needless estate taxes would have to be paid on the excess. So, be sure to consider this avoidable outcome when that time comes.

- *Gift taxes:* You may be aware that you can give any number of individuals up to $15,000 tax free every year and an unlimited amount to your spouse. In addition, there are special rules for tuition and medical expense gifts. Gifting is a good way to get excess funds to children, other relatives, or special friends. Keep in mind that annual gifts over $15,000 to any one party are both reportable and taxable. But the tax is not due currently, as it is lumped together with your net assets when you die and is part of the $11.2 million exclusion (estate and gift taxation is viewed as one combined amount under federal law). So, you can actually give away a lot over your lifetime without any tax consequences.

- *Trusts:* A trust is simply a separate legal entity into which are put assets that are managed by a trustee, and the income and principal are paid out according to the instructions in the trust agreement. In other words, assets go in, someone manages them and pays out the income and/or principal per the trust's instructions. These instructions, for the most part, are specified by the person(s) creating the trust.

For a believer, there are two important uses for a trust. The first one is a very practical response to Proverbs 20:21:

> *An inheritance claimed too soon will not be blessed at the end.*

The New Living Translation puts it a bit more succinctly:

> *An inheritance obtained too early in life is not a blessing in the end.*

In simple terms, it's not a blessing because it is usually blown! The well-known investor Warren Buffett, who believes in giving inheritances *before* he dies—since he can watch and advise the recipient—puts this issue in a nutshell:

> A very rich person should leave his kids enough to
> do anything but not enough to do nothing.

Whether set up to provide income to someone while you are still living or activated via your will when you die, the first use of trusts is to provide control over and management of assets. For example, a trust can let you specify when your kids will get their legacy, and you can authorize payout of portions of the assets at different ages, hopefully when they are more able to manage the funds on their own. So, trusts can be useful no matter what the size of your estate.

Second, certain kinds of trusts can be used to avoid probate, with all its attendant costs, publicity and delays. Lower costs mean that more of your estate goes to your heirs, and less delays means it gets to them more quickly after your death.

Besides using trusts to care for your kids, you should know about two other useful types of trusts:

Revocable Living Trusts: Rather than being activated via your will when you die, revocable living trusts are put in effect while you are still living. In simple terms, you transfer assets—often your home, life insurance and retirement plans—into the trust and you can name yourself as trustee and make changes when appropriate. As a result, you manage the assets just as you did previously. Upon your death, a successor trustee—a remaining spouse, for example—distributes the assets according to the trust's instructions, which could be into the surviving spouse's revocable living trust. And remember, these assets avoid the probate process and costs, and you can change the trust at will.

Are there drawbacks to a living trust? It can cost anywhere from about two hundred to a thousand dollars to set one up—more than a simple will—and title to whatever is put into the trust must be transferred to the trust. But once it's done, life goes on as before. The benefits of sharply lower probate costs and virtually immediate transfer of the assets to the beneficiary (remember that assets going through probate can take six months to two years to finally get distributed) far outweigh the setup costs. It may appear complicated, but really it's not. Most competent financial advisors will recommend setting up a living trust when you reach fifty-five to sixty years of age.

Charitable Trusts: The other type of trust that you should be aware of is a charitable trust. These are used to give to charities and can be set up and activated either during your lifetime or upon your death. If activated during your life, however, they can provide two sure-fire money-saving benefits and possibly a third!

- First, there is an actuarially calculated income tax deduction based on the present value of the gift, or the value in today's dollars of your future gift.

- Second, after your death, your estate will be smaller, since you gave away the assets, thereby reducing any potential probate fees.
- And third, if your estate is large enough to be subject to federal estate taxes, the tax will be less since your estate is smaller. This is significant as estate tax rates quickly reach forty percent.

If these types of trusts are only activated via your will, then the income tax deduction is lost forever. In a simple phrase:

Giving while living beats donating after dying.

There are two types of charitable trusts, the difference being who gets the income or "lead", and who gets the principal or "remainder."

Charitable lead trusts: This type of trust gives the "lead," or current income, to a charity, and then upon the occurrence of a specified event—usually the death of the grantor—the principal, or the asset itself, goes to the named beneficiary(ies), likely your children or grandchildren. It is very useful for those who do not need the income to fund their retirement.

Charitable remainder trusts: If you are like most folks, however, you will need the income. With this type of trust, the income goes to the beneficiary, which can be yourself if done during your lifetime, and then upon your death, the "remainder," or principal, passes to the charity. So, you can retain the right to receive the income, just as if you had full control over the asset. You receive an income tax deduction based on the actuarially computed value of the future gift to the charity and you remove the asset from your estate, potentially lowering your estate taxes. Pretty nifty, don't you think?

Summary

We have, admittedly, covered a lot of technical information. In terms of the bigger picture, there are really only two main points: First, get a will, power of attorney, and advanced medical directive prepared. And second, if you have minor-aged children, name a guardian in your will. As I said before:

> Now's the time ... hindsight is impossible.

Beyond that, we talked about the importance of trying to have as little as possible of your estate go through the probate process, which is expensive, time-consuming and public. We also talked about life insurance and how a reasonable amount of term insurance is consistent with Paul's instruction of providing for the family. Finally, we talked about trusts and how they can be effectively used to avoid the probate process, protect minor-aged children from getting their share of the inheritance too quickly, and provide income tax benefits for charitable giving before the assets are distributed upon your death.

So, put this book down, get your calendar out, and set a date within the next week to call an estate planning attorney to get this ultimate stewardship process in the works. Don't put off until tomorrow what you can do today. Become a member of that elite group that truly has their affairs in order.

Final Thoughts

Paul wrote in 2 Timothy 4:7: "I have fought the good fight, I have finished the race, I have kept the faith." May you strive to live the remainder of your days here on God's earth to be the best *oikonómos* possible, to give away as much as possible and to make the transference of whatever is left as smooth as possible. If you do, when you meet Him face-to-face, you *will* hear those magical words,

"Well done, good and faithful servant! You have been faithful with a few things; I will put you in charge of many things. Come and share your master's happiness!"

There is one final incredible verse I would like to leave you with. Remember that in trying to be that exemplary *oikonómos* of whatever time, talents, and financial resources He has entrusted to you, we are all imperfect and live in an imperfect world. But fear not, for listen to what God Almighty, the Creator of the Universe, promises to each one of us in Isaiah 46:4—and I would encourage you to not only say it aloud but to underline it in your Bible and etch it deeply into your mind and heart:

> *Even to your old age and grey hairs*
> *I am he.*
> *I am he who will sustain you.*
> *I have made you and I will carry you;*
> *I will sustain you and I will rescue you.*

May God bless you richly!

INFORMATION REGARDING THE SEMINAR

What the Bible *Really* Says About Money and Giving is also presented as a six-session, nine-hour highly-interactive, live seminar usually offered Friday night and all-day Saturday. Generally following the contents of this book, participants learn timeless truths on how God wants His people to view and handle what His Word calls *mammon*. Covering many topics that pastors may feel inadequate or unwilling to present from the pulpit, the seminar provides both head and heart-instruction on the wealth of input contained in His Word that many believers never even knew existed.

Should sponsoring entities desire, the author can be available for sermons and/or individual financial counseling the week immediately following the seminar.

For further information on the seminar, including costs and timeframe for advance planning, please use the contact information below. Due to the author's business involvements in the summer, the seminar is only able to be offered during mid-October through mid-April.

Contact Information:

Webpage: BibleBasedFinances.com
Email: mike@BibleBasedFinances.com

ENDNOTES

1. Gregg Valentino, reprinted with permission
2. Original quote uses "man" in place of person; italics added
3. http://www.themasonictrowel.com/Articles/Symbolism/the_temple_files/king_solomon_temple.htm noteworthy fact #6 suggests a cost in today's dollars of $174 billion!
4. http://press.careerbuilder.com/2017-08-24-Living-Paycheck-to-Paycheck-is-a-Way-of-Life-for-Majority-of-U-S-Workers-According-to-New-CareerBuilder-Survey
5. Using 2013 for accurate comparison
6. US Cenus Bureau, September 2017, looking at 2016 amounts – actual $59,039
7. FINCA.ORG 8-18-16; world population in 2013 = 7.1 billion
8. Max Roser and Esteban Ortiz-Ospina (2019) - "Global Extreme Poverty". Published online at OurWorldInData.org. Retrieved from: 'https://ourworldindata.org/extreme-poverty' [Online Resource]
9. Parallel passages: Matthew 19:16-30, Luke 18:18-30
10. NIV comment on Matthew 25:15.
11. Did you know that the most loyal Starbucks customers visit 18 times per month (10-6-04, http://starbucksgossip.typepad.com/_/2004/10/average_custome.html)? Add to that the cost of a newspaper, a snack and ...
12. How other translations word the second half of Ps 25:12:
(Amplified, KJV) Him shall He teach in the way that he should/shall choose.
(Harrison – The Psalms for Today) He will point out to him the direction which he should take.
(New English Bible) He shall be shown the path that he should choose.

13 Ibid; the Phoenicians became a people in 3000 BC, also known as the Canaanites the Carthaginians were circa 800 BC.
14 https://wealthwithpurpose.com/generosity/what-is-the-tithe/.
15 Genesis 47:24
16 Even in churches the strongly preach the tithe, the average is still only about 3%.
17 In the Old Testament, God set a couple of basic guidelines under the Law: First, no interest was to be charged to fellow Israelites and second, only normal interest (not usurious) rates to foreigners.
18 See also Luke 6:35.
19 May 2018 at this writing
20 https://clark.com/cars/auto-car-loan-maximum-length-72-60-month; May 9, 2018
21 "Bank Tells All – By Mistake," *USA Today*, February 19, 1988
22 Liability can be up to $500 vs. $50 for credit cards. However, if you don't report your lost or stolen card within 60 days, you could be responsible for all of the damages or loss.
23 Allentown, PA *Morning Call*, May 5, 1988.
24 Pages 144-45 of reference cited two notes down
25 Pages 10, 11, 83, reference in next note
26 The Folly of Instalment Buying, Roger Ward Babson, Frederick A. Stokes Company, 1938
27 I'm assuming no repayment on loan. If repayment made over 1 year, asset must increase 4.4%, as payments, after tax, total $104.40.
28 Babson, page 237.
29 *Money*, Special Issue 1987, page 188.
30 Under new rules passed in 2017, if the proceeds are used to improve your home, interest on up to $750,000 of mortgages and home equity loans is deductible. However, amounts used for personal living expenses are not.
31 See also Proverbs 13:33, 15:6a, 21:20a, 2 Corinthians 12:15b
32 See also Proverbs 13:22b, 27:20, 1 Timothy 6:5b
33 https://www.google.com/search?biw=1520&bih=704&tbm=isch&sa=1&ei=G-nhXJy3KtLe0wLLjYmQDQ&q=cirrus+sr22&oq=cirr&gs_l=img.1.3.0l10.237126.237845..243243...0.0..0.90.355.4......0....1..gws-wiz-img.......0i67.oZ9yWWmDZe0#imgrc=-S2u0VgqXHVSoM:
34 *Your Finances in Changing Times*, Larry Burkett, Crown Financial Ministries 1975, pages 113-23.
35 "A brief history of retirement: It's a modern idea," Seattle Times, December 31, 2013

36   "How Retirement was Invented," The Atlantic, October 24, 2014
37   Parade, May 17, 1987, Do The Best You Can With What You've Got; by the way, he "retired" from the pulpit at age 85)
38   November 7-13, 2011, pages 76-81
39   Genesis 2:15, Exodus 20:9, Colossians 3:23-24, 2 Timothy 2:6, 2 Thessalonians 3:10-12, Ephesians 4:28, 1 Timothy 5:8
40   Although most of these studies only involved men, the results will likely be similar for women who pursue these types of jobs also.
41   https://www.cnbc.com/2018/05/15/how-much-americans-have-saved-for-retirement.html
42   https://www.cnbc.com/2018/04/23/how-much-us-families-have-in-retirement-savings-and-how-much-they-need.html
43   https://www.cnbc.com/2017/04/07/how-much-the-average-family-has-saved-for-retirement-at-every-age.html
44   For you math whizzes, time value of money considerations have been left out. Depending on interest rates, that time period could easily be stretched to 15-20 years.
45   For a good example, see *Money*, December 1983, page 157.
46   The only other time a similar thought is uttered in God's Word is in **2 Sam 17:23**, when Ahithophel, a formerly trusted advisor of King David who defected to the enemy, "put his house in order" just prior to hanging himself.
47   The Wall Street Journal, May 15, 1987, "Who Gets the Kids? Parents Fail to Designate Guardians in Wills."
48   Ibid.
49   *Money*, June 1984, "Drafting an Heir-tight Will," editorial comment added.
50   Ibid.
51   *Money*, August 1981, "No Way Without a Will," emphasis added.
52   For more information, see https://www.thebalance.com/how-to-calculate-the-value-of-your-gross-estate-3505635
53   The Wall Street Journal, "Who Gets the Kids...," May 15, 1987
54   As mentioned by my editor, this process is not always so "clean and simple." She had an aunt who was suddenly widowed at age thirty-eight and was shocked to learn that she had to endure the uncomfortable process of going to the courthouse to literally be "granted" custody of her two boys. This in addition to bereaving the untimely loss of her husband.
55   All Wall Street Journal, May 15, 1987.

56 Biblegateway.com has fifty-nine English translations. Only The Passion translation contains the word "insurance" one time—Proverbs 29-14—and it has nothing to do with insurance.
57 G. Kittle, *Theological Dictionary of the New Testament*, page 64.
58 https://www.google.com/search?biw=1520&bih=704&tbm=isch&sa=1&ei=yefhXJzbINKBk-4P2t6f8As&q=man+on+tightrope&oq=man+on+tightrope&gs_l=img.3..0j0i8i30l4j0i24.330903.335187..337149...3.0..0.242.1855.17j1j1......0....1..gws-wiz-img.......0i67j0i10j0i5i30.ABd1XH0VHhg#imgdii=4S73yM2rcGqqJM:&imgrc=qrSGrJv-Uhjk_M:

CPSIA information can be obtained
at www.ICGtesting.com
Printed in the USA
LVHW032100100221
678988LV00007B/148